THE LIVING ARTIFACT

by

Floyd Collins

STEPHEN F. AUSTIN STATE UNIVERSITY PRESS

Production Manager: Kimberly Verhines

IBSN: 978-1-62288-922-8

For more information:
Stephen F. Austin State University Press
P.O. Box 13007 SFA Station
Nacogdoches, Texas 75962
sfapress@sfasu.edu
www.sfasu.edu/sfapress
936-468-1078

Distributed by Texas A&M University Press Consortium
www.tamupress.com

ACKNOWLEDGMENTS

Grateful acknowledgment is extended to the following journals, in which these chapters first appeared, some in slightly different versions:

"Richard Wilbur: A Retrospective and Appreciation": *Kenyon Review*

"Forms Open and Closed: The Poetry of W.S. Merwin": *Gettysburg Review*

"Derek Walcott: Caribbean Nobel Laureate": *Gettysburg Review*

"Metamorphosis Within the Poetry of Charles Wright": *Gettysburg Review*

"Stanley Plumly: An Appreciation": *Gettysburg Review*

"Pattiann Rogers: Motives for Metaphor": *Gettysburg Review*

"Blear-Eyed Wisdom Out of Midnight Oil": *Gettysburg Review*

"Vexed Heritage: Two Southern Poets": *Georgia Review*

"Auspicious Beginnings and Sure Arrivals: Beth Ann Fennelly and
        Eavan Boland": *West Branch*

"Esperanza and Hope: I Am My Own Country": *Free State Review*

"Carolyn Forché: A Poetry of Witness": *Georgia Review*

"Michael Waters: Wit and Wordplay": *Gettysburg Review*

"Elizabeth Spires: *Annociade* and *Worldling*": *Gettysburg Review*

"David Baker: Midwestern Counter-Sublime": *Gettysburg Review*

"Eric Pankey: The Crisis of Faith": *Gettysburg Review*

for my sister Becky

CONTENTS

The Living Artifact

Three eminent critics belonging to the generation before the author of the present study—Harold Bloom, Helen Vendler, and Peter Stitt—inform the methodology and prose style adopted in this opus. In his seminal text titled *The Western Canon* (1994), Bloom espouses an agonistic and hierarchical approach to the language arts, one in which all poets suffer from a sense of belatedness, inevitably foundering in the wake of Homer, Dante, and Shakespeare. His insistence upon measuring all the poetry written in the twentieth century and beyond against the achievements of the great granite dead is compelling but, for the most part, counter to the purposes of this book. However, there is no gainsaying his extraordinary erudition, a quality every student of literature should strive to emulate. Helen Vendler's *Part of Nature, Part of Us: Modern American Poets* (1990), while unquestionably a learned text, stylistically proves to be the work of a self-confessed rhapsode whose exemplar is that euphonic genius Wallace Stevens. She, therefore, enters into a dialogical relationship with the poets whose works she explores, seeking entrance to their singular lyric acumen through a linguistic mimesis of her own. Yet her uncanny knack for closely analyzing various modes of versification is commensurate to Bloom's. More influential than either Bloom or Vendler with regard to the present book-length assessment of contemporary poets is Peter Stitt's *The World's Hieroglyphic Beauty.* While still an undergraduate, I avidly perused the current periodicals section of the University of Memphis library in an effort to discover someone whose critical philosophy was at once perspicacious and readily accessible to a comparative neophyte who aspired to become a man of letters. I chanced on *The Georgia Review,* then edited by Stanley Lindberg, who published on a quarterly basis Stitt's essay-reviews from the late seventies to the late eighties. Every piece brought together four or five disparate volumes of poetry under a single unifying thesis that tapped into the Western literary tradition. Most engaging of all was Stitt's sacramental vision contending that the realms of the spirit and flesh are ultimately one.

After a decade of writing for Lindberg, Stitt resigned his faculty position at the University of Houston and founded *The Gettysburg Review* at Gettysburg College in Pennsylvania. Concerning artwork, design, and belletristic content, his new journal took *The Georgia Review* as its template. In the summer of 1989, after completing my M.F.A. at the University of Arkansas, I submitted several poems to a special railroad issue of *The Gettysburg Review.* When Stitt selected for publication in his pages a poem called "Piano Player," he invited me to write a critical essay modeled on those he had amassed over the previous ten years. He soon accepted an 8,000-word article titled "The Language of Illumination" for his winter 1990 issue and proposed that I become his regular poetry reviewer, an appointment I held with an occasional hiatus until his retirement in 2016. During the ensuing years, I also took on assignments from *The Arkansas Review, The Free State Review, The Georgia Review, The Kenyon Review, The Sewanee Review,* and *West Branch*. Moreover, the University of Delaware Press published my book-length critical study titled *Seamus Heaney: The Crisis of Identity* in 2003.

But for those involved in literary pursuits, the present cultural landscape is not without certain pitfalls. As poet and critic David Baker so astutely observes in *Heresy and the Ideal: On Contemporary Poetry* (2000), academia is no longer a haven for people whose appreciation of any linguistic artifact derives primarily from its aesthetic worth: "The marketplace has always been an unfriendly site for poetry. But the contemporary academy is not very enthusiastic about the art, either. For the last two decades, the literary professorate has disengaged itself from the literary text as a whole. I have colleagues who don't read literature anymore, although they read earnestly about theories of literature." Perhaps a few socio-political discourses have a certain intrinsic merit, Feminism and New Historicism being primary examples. But proponents of Jacques Derrida's Deconstructionist theories have yet to discern that *Of Grammatology* (1967) is downright farcical in many of its basic tenets, and its only real use is to enable Marxists, for example, to dismantle the rhetorical strategies of opposing disciplines. One of the purposes of this critical study is to incorporate more coherent approaches to evaluating literature that lend depth and clarity to close readings of poems evoking both spiritual and empirical realms. Roland Barthes, who proclaims "The Death of the Author," I cheerfully consign to those refining fires that are banked in the nether regions rather than Byzantium.

During the 2000-2001 academic year, I was Shakespeare Seminar Scholar and Poet-in-Residence at Wabash College in Crawfordsville, Indiana, a post once held by Ezra Pound until the eventual expatiate was dismissed by the administration because the ladies of the community objected to his "Latin Quarter ways." Before I was invited to interview for the position, the English Department chairman Warren Rosenberg called and remarked: "I see on your resume that you lectured on Renaissance literature at Quincy University last fall and spring; did you happen to teach Shakespeare? More than a little non-plussed, I responded: "How do you teach Elizabethan and Jacobean literature if the leading dramatist of the seventeenth century is not on your syllabus?" Apparently, the playwright who scratched from parchment *A Midsummer Night's Dream, Twelfth Night, Romeo and Juliet, Julius Caesar, Richard II, 1 Henry IV, 2 Henry IV, Henry V, Hamlet, King Lear, Othello, Macbeth, A Winter's Tale,* and *The Tempest* was already being supplanted in the curriculum by Restoration mediocrities such as Aphra Behn. I'm not raising a gender issue here. I number among the most accomplished poets of my generation C.D. Wright, Carolyn Forché, Brigit Pegeen Kelly, and Elizabeth Spires, to name but a few. Natasha Trethewey and Beth Ann Fennelly bode well for the future. Pattiann Rogers, Eavan Boland, and Louise Glück set the benchmark for those born shortly before or during World War II.

Nevertheless, I feel obliged to begin primarily with those male artists who dominated contemporary poetry during the second half of the twentieth century: Richard Wilbur, W.S. Merwin, Derek Walcott, Charles Wright, Seamus Heaney, and Stanley Plumly. But even if we exempt the preternaturally gifted Sylvia Plath, who has been the subject of so many critical biographies that any commentary here would be redundant, that still leaves us with Pattiann Rogers and Eavan Boland. Excluding laudable voices such Amy Clampitt and Margaret Atwood was more or less a matter of personal taste and inclination than willful neglect. Critics bent on revising the canon prefer to dismiss Harold Bloom's amalgam for literary excellence—"mastery of figurative language, originality, cognitive power, knowledge, [and] exuberance of diction"—yet these are felicitous traits that Charles Wright and Pattiann Rogers share in abundance. To be sure, Bloom's insistence on ranking poets insofar as each meets his various criteria for genuine distinction borders on caprice, but separating the proverbial wheat from the chaff is inevitable when evaluating the language arts. I would add to this formulation the dual elements of beauty and strangeness, the capacity to endow language with a sense of the numinous that derives from some singular experience, which is perhaps best put forward in the concluding stanza of T.S. Eliot's "Little Gidding": "And the end of our exploring / Will be to arrive where we started / And know the place for the first time."

Another conundrum that David Baker addresses in *Heresy and the Ideal* is the woeful indifference of the reading public to poetry focusing on subjects that practitioners of the craft would have deemed essential during the English Renaissance and the Era of the Romantic Triumph (1798-1832): among these are life, death, time, and mutability. For instance, the theater of Shakespeare's day was considered popular entertainment; therefore, the man from Stratford-on-the-Avon staked his reputation as the quintessential wordsmith on his sonnets dedicated to the young Earl of Southampton. Conversely, twentieth-century film directors and screenwriters, including David Lean, Frederic Raphael, Stanley Kubrick, Francis Ford Coppola, Steven Spielberg, Spike Lee, and Kathryn Bigelow are already garnering an impressive body of cinematic scholarship. Songwriter Bob Dylan has no formal education beyond high school, but the Swedish Academy in Stockholm awarded him the 2016 Nobel Prize for Literature "for having created new poetic expressions within the great American song tradition." Yet some of the nation's finest M.F.A. programs in creative writing—the University of Iowa, Johns Hopkins University, the University of California at Irvine, and the University of Arkansas—have distinguished faculty and alumni who remain unknown within the cultural mainstream. Ask someone on any street corner if he or she has read Louise Glück's *The Triumph of Achilles* (1985). Notwithstanding these paradoxes past and present, Baker asserts: "College students are more interested in poetry and creative writing than ever before, and writing classes are plentiful, the programs rich and diverse. Accusations that poetry has become more insular, restrictive, or complacent are simply wrong." These are "singing schools" of the sort that Yeats, for all his visionary brilliance, could scarcely imagine when he published *The Tower* (1928), and if his limestone bastion of Thoor Ballylee is not overgrown with ivy, neither is the masonry of the University of Iowa, whose earliest M.F.A. graduates often enrolled on the G. I. Bill. But education is not just a process, it is also an experience, and that does not always guarantee a positive one: "I could write nothing at all that pleased Lowell," complained Philip Levine, eventual recipient of the Pulitzer Prize, about a poetry workshop he took with Robert Lowell at Iowa. "Arbitrary, petty, and cruel" is how another former student at Harvard described the author of *Lord Weary's Castle* (1946). But students at the University of Maryland almost invariably regarded the late Stanley Plumly as a dedicated and nurturing teacher. Moreover, I would not trade anything for the years I worked under the auspices of Miller Williams and James Whitehead in Fayetteville, Arkansas.

Of course, poetry is also a sacred encoding, and the technical skills one hones and refines through formal schooling are only part of the equation for those who wish to become accomplished poets. Many successful writers of verse are in some measure autodidacts who began to read vital texts during their formative years. My own passion for Homer was kindled by the enormous wooden horse depicted on the glossy cover of a mass-circulation magazine that I chanced on while still a child. By age eleven, I was reading the Ionian bard's *Iliad* in Richmond Lattimore's translation. Although I never learned the Greek dialect adapted from the linear *B* script that preserved ancient Mycenaean culture, I went on to read Robert Fagles's version and then Christopher Logue's Modernist rendition titled *War Music* (2016).

From the popular cinema of my youth, I conceived an enthusiasm for siege and battle of the Alamo. I took language courses as an undergraduate that enabled me to read the purported field diary of Jose Enrique de la Peña, a young officer in the 1836 Mexican Army of Operations who provided evidence that David Crockett may have been compelled to surrender, only to be executed along with four other wounded members of the garrison at the command of Generalissimo Antonio López de Santa Anna. After that, I began to read in the original Spanish the poems of Juan Ramón Jiménez, Federico García Lorca, Rafael Alberti, and Pablo Neruda. I subscribed to Robert Bly's literary journal *The Sixties* and perused not only his translations of the Swedish poet Tomas Tranströmer and the poems of German

Expressionist Georg Trakl carried over into English by the editor's friend James Wright, but I also delighted in the publication's iconoclastic reviews and the lively debate engendered by those articles. (I realized decades later that W. H. Auden was correct when he said that reviewing bad books is bad for one's character.) I submitted my early efforts to the "little magazines," and by the time I turned twenty, I had placed perhaps a score of poems in several periodicals that typically ceased to appear after only a few issues. But before I earned my baccalaureate degree, I had published a limited edition collection with a good regional house and served as poetry editor of the English Department's professional journal at the University of Memphis. When I subsequently enrolled in one of the more reputable M.F.A. programs in the South, I was told by my thesis director that my apprenticeship as a writer was at an end, but before I finished graduate school, I realized it had hardly begun.

The second generation of poets that come under scrutiny in this study present the reader with dichotomies peculiar to their own age group. During a one-on-one conference with Caribbean poet and eventual Nobel laureate Derek Walcott in the spring of 1985, he asked me why young American poets were compelled to wait longer than their predecessors had before receiving any significant recognition. A decade later, I noticed that among those authors born in the late 1940s and early-to-middle 1950s, only Yusef Komunyakaa and Rita Dove had been awarded the Pulitzer Prize. R.T. Smith, editor of the journal *Shenandoah* at Washington and Lee University and Komunyakaa's coeval, has not garnered such accolades, despite his being no less talented than the Vietnam veteran who wrote *Neon Vernacular: New and Selected Poems* (1994). Frank Stanford, the Mississippi Delta and Ozark prodigy, who was born in 1948, took his own life at age 29, banging off into his heart three rounds from a .22 caliber target pistol with imitation pearl grips. He left behind a 15,283-line stream-of-consciousness epic titled *The Battlefield Where the Moon Says I Love You* (1977) and a cult following, but he remains virtually unknown outside of the Southeastern United States.

Carolyn Forché won the Yale Series of Younger Poets Award for her first volume, *Gathering the Tribes* (1976), and the Lamont Selection from the Academy of American Poets for her second titled *The Country Between Us* (1981), but she has not received the Pulitzer Prize as W.S. Merwin did in 1971, or the National Book Award bestowed on Adrienne Rich in 1974. Despite Forché's having been nominated for National Book Award for *What You Have Heard Is True* (2019), a memoir about her years as a human rights advocate in war-torn El Salvador during the late seventies, this signal honor was ultimately conferred on Sarah M. Broom. Michael Waters was born in 1949, graduated from the heralded University of Iowa Writers Workshop and is arguably the ablest poet of his generation. Still, he has failed to receive the Pulitzer accorded Mark Strand and Charles Wright before age sixty-five. Elizabeth Spires attended Vassar and Johns Hopkins; her second volume titled *Annonciade* (1989), and her third collection *Worlding* (1992) were both quite extraordinary, but the critical acclaim conferred on Sylvia Plath's posthumous *Ariel* (1965) continues to elude her. Moreover, Spires's children's book, *The Mouse of Amherst* (2001), is superior to anything in that genre that Plath ever turned her hand to.

David Baker is the poetry editor of *The Kenyon Review*, and Eric Pankey directs the creative writing program at Washington University in St. Louis, but both poets merit more attention than they have thus far accrued. Alan Dugan belonged to the same generation as Howard Nemerov and James Dickey; although his first collection titled simply *Poems* (1961) won the Yale Series of Younger Poets Award, the National Book Award, the Pulitzer Prize, and the Prix de Rome, his subsequent output was comparatively mediocre, and few students of literature read his poetry today. His most enduring legacy might be the fact that he championed Frank Stanford's work before the latter's untimely death. It could be argued that American poets born in the mid-twentieth century are obliged to await recognition to avoid Dugan's fate, but the assertion seems a specious one, considering the prodigious gifts of R.T. Smith, Michael Waters, Carolyn Forché, David Baker, Eric Pankey, and Natasha Trethewey (who has won a Pulitzer), to name but a few.

In his milestone (as opposed to monolithic) essay defining the metiér of the poet titled "Tradition and the Individual Talent," T.S. Eliot elucidates his theory of "the historical sense" that he considers "indispensable to anyone who would continue to be a poet beyond his [or her] twenty-fifth year." He affirms that "the whole of the literature of Europe from Homer and within it the whole of the literature of his [or her] own country has a simultaneous existence and composes a simultaneous order." Moreover, in his six-hundred page study on Modernism, *The Pound Era* (1971), Hugh Kenner claims that "a cosmos had altered" the moment German archaeologist Heinrich Schliemann's spade struck a limestone citadel deep in the mound of Hissarlik in April 1870: "Troy after Schliemann was no longer a dream, but a place on the map." Indeed, the low promontory in present-day northwest Turkey still overlooks the plain above the glittering Dardanelles, the rumored site of Homer's legendary Troy for over three millennia. For the first time in our age, heroes of flesh and blood quickened the dactylic hexameter of the *Iliad*. Schliemann's discovery and the artifacts unearthed there brought details of the lives Homer described to light, connecting world and word in a way that would have far-reaching effects on modern and contemporary writers. Kenner furthermore articulates the new premium placed on "particularity" in poetry—the hard, clear, precise imagery initially urged by T.E. Hulme and Ezra Pound, later espoused by Harold Bloom, Helen Vendler, and Peter Stitt. Of course, theorists would scoff at the notion that past and present comprise a seamless continuum.

Still, Eliot anticipated this skepticism in "Tradition and the Individual Talent": "Someone said: 'The dead writers are remote from us because we *know* so much more than they did.' Precisely, and they are that which we know." The great bastion unearthed by Schliemann's successor Wilhelm Dörpfeld on the eastern circuit of Troy VI became a symbol for the primacy of the human spirit in twentieth century literature—from Yeats's Thoor Ballylee to Joyce's Martello Tower in *Ulysses* (1922). The Ionian bard's "great tower of Ilion" also presages the apocalypse in T. S. Eliot's *The Wasteland* (1922): "Falling towers / Jerusalem Athens Alexandria / Vienna London." Henceforth, war would be waged on a scale that would dwarf the Greek confederation assembled by Agamemnon on the shores of Asia Minor. But Kenner goes a step beyond Eliot's "historical sense" when he implies that Homer's Troy provides the cornerstone for archaeology as well as Western literature. Schliemann took from the rubble at Hissarlik lanceheads of "pitiless bronze" (an alloy of copper and tin worried from the rocky terrain at Cypris), wooden spindle whorls, electrum pins, sixteen thousand bits of gold stitched into a diadem that supposedly adorned the head and shoulders of the Spartan queen, Helen. To Kenner—and hardly less so to Derek Walcott and Seamus Heaney—it seems a revelation "to believe that the *Odyssey* was composed by a real person in touch with the details of real cities, real harbors, real bowls and cups and pins and spoons, real kings, real warriors, real houses." In his magnum opus *Omeros* (1990), Derek Walcott employs the names of heroes from Homer's *Iliad*, thus imparting both a historical and a mythic dimension to his characters, the St. Lucian fishermen, Achille and Hector. His female protagonist Helen, for whose love the two native islanders contend, Walcott depicts as a waitress in his epic poem's final chapter:

> You can see Helen from the Halcyon. She is dressed
> in the national costume: white, low-cut bodice,
> with the frilled lace at the collar, just a cleft of breast
>
> for the customer when she places their orders
> on the shields of the tables. They can guess the rest
> under the madras skirt with its golden borders.

Throughout *Omeros*, Walcott displays a narrative gift rivaled only by Christopher Logue's among poets living into the twenty-first century. But the latter's prosodic skills in *War Music* do not match those of the Caribbean virtuoso. Note the repetition of aspirate *h* in the phrasal turn "Helen at the Halcyon," the speaker's breath seemingly caught in his beard at the sight of the island girl's "cleft of breast" exposed when she bends to set rum and Coke on the polished table. But there is nothing servile in this young woman's demeanor;

perhaps only a few generations removed from the African continent, the more chains you put on her the less like a slave she looks. Consider the end-stopped off-rhymes in "dressed," "breast," and "rest," in addition to the well-rounded *o* sounds in "orders" and "borders." Her subtle enticements lent full definition by the "madras shirt with its golden borders," Helen endows the shopworn adjective-noun combination "tourist-trap" with a new meaning. She is the living embodiment of the sobriquet "Helen of the West Indies," which connotes the broadsides fired by French and British galleons at one another until the tropical isle was declared a Crown Colony in 1814. In a scant six lines, Walcott rehearses the plight of a culture that failed to gain political independence until 1979.

Seamus Heaney, another Nobel Prize-winning poet discussed in this book, also resorts to the matter of Troy in a search for parallels between the Troubles in Northern Ireland and various crises in the past. "Mycenae Lookout," which probably owes its inception to his earlier version of Sophocles' *Philoctetes* (1991), draws on the fall of Homer's windswept Ilium, infusing his poem with what Eliot termed "the mythic method." Indeed, "Mycenae Lookout" enacts desire in a language of bloodlust and turmoil. Heaney's speaker is the sentry in Aeschylus's *Agamemnon*, a common soldier sent aloft by Clytemnestra to watch for the victory beacon from Troy. Like a number of Heaney's speakers from his earlier work, the sentry expresses both reluctance and complicity; his position in the watchtower affords alienation, but little detachment. His knowledge of the queen's protracted affair with Aegisthus, Agamemnon's cousin, pricks his conscience as much as the war's eventual outcome:

> And [I] saw it coming, clouds bloodshot with the red
> Of victory fires, the raw wood of that dawn
> Igniting and erupting, bearing down
> On a fleeing population. . . .
> Up on my elbows, head back, shutting out
> The agony of Clytemnestra's love shout
> That rose through the palace like the yell of troops
> Hurled by Agamemnon from the ships.

Through metaphor, Heaney compares the final conflict to seething magma bearing down on the Trojan citadel. For the speaker, both the war and the royal liaison are a carnal nightmare: "I'd dream of blood in bright webs in a ford / Of bodies raining down like tattered meat."

In part 2, we never see Agamemnon struggle in the web and tackling of Aegisthus's net or the fatal blow struck home by Clytemnestra. Instead Heaney focuses on the young Cassandra, "a lamb at lambing time, // the bleat of clair— / voyant dread," dubbing her the "little rent / cunt of their guilt." The cruel metonym refers not only to the brutal rape of the Trojan priestess, but also the gruesome wounds inflicted upon her while attending Agamemnon's bath. In a savage mingling of Eros and Thanatos, the Irish poet enacts the perverse fate that overtakes both the sacker of Troy and his lovely spoil:

> in she went
> to the knife
> to the killer wife,
>
> to the net over
> her and her slaver
> to the Troy reaver
>
> saying, "A wipe
> of the sponge
> that's it.
>
> The shadow hinge
> swings unpredict-
> ably and the light's
>
> blanked out."

The terse enjambment and trickling metric suggest blood seeping across the glazed tiles. In part 3, Heaney's narrative harks back to the war, and the speaker's visual acuity sharpens to a foreknowledge similar to Cassandra's. The sentry conjures the Trojan plain during brief periods of armistice with startling clarity: "The little violet's heads bowed on their stems, / The pre-dawn gossamers all dew and scrim / And star-lace." The lulls are all the more painful for what they presage. He describes the blood-letting on the battlefield as a series of isolated vignettes, each confrontation a choreographed horror:

> I saw cities of grass,
> Valleys of longing, tombs and a wind-swept brightness,
> And far off, in a hilly, ominous place,
>
> Small crowds of people watching as a man
> Jumped a fresh earth-wall and another ran
> Amorously, it seemed, to strike him down.

The individual combats between warriors, recast in the language of desire, become brutal trysts with death.

In part 4, the speaker remembers his inability to dispel his image of the doomed Mycenaean king: "My own mind was a bull-pen / where horned King Agamemnon / had stamped his weight in gold." As lord marshal of the Greek coalition, Agamemnon puts on the aspect of a bull, but his helmet-ridge also bears the cuckold's horns. Indeed, nothing will assuage the speaker's conscience for his silent complicity in the regicide plotted by Aegisthus and Clytemnestra: "I moved beyond bad faith: / for his bullion bars, his bonus / was a rope-net and a blood bath." Throughout "Mycenae Lookout" memory perverts desire: the queen yearns for Agamemnon's death because he sacrificed their daughter Iphigenia to gain a fair wind for Troy; the Greeks crave vengeance for the abduction of Helen. Some Irish critics have suggested that Heaney's rewriting of Aeschylus is an analogue for the endless cycle of sectarian reprisals in Northern Ireland.

I have devoted this much space to close readings of poems by Seamus Heaney and Derek Walcott because they are the only Nobel laureates included in this book. Moreover, I have examined Heaney's "Mycenae Lookout" at greater length than I did the brief passage from Walcott's *Omeros* for the simple reason that I've already published a book-length critical study on Heaney's oeuvre and consequently his poetry will receive but a cursory glance in *The Living Artifact*. Like David Baker, I deplore the recent trend toward privileging theory over close engagement with the literary text. For me, a poem is first and foremost a language artifact, and if that conjures an image of the kiln-fired urn with its fast-glazed surface that Cleanth Brooks conceived in his own study titled *The Well Wrought Urn* (1947), then the abstractionists who dominate scholastic discourse today can simply read and recant.

Richard Wilbur:
A Retrospective and Appreciation

At the time of his death on October 14, 2017, ninety-six-year-old Richard Wilbur might well have been what the more conservative elements of the contemporary literary scene would term a national treasure. His third collection of original verse, *Things of This World* (1956), garnered him his first Pulitzer Prize, as well as the National Book Award, at the age of thirty-six. His *New and Collected Poems* (1988) earned Wilbur his second Pulitzer, and made him for almost two decades the only living poet to have attained America's highest belletristic award not once, but twice. He succeeded the nation's first Poet Laureate, Robert Penn Warren, in 1987. Add to this a Bollingen in 1963 for his translation of Molière's *Tartuffe* and a plethora of other achievements in the language arts, and no one could gainsay his stature as a man of letters.

Generally considered as belonging to a generation of poets that includes Elizabeth Bishop, John Berryman, Randall Jarrell, and Robert Lowell—all of whom eventually broke from the New Critical tenets espoused by American formalists such as John Crowe Ransom and Allen Tate—Wilbur alone shunned the solipsistic maunderings of the Confessional mode. From beginning to end, he preferred to write a poetry of wit, candor, and grace, developing in the process an aesthetic that embraced a delicate equipoise between realms both spiritual and empirical. Indeed, Jarrell (usually thought to be ablest critic of the lot) asserted that Wilbur "never goes too far, but he never goes far enough." To redress Jarrell's contention one may well cite the first couplet of Wilbur's "Epistemology":

> Kick at the rock, Sam Johnson, break your bones
> But cloudy, cloudy is the stuff of stones.

Here the sage and serious Dr. Samuel Johnson, in order to deny Bishop George Berkeley's assertion that "there are no material objects, only minds and ideas in those minds," resorts to his famous *Argumentum ad lapidum* by striking the brunt of a boulder with the toe of his boot to the delight and edification of his youthful companion James Boswell. But many believe that Johnson's famous "*Thus* I refute it" only dismisses rather than disproves the cleric's theorem. Wilbur adroitly deploys vowels—short *i* and *o* in "kick" and "rock" followed by long *a* in "break," all bracketed by consonantal *c* and *k* sounds—in order to lend the first line a brutal ire that confirms the English philosopher's position. However, Wilbur seems to demur when he states outright "cloudy, cloudy is the stuff of stones."

Only in the second couplet of "Epistemology" do we encounter an allusive irony missed by many of the poem's commentators:

> We milk the cow of the world, and as we do
> We whisper in her ear, "You are not true."

The phrase "cow of the world" serves as metaphor for what can be apprehended through the five senses, and yet even as she pays out a vital sustenance we intimate or "whisper" our denial of such rich and bountiful concord. But here Wilbur introduces a piquant barb that brings Samuel Johnson back into the picture. When Boswell inquired as to his opinion of certain French metaphysicians, he replied: "Truth will not afford sufficient food to their vanity; so they have betaken themselves to error. Truth, Sir, is a cow which will yield such people no more milk, and so they have gone to milk the bull." Like Johnson, Wilbur apparently believes that the theorist's tendency to over-intellectualize is tantamount to idly disporting oneself.

First and foremost a poet of balance and proportion, Wilbur chooses to avoid extremes, granting equal validity to both corporeal and spiritual worlds. Many observers have noted his affinities with fellow New England poet Robert Frost, but few nowadays address his *agon* with the shade of Edgar Allan Poe. Wilbur cites Poe's aesthetic as one in which "the poet's only escape from a 'fallen planet' is a deliberate retreat from the temporal, rational, physical world into the visionary depths of his mind." He sees Poe as nurturing a blatant *contemptus mundi* in poems such as "The Bells," "To One in Paradise," and "Ulalume." Unlike his predecessor, Wilbur refuses to debase the physical in a fervent desire for the spiritual. Here is the first stanza of "The Death of a Toad":

> A toad the power mower caught,
> Chewed and clipped of a leg, with a hobbling hop has got
> To the garden verge, and sanctuaried him
> Under the cineraria leaves, in the shade
> Of the ashen and heartshaped leaves, in a dim,
> Low, and a final glade.

The dramatic situation is simple enough. Perhaps in all innocence, the third-person speaker has run over a toad in his haste to finish mowing the lawn before dusk settles. Yet certain hierarchical values are implicit in the poet's word choice. Significantly, it is a "power" mower that has overtaken the hapless reptile, its metabolism already slowed by the first onset of evening. The toad, "[c]hewed and clipped of a leg," shakes off its natural torpor long enough—notice the repetition of initial *h* and consonantal *o* in the participle "hobbling hop has got"—to seek asylum, not in some primeval splendor, but rather in a carefully tended garden plot. Of particular interest is Wilbur's transitive verb-object construction "sanctuaried him." The maimed toad settles into himself like monastery stone, at first alert and watchful in the shelter of "cineraria leaves," a plant native to the Canary Islands and southern Africa. The poet relies on various internal rhymes such as "shade," "heartshaped," and "glade" to hold his place in each line; moreover, he establishes an end-stopped pattern of *aabcbc* that remains unobtrusive, so skillful is his knack for enjambment. In fact, most critics agree that Wilbur was the master prosodist of his generation. In the second stanza, the toad, having attained refuge and a momentary equilibrium, begins to feel the onset of the inevitable:

> The rare original heartsblood goes,
> Spends in the earthen hide, in the folds and wizenings, flows
> In the gutters of the banked and staring eyes. He lies
> As still as if he would return to stone,
> And soundlessly attending, dies
> Toward some deep monotone.

The locution "heartsblood" denotes the few drops hoarded in the purple knot of the amphibian's heart, a sticky infusion that now "spends" over a "hide" described as "earthen," one about to return, not to unregenerate clay, but to "stone." Paradoxically, it is also a pouring forth almost sacramental, a liquescence that seeks out "folds" and "wizenings," and replenishes the metaphorical "gutters" of eyes now "banked" and "staring." But the toad feels his life-force begin to ebb, and so listens intently for what lies on the other side of that "deep monotone":

> Toward misted and ebullient seas
> And cooling shores, toward lost Amphibia's emperies.
> Day dwindles, drowning and at length is gone
> In the wide antique eyes, which still appear
> To watch, across the castrate lawn
> The haggard daylight steer.

The cold-blooded little denizen of gardens, rocks, and new-mown lawns breathes in the particle "mists" of other shores, and finds itself ensconced at last in "lost Amphibia's emperies." One catches the glint of precious ore in the short *i* sounds in "misted" and "ebullient," as if the diminutive amphibian had arrived at a veritable El Dorado. Wilbur's subtle variations on a decasyllabic line rife with apt substitutions and inversions is once more in evidence, but even this pales beside his innate capacity for lyrical élan and brilliant wordplay. For example, note the proximity of the adjective "castrate" and the verb "steer," which concludes "The Death of a Toad." The dark witticism addresses the plight of the grey reptile "clipped" by a "power mower" in the first stanza, and comes to rest in the poignant stare, those "wide antique eyes" that behold, in the words of Wallace Stevens, "[n]othing that is not there and the nothing that is."

Perhaps Wilbur's most direct confrontation with Poe's long and foreboding shadow occurs in "The Undead." In "The Fall of the House of Usher," the nineteenth-century fiction writer and poet broaches the subject of vampirism when his narrator is summoned to the ancestral mansion of a schoolfellow named Roderick Usher whose sister, Madeline, is a succubus. Of course, we learn this gradually through Poe's penchant for Gothic imagery, phantasmagoria, and the brother's increasing "mad hilarity" after he "encoffins" the still-living lady Madeline in the family crypt. In the penultimate paragraph, with "blood upon her white robes," she falls on her brother and bears him "to the floor a corpse, and a victim to the terrors he had anticipated." In short, anxiety betokens a wish. Wilbur's approach to the same topic appears to be meditative, occasionally downright whimsical, and he shuns Poe's tendency to degrade the things of this world in an effort to achieve a spiritual sublime. "The Undead" consists of eleven unrhymed tetrastichs and, as one scholar has already observed, each stanzaic pattern resembles a bat on the wing. Moreover, Wilbur's frequent recourse to alliterative stresses calls to mind Old English and early medieval Germanic poetry, thus conjuring the boreal cold of northwest Europe and the Balkan states. Here are the first two stanzas:

> Even as children they were late sleepers,
> Preferring their dreams, even when quick with monsters,
> To the world with all its breakable toys,
> Its compacts with the dying;

> From the stretched arms of withered trees
> They turned, fearing contagion of the mortal,
> And even under the plums of summer
> Drifted like winter moons.

Wilbur's opening is somewhat akin to a psychological profile, although the haunting loveliness of his apt diction and evocative imagery precludes the clinical detachment necessary to such an undertaking. According to the poem's speaker, even the Nosferatu have a childhood, albeit strange and secretive, evoking none of the spontaneity and luminous joy that Wordsworth ascribes to that brief interlude. They prefer dreams begotten of little other than vain fantasy, and "quick with monsters" to this perishable world of "breakable toys," and hence decline to make peace with the notion of mortality, "[i]ts compacts with the dying." The undead shrink from "withered trees," the fruitless beseeching that connotes "contagion of the mortal"; even under "the plums of summer" bruised and ripe to succulence, these pasty wraiths drift cold as melons or "winter moons." In the following stanza, Wilbur offers a cogent explanation of his dubious protagonists' essential plight:

> Secret, unfriendly, pale, possessed
> Of the one wish, the thirst for mere survival,

> They came, as all extremists do
>   In time, to a sort of grandeur.

Possessed by an insatiable thirst, not so much for life as "mere survival," the vampire in his dire extremity comes "[i]n time, to a sort of grandeur." As a consequence, however, the proverbial children of the night have taken on a number of undesirable attributes: "Secret, unfriendly, pale," these solipsists have no current sense of identity with any living thing:

> Now, to their Balkan battlements
> Above the vulgar town of their first lives,
>   They rise at the moon's rising. Strange
>   That their utter self-concern

> Should, in the end, have left them selfless:
> Mirrors fail to perceive them as they float
>   Through the great hall and up the staircase;
>   Nor are the cobwebs broken.

Unlike the Lord Hamlet, whose father's shade "in complete steel" paces the mist-shrouded north bastion of Elsinor, the undead are not "to the manor born" but have transcended "the vulgar town of their first lives" through a spiritual asceticism and an unmitigated desire to be something wholly other. Wilbur's accentual meter, replete with alliterative stresses such as "Balkan battlements," enlivens the resurrection of these spectral figures—note the luminescent double *u* in "moon"—who seem answerable to some ghostly summons. Yet the speaker reminds us that their "utter self-concern" or abject narcissism has ultimately left them "selfless." The gilt mirrors of the great hall deny any semblance of their passing, and the spider's dusty spittle-strings, the frail "cobwebs," remain unbroken.

Wilbur's next two stanzas put one in mind of the horror films so much in vogue during the late fifties and early sixties; indeed, the poet seems at once amused and bemused when relating the following vignette:

> Into the pallid night emerging
> Wrapped in their flapping capes, routinely maddened
>   By a wolf's cry, they stand for a moment
>   Stoking the mind's eye

> With lewd thoughts of the pressed flowers
> And bric-a-brac of rooms with something to lose,—
>   Of love-dismembered dolls, and children
>   Buried in quilted sleep.

The oxymoron "pallid night" is a subtle touch, but the wind-rumpled cadence and repetition of plosive *p* in the phrase "[w]rapped in their flapping capes" proves genuinely sublime. This is a cinematic vampire, one "routinely" alive to the enraptured keening of wolves in the hills, who "stand[s] for a moment" as if waiting for the proper cue and the camera to begin rolling. Wilbur revives a dead metaphor when he zooms in on the Nosferatu "[s]toking the mind's eye," and allows us a moment to savor his pun on the appellation Bram Stoker, author of *Dracula* (1897). In the ensuing stanza, the poet adopts a more whimsical tone as he contemplates the memorabilia of those about to fall prey to the incubus. Here the sonic properties of certain locutions—"lewd," "room," "lose"— resonate with the alliterative tempo of "bric-a-brac" to telling effect. Moreover, the mention of "love-dismembered dolls" seems all the more poignant when we realize that such passionate attachment to the things of this world is beyond the vampire's purview.

Wilbur's reanimated corpse plies between the ethereal nothingness that "the mirrors fail to perceive" in stanza five and the frenetic creatures of the eighth tetrastich: "Then they are off in a negative frenzy, / Their black shapes cropped into sudden bats / That swarm, burst, and are gone." Here the poet resorts to the argot of cinematography, words such as "negative" and "cropped," to designate bats bursting like caped riders from a rook-haunted wood. But then the poet abruptly brings us back to the temporal world:

> Thinking
> Of a thrush cold in the leaves
>
> Who has sung his few summers truly,
> Or an old scholar resting his eyes at last,
> We cannot be much impressed with vampires,
> Colorful though they are.

Although cold among the foliage, the thrush stands as a counter-sublime to the volatile and "cropped" figure of the vampire in its winged permutation; unlike the undead, he is a creature of time and chance singing his "few summers truly" with nothing plangent in the mellifluous air. By sheer proximity, the "old scholar," his lamp quenched and his intellectual labors relinquished for one evening, shares the avian spirit's knowledge (in the thrush's case instinctual) of inevitability and the eventual lot of all sensate beings. The vampire has been free for centuries from "contagion of the mortal," but can never partake of this wisdom whether innate or earned. Therefore, "[w]e cannot be much impressed with vampires, / Colorful though they are." Wilbur's concluding stanzas put all in perspective:

> Nevertheless, their pain is real,
> And requires our pity. Think how sad it must be

> To thirst always for a scorned elixir,
>   The salt quotidian blood
>
> Which, if mistrusted, has no savor;
>   To prey on life forever and not possess it,
>   As rock-hollows, tide after tide,
>   Glassily strand the sea.

Pain is the one mortal extremity yet available to the undead, and if it "requires our pity," we must remember that pathos is an emotion not unmixed with contempt. Thus, there will be no stakes of ash or solar incinerations. Their ilk's craving for "the salt quotidian blood" puts them beyond the pale insofar as fellow-feeling is concerned, and leaves us to reflect significantly on the "rock-hollows" that with the tide's diurnal ebb and flow "[g]lassily strand the sea." Some critics claim that "The Undead" is a thinly veiled look askance at Confessional poets like Robert Lowell with his earnest imploration in "Florence" that we "[p]ity the monsters!" or Sylvia Plath's strident harangue in "Daddy"—"[t]here's a stake in your fat black heart"—but more probably it stems from Wilbur's need to engage and dispel Poe's antithetical influence.

In *The World's Hieroglyphic Beauty* (1985), the late Peter Stitt designates Thomas Traherne as another poetic forebear with whom Wilbur must come to terms. One among a number of seventeenth century Anglican lyricists— including John Donne, George Herbert, and Henry Vaughan—labelled by Samuel Johnson as the "Metaphysical Poets," theologians whose abiding aim was to couple fervent emotion with intellectual rigor, Traherne lived as an obscure country priest and did not move in literary circles. His contribution to English letters was rescued by William T. Brooke late in the nineteenth century when he discovered several of Traherne's works in "a barrow of books to be trashed," euphemistically referred to as a London "street bookstall." In retrospect, Traherne's passionate love of the natural world that anticipated the Era of the Romantic Triumph by a hundred and thirty years may well be his true legacy to literature.

The title and some of the perceptions in Wilbur's "A World Without Objects IS a Sensible Emptiness" derive from Traherne's *Centuries of Meditations* (1908), in particular "Second Century, Meditation 65." Here Traherne insists that love is a necessary condition of the full and complete life: "The whole world ministers to you as the theatre of your love. It sustains you and all objects that you may continue to love them. Without which it were better for you to have no being. Life without objects is a sensible emptiness, and that is a greater misery than Death or Nothing." Interestingly enough, like T. S. Eliot's "Journey of the Magi," Wilbur's poem involves a setting forth into regions unknown:

> The tall camels of the spirit
> Steer for their deserts, passing the last groves loud
> With the sawmill shrill of the locust, to the whole honey of the arid
> Sun. They are slow, proud
>
> And move with a stilted stride
> To the land of sheer horizon, hunting Traherne's
> *Sensible emptiness,* there where the brain's lantern-slide
> Revels in vast returns.

Wilbur's "tall camels of the spirit" are metaphorical beasts, not the "galled, sore-footed, refractory" dromedaries of Eliot's poem. Notice how the mellifluous *l* sounds in the first stanza take on a fierce somnolence in the adjective-noun combination "sawmill shrill" as these draft animals and their riders, who are presumed abstractionists, quit the precincts of the mutable world for the languorous "whole honey of the arid / Sun." Wilbur's syllabic gait corresponds to the "proud" and deliberate "stilted stride" of this caravan bent on "sheer horizon," the utter vacuity or *spiritus mortem* that Traherne calls a "*Sensible emptiness.*" As Peter Stitt remarks, "the light source for the 'brain's lantern-slide' is self-generated and abstract, unattached to corporeal reality." Wilbur's vocative "O" seeks to reprove the nihilistic impulse to "drink / Of pure mirage":

> O connoisseurs of thirst,
> Beasts of my soul who long to learn to drink
> Of pure mirage, those prosperous islands are accurst
> That shimmer on the brink
>
> Of absence; auras, lustres,
> And all shinings need to be shaped and borne.
> Think of those painted saints, capped by the early masters
> With bright, jauntily worn
>
> Aureate plates, or even
> Merry-go-round rings. Turn, O turn
> From the fine sleights of the sand, from the long empty oven
> Where flames in flamings burn.

Wilbur decries the refined aspirations of those who would drink of a pure sublime or "mirage" that betokens nothingness; the disembodied if affluent archipelagos of longing offer little succor to those who divest themselves of any corporeal presence. "Auras" and "lustres"—the play on "lust" is compelling—must be lent a certain heft or definition, a malleable and substantive being. Wilbur invokes the knowing hands of Quattrocento "masters" to adorn the heads of "painted saints" nimbus-lit with "[a]ureate plates." The ideogrammatic "[t]urn, O turn" leads to the desired corrective:

Back to the trees arrayed
In bursts of glare, to the halo-dialing run
Of the country creeks, and the hills' bracken tiaras made
Gold in the sunken sun,

Wisely watch for the sight
Of the supernova burgeoning over the barn,
Lampshine blurred in the steam of beasts, the spirit's right
Oasis, light incarnate.

These concluding stanzas demonstrate not only Wilbur's preternatural prosodic skills, but also his uncanny knack for figurative language and memorable tropes. The poet's visionary yen for the radiant verdure of boughs—kindled by the plosive *b* in "bursts"—culminates in an insistent "glare" that fails to consume the branches it is engrafted to. The rustic "country creeks" go on "dialing" up the sun-refracted and chill rainbows that span them bank to bank. The hills are crowned with "bracken tiaras" transmuted to "[g]old" as the sun lies "sunken" on the horizon. Significantly, Wilbur enjoins us to "[w]isely watch"—an unmistakable allusion to Eliot's magus—for "the supernova burgeoning over the barn" like the Star of the Nativity burning over the hayricks and stables of Bethlehem Ephrata in the first century A. D. When he speaks of "lampshine blurred in the steam of beasts," one breathes deep the ammonia rising off the liquid excrement of livestock in the shadow of the manger. As Peter Stitt avers, "the lampshine (final answer to the 'brain's lantern-slide') is projected through the steam from farm animals—this is "the spirit's right / Oasis, light incarnate." The "spirit's right / Oasis" proffers both balm and benediction, a commingling of the spiritual and corporeal that Wilbur deems crucial to our ultimate well-being. Without the condition of "light incarnate," the spirit made flesh, we face what Thomas Traherne labels "a greater misery than Death or Nothing," a notion with which Wilbur wholeheartedly concurs.

Perhaps "Cottage Street, 1953," affords the student of Richard Wilbur's poetry the most salient instance of his belief that artists should lead lives of balance and due proportion, and thereby avoid the fate of second-generation Confessional poets like Sylvia Plath and Anne Sexton, both of whom eventually committed suicide. The poem's setting is the home of Edna Ward, a long-time resident of Wellesley, Massachusetts, and close friend of Aurelia Plath, mother of the troubled and sublimely gifted Sylvia. Following her junior year at Smith College, the fledging poet spent the summer in New York City as a guest editor at *Mademoiselle*. The stress of editorial board responsibilities and the attendant social obligations led to a complete mental and emotional collapse, and thence to the first medically documented attempt on her own life. On August 24, 1953, she took a lethal overdose of sleeping pills and made her way into the crawlspace beneath her mother's house. The subsequent discovery and resuscitation is chillingly recounted by Plath in "Lady Lazarus," which appeared in the posthumous *Ariel* (1965). Wilbur's "Cottage Street, 1953," begins in Edna Ward's parlor:

> Framed in her phoenix fire-screen, Edna Ward
> Bends to the tray of Canton, pouring tea
> For frightened Mrs. Plath; then, turning toward
> The pale, slumped daughter, and my wife, and me,
>
> Asks if we would prefer it weak or strong.
> Will we have milk or lemon, she enquires?
> The visit seems already strained and long.
> Each in his turn, we tell her our desires.

When "Cottage Street, 1953" was first published in *The Mind-Reader: New Poems (1976)*, a new method of critical reading was putting feminism and women's rights at the foreground of literary texts. Here is where Plath began to be viewed as a victim of patriarchal power. The poem consists of seven quatrains measured out in a symmetrical and virtually flawless iambic pentameter. Wilbur begins with a participial phrase—"[f]ramed in her phoenix fire-screen"—that seethes with fricative *f* and long *e* sounds, and is at once allusive and brilliantly anachronistic. Not yet written in 1953, the closure of Plath's strident and holocaustal "Lady Lazarus"—"Herr God, Herr Lucifer, / Beware / Beware // Out of the ash / I rise with my red hair / And I eat men like air"—conjures the bird from Arabian mythology that dies in the flames of a cinnamon pyre and is reborn amid the ashes. By way of contrast, the genteel and gracious hostess, Edna Ward, moves attentively among her guests, framed by the cold iron of a fire-screen behind which the natal embers settled and winked out two seasons ago. The tea she pours is a Chinese gourmet blend, and she ministers to her guests—Aurelia and Sylvia Plath, Richard and Charlee Wilbur—in an almost ritualistic manner, offering first milk to ameliorate or perhaps a twist of lemon for zest. Only the reclining posture of "the pale, slumped daughter," dazed in the spark-littered aftermath of electroshock therapy, violates the poise of Wilbur's balanced metric and urbane dismay. Indeed, he feels impotent to help by either example or precept:

> It is my office to exemplify
> The published poet in his happiness,
> Thus cheering Sylvia, who has wished to die;
> But half-ashamed, and impotent to bless,
>
> I am a stupid life-guard who has found,
> Swept to his shallows by the tide, a girl
> Who, far from shore, has been immensely drowned,
> And stares through water now with eyes of pearl.

In the first of the two stanzas above, Wilbur states his purpose or "office" within this setting of consummate domesticity, and frankly owns that he is not equal to the task. In his poetry, the ocean represents Chaos or oblivion, and here is this youthful prodigy, "immensely drowned," washed onto the shoals or "shallows" of his more or less secure demesne (of course, we must remember that Wilbur saw combat in the European Theater of World War II). Now the poet's intertextual resonances become multilayered and complex. He ventures that Sylvia "stares through water now with eyes of pearl," and awakens us to the song of the erring spirit Ariel in Shakespeare's *The Tempest*: "Full fathom five thy father lies / Of his bones are coral made; / Those are pearls that were his eyes." If Plath's eyes have taken on a visionary luster, we recall too the nacreous night crawlers in "Lady Lazarus": "The second time I meant / To last it out and not come back at all. / I rocked shut / As a sea shell. / They had to call and call / And pick the worms off me like sticky pearls." In the fifth stanza, Wilbur concedes a moral defeat:

> How large is her refusal; and how slight
> The genteel chat whereby we recommend
> Life, of a summer afternoon, despite
> The brewing dusk which hints that it may end.

Despite the well-intentioned affability and refined largesse of her interlocutors, Plath's "large" refusal makes all the more ominous the "brewing dusk," the prospect of Sirius breaking clear in the blue vault of heaven. Wilbur ends with a short paean to his hostess and a succinct appraisal of Plath's artistic merit:

> And Edna Ward shall die in fifteen years,
> After her eight-and-eighty summers of
> Such grace and courage as permit no tears,
> The thin hand reaching out, the last word *love*,
>
> Outliving Sylvia who, condemned to live,
> Shall study for a decade, as she must,
> To state at last her brilliant negative
> In poems free and helpless and unjust.

Wilbur compares the purposive decorum and heartfelt solicitude of his mother-in-law Edna Ward over and against the as-yet-unstated "brilliant negative" of the twenty-two-year-old Sylvia Plath. He sees the courage and dignity that the older woman embodied as optimal inasmuch as we are all destined to vanish through the star-filter of memory; but her final utterance "*love*," is one that befits our remembrance. Of course, Wilbur must have been aware that "Love" is the first word of "Morning Song," the poem that opens *Ariel*: "Love set you going like a fat gold watch." Nothing could be more affecting than the observation that

Plath has been "condemned to live," to immerse herself "for a decade" in the Western canon before taking her rightful place on the steep slopes of Parnassus. Wilbur's final assessment is three-tiered—"free," "helpless," "unjust"—the last adjective rankling Plath's adherents most.

One of the truly engaging entries in Wilbur's *Collected Poems: 1943-2004*, "Beowulf" shows the gifted stylist confronting the canonical Old English epic in his own inimitable manner. He foregoes the traditional Germanic prosodic measure, the four-stress alliterative line with each hemistich separated by a medial caesura, in favor of a quantitative meter variously truncated or extended a half-foot. In contrast to the anonymous *scop* who focused on the violence-prone heroic culture of Scandinavian forebears whose fifth and sixth-century migrations from the northwest European continent eventually led to the formation of the Anglo-Saxon Heptarchy that included the insular petty kingdoms of East Anglia, Kent, Mercia, Northumbria, Essex, Sussex, and Wessex, Wilbur presents us not with a merely transcriptive, but rather his own deeply introspective retelling of the Geatish prince's story. Indeed, we see little of what the chroniclers dubbed "a wind-age, a wolf-age" in the first two stanzas:

> The land was overmuch like scenery,
> The flowers attentive, the grass too garrulous green;
> In the lake like a dropped handkerchief could be seen
> The lark's reflection after the lark was gone;
> The Roman road lay paved too shiningly
> For a road so many men had traveled on.
>
> Also the people were strange, were strangely warm.
> The king recalled the father of his guest,
> The queen brought mead in a studded cup, the rest
> Were kind, but in all was a vagueness and a strain,
> Because they lived in a land of daily harm.
> And they said the same things again and again.

From the speaker's perspective, the very landscape seems a large contrivance, too self-consciously worked up, the "grass too garrulous green," and paradoxically figured in the jog-trot alliterative rhythms of the Old English original. The lark is an afterimage in a transfer of sky on the lake's surface, and the rheum-glistening brick has been trod impossibly smooth under the boots of Hadrian's legions. Wilbur's version is plainly meant for those who have more than a nodding familiarity with the pagan Germanic saga belonging to a centuries-old oral tradition recast and scribed down in Old English by an imaginative writer living in the Judeo-Christian dispensation instituted by the Synod of Whitby in 664 A. D. Conspicuously missing is the compound metaphor or kenning—whale-road (sea), sea-steed (ship), wound-dew (blood), battle-kite (carrion hawk)—a device or lack thereof that literally makes "strange" the whole scenario that begins stanza two of Wilbur's recitation. The Danish ring-lord, King Hrothgar, recalls to Beowulf his father's visit as a youthful refugee to Heorot, and his queen fetches mead in a "studded cup"—the beautifully chiming assonantal *u* sounds awakening dim memories of Old High German cadences—and the people seek to ingratiate themselves in the name of some inchoate fear.

In the ensuing stanzas, Wilbur relates with a synoptic clarity the midnight confrontation between Beowulf and the moor-walking Grendel. The New England poet does not elaborate on the Geatish warrior's *beot* or binding oath to meet the hell-thane hand-to-hand and without weapons in Hrothgar's horn-rigged manor. Oddly enough, he depicts Grendel, not as some ghoulish aberration, but as a child bereft of love and doomed to the loneliness of all pariahs:

> It was a childish country; and a child,
> Grown monstrous, so besieged them in the night
> That all their daytimes were a dream of fright
> That it would come down and own them to the bone.
> The hero, to his battle reconciled,
> Promised to meet the monster all alone.
>
> So then the people wandered to their sleep
> And left him standing in the echoed hall.
> They heard the rafters rattle fit to fall,
> The child departing with a broken groan,
> And found their champion in a rest so deep
> His head lay harder sealed than any stone.

Wilbur's assertion that "[i]t was a childish country" amounts to a cultural indictment; Grendel, "a child, / Grown monstrous" is the product of a milieu based on a score-taking reciprocity, an era of the *wergild* or man-price exacted more in the spirit of the Old Testament tribal values of "an eye for an eye, a tooth for a tooth" than on Christian doctrine. An exile from the hearths of men, Grendel battens on the surrounding countryside both psychically and physically, his impulse to rend and devour captured in the incisive *n* sounds that Wilbur implements in the passage "come down and own them to the bone." Beowulf also undergoes an isolation and dark night of the soul; the retainers of his own warrior elite or *comitatus* are nowhere at hand as he waits in the deep "echoed hall." Wilbur does ring up deft variations on the alliterative register when Beowulf and Grendel come to grips: "[t]hey heard the rafters rattle fit to fall," and one cannot fail to notice that it is "[t]he child departing with a broken groan," hell's fosterling sundered even from himself with a soul-belittling mortal hurt. Even the stalwart Geatish warrior lies catatonic in the aftermath of such a desperate encounter. The Spear-Danes find "their champion in a rest so deep / His head lay harder sealed than any stone."

Rhyming *abbcac*, stanza five recapitulates the first, although the people seem strangely aloof now that danger is no longer in the offing:

> The land was overmuch like scenery,
> The lake gave up the lark, but now its song
> Fell to no ear, the flowers too were wrong,
> The day was fresh and pale and swiftly old,
> The night put out no smiles upon the sea;
> And the people were strange, the people strangely cold.

Now no one hearkens to the fell accents of the lark; the bounteous floral offshoots of the countryside seem askew, and the shadows lengthen as the day sublimes into evening. Wilbur makes no mention of Grendel's mother, the tarn-hag who hankers for revenge, nor does he touch on the dragon, the winged firedrake, that later scorches the thatched roofs of all Geatland. Nevertheless, the Danes bid Beowulf a hero's farewell:

> They gave him horse and harness, helmet and mail,
> A jeweled shield, and ancient battle-sword,
> Such gifts as are the hero's hard reward
> And bid him do again what he has done.
> These things he stowed beneath his parting sail,
> And wept that he could share them with no son.
>
> He died in his own country a kinless king,
> A name heavy with deeds, and mourned as one
> Will mourn for the frozen year when it is done.
> They buried him next the sea on a thrust of land:
> Twelve men rode round his barrow all in a ring,
> Singing of him what they could understand.

Wilbur devotes a scant two lines to Hrothgar's generous tokens, never alluding to those precious artifacts that include a torque of twisted gold fit to rival "the Brosings' neck-chain." However, Beowulf does receive "horse and harness, helmet and mail," Wilbur's initial aspirates—interspersed with *r* and rolling *l*—evoking the palpable surfaces and textures that inhere in all Germanic tongues. The hero also gets a richly embossed shield and a "battle-sword," the latter sadly lacking the engraved runes of the traditional patrilineal blade. Thus his hard-won trophies are destined to become grave-goods: "[T]hese things he stowed beneath his parting sail, / And wept that he could share them with no son." As he feared, Beowulf returns to the land of the Weather-Geats, and eventually dies "a kinless king," neither *scop* nor *skald* singing his apotheosis. The lay falls instead to a dozen mounted hearth-companions in full war-graith: "Twelve men rode round his barrow all in a ring, / Singing of him what they could understand." Except when he finds it expedient to do otherwise, Wilbur not only tends to eschew the alliterative template of the original *Beowulf*, but he also strives to reimagine the tale in terms of a millennial strangeness that knows no sovereign spirit bent on living forever in the choicest gleanings of the word-hoard.

So far in this retrospective and appreciation of Richard Wilbur's career, this critic has dealt only peripherally with the mundane particulars of the poet's day-to-day existence, but "Security Lights, Key West" offers a few signal opportunities to do so. America's southernmost inhabited island, Key West's notoriety as a writer's retreat began on the cusp of the Great Depression when John Dos Passos invited Ernest Hemingway down for some deep-sea fishing. Other literary luminaries followed suit, and soon Hemingway, Tennessee Williams, Robert Frost, and Wallace Stevens were guests in the opulent gardens adjoining the old colonial homestead of Miss Jessie Porter, a fifth-generation inhabitant and island conservationist. During the sixties, Key West's subtropical enticements proved irresistible to Richard and Charlee Wilbur, John and Judith Ciardi, as well as James Merrill and his partner David Jackson. Perhaps Charlee described best the ethnic and cultural diversity that was part and parcel of the south Florida isle's intrinsic charm: "Everyone got along well there. It was Navy / civilian, gay / straight, black / white, Cubans. Benign funny jokes being told, each group to the other." But over the decades everything changed tone and tint as the restored "conch houses" of the Old Town yielded to spacious condominiums; thereafter came a new generation of writers with their carefully nurtured antagonisms and shoals of groupies. Wilbur's mood is at once nostalgic and pensive as he ponders Key West's last vestiges of magic:

> Mere minutes from Duval Street's goings-on,
> The midnight houses of this quiet block,
> With their long-lidded shutters, are withdrawn
> In sleep past bush and picket, bolt and lock,
>
> Yet each façade is raked by the strange glare
> Of halogen, in which fantastic day
> Veranda, turret, balustraded stair
> Glow like settings of some noble play.

Duval Street was the hub of Key West nightlife, including restaurants like Le Mistral; not too far distant stood Logun's Lobster House with its ragtime pianist Billy Nine Fingers, and the porn emporium, Munro Theater. The poet summons and banishes the neon-lit boulevard from the fog-shrouded past with the noun "goings-on." For now, he broods on the "midnight" houses of the residential quarter, conscious of the decent lives within them. The glottal stops in the end rhymes "block" and "lock" seem to forestall abruptly any sort of intrusion. Indeed, one listens for the tumblers falling into place. But security lights bathe the slumbering neighborhood in a halcyon "glare," the ethereal illumination singling out "[v]eranda, turret, balustrated stair," and setting the stage for the "fantastic" reenactments of a literary collective unconscious:

> As if the isle were Prospero's, you seem
> To glimpse great summoned spirits as you pass.
> Cordelia tells her truth, and Joan her dream,
> Becket prepares for the sacrifice of Mass,
>
> A dog-tired watchman in the mirador
> Waits for the flare that tells of Troy's defeat,
> And other lofty ghosts are heard, before
> You turn into a narrow, darker street.

Wilbur identifies with Shakespeare's necromancer who could, from his island promontory, command the dark cloud masses walling on the horizon and dispatch his "tricksy" minion Ariel to do his bidding. A cavalcade of transcendent "spirits" passes beneath his gaze. Cordelia refuses to flatter, and her lack of unctuousness costs her both patrimony and life. Shaw's Joan raises the siege of Orleans at the behest of Saints Michael, Margaret, and Catharine, crowning the exiled dauphin Charles VII at Reims Cathedral. Eliot's Thomas à Becket removes from one finger the golden triple lions of England's Chancellor and slips onto the other the purple stone designating him Archbishop of Canterbury. Aeschylus's lone sentinel scans the night Aegean for the watch-fires signaling the fall of Troy's citadel. All of these apparitions belong to a painstakingly earned inheritance, a lifetime spent in service to the republic of letters. Only when Wilbur turns "into a narrow, darker street" does he enter *terra incognita*.

> There, where no glow or glare outshines the sky,
> The pitch-black houses loom on either hand
> Like hulks adrift in fog, as you go by.
> It comes to mind that they are built on sand,
>
> And that there may be drama here as well,
> Where so much murk looks up at star on star:
> Though, to be sure, you cannot always tell
> Whether those lights are high or merely far.

Unlike Frost stopping at the margin of a snowy hinterland for a moment of solitary reflection before moving on, Wilbur wanders through a shantytown of "pitch-black houses" toward what ends he cannot possibly know. No landmark or touchstone guides his progress; indeed, the poor domiciles resemble "hulks adrift in fog," and it occurs to the poet that these dim precincts "are built on sand," without any cultural or historical bent toward affirmation. But Wilbur concedes "there may be drama here as well," some psychic or interstellar epiphany ("[w]here so much murk looks up at star on star") available even to those living on the threshold of awareness. The poet's technical virtuosity—his tonal felicities and regular metric—enhances his overall meaning: "Though, to be sure, you cannot always tell / Whether those lights are high or merely far."

If "Security Lights, Key West" speaks to the mutable nature of life's most cherished interludes, many of Wilbur's later poems contemplate the prodigal delights and ineffable sadness that inform our most intimate connections. Unlike many another poet in his soul's fecklessness and heart's caprice, his wife Charlee and his Muse were one and the same. Most of the poems about her are marked by a tender regard and genuine affection, as in "A Late Aubade." A traditional poem wherein lovers greet the dawn, the very belatedness of Wilbur's morning song renders superfluous any *carpe diem* exhortations, and summarily dismisses such clichéd feminine pursuits as "rising in an elevator cage / Toward Ladies' Apparel" or engaging at luncheon in "a screed of someone's loves / With pitying head":

> Think of all the time you are not
> Wasting, and would not care to waste,
> Such things, thank God, not being to your taste.
> Think what a lot
>
> Of time, by woman's reckoning,
> You've saved and so may spend on this,
> You who would rather lie in bed and kiss
> Than anything.

Wilbur's speaker counts himself most fortunate that the lady of his choosing would rather beguile the forenoon sharing wild plum kisses in his casual embrace than browsing the racks of Victoria's Secret or commiserating with another woman regarding affairs of the heart. But a gentle reminder brings the erstwhile amorist around:

> It's almost noon, you say? If so,
> Time flies, and I need not rehearse
> The rosebuds-theme of centuries of verse.
> If you *must* go,

Wait for a while, then slip downstairs
And bring us up some chilled white wine,
And some blue cheese, and crackers, and some fine
Ruddy-skinned pears.

Charlee's input is brief, an observation that the day is nearing its meridian. Wilbur implores her to dally a bit longer, to fetch up a carafe of ice-hot Rhine wine, some aged "blue cheese," and pears rouged to the fleshly hues of connubial bliss. His gustatory imagery amounts to nothing less than a subliminal invitation to yet another tryst. For some, the lexical moderation of "A Late Aubade" makes the glib accents of Berryman's risqué "Dream Song 4" read like those of a fumbling adolescent.

On April 2, 2007, Charlee Wilbur, who had been suffering from pneumonia and pleurisy, had a nurse call her husband from the Cooley Dickinson Hospital in North Hampton, Massachusetts: "Tell him to come earlier today, and that I've asked for a priest." According to a recent biography, the poet arrived in time for his wife of sixty-five years to look for a brief moment into his eyes: "Then she peacefully lay back and I scarcely knew she had died." However, Wilbur's creative life did not end with Charlee's passing; he continued giving public readings and translating from French, Russian, and Latin (including gnomic and riddling verse from Symphosius's *Aenigmata*), and in 2010, he published *Anterooms* with Houghton Mifflin Harcourt. In lieu of a dedication to Charlee, the slim volume opens with "The House":

Sometimes, on waking, she would close her eyes
For a last look at that white house she knew
In sleep alone, and held no title to,
And had not entered yet, for all her sighs.

What did she tell me of that house of hers?
White gatepost; terrace; fanlight of the door;
A widow's walk above the bouldered shore;
Salt winds that ruffle the surrounding firs.

Is she now there, wherever there may be?
Only a foolish man would hope to find
That haven fashioned by that dreaming mind.
Night after night, my love, I put to sea.

In "The House," Wilbur addresses the affinities between dreams and the hereafter; he recollects a modest double-decked edifice that Charlee knew from reveries both waking and sleeping, a domestic retreat that had its foundation in the wish-fulfillment of childhood. He recognizes certain features that she imparted to him over the years: the gatepost (significantly whitewashed), the terrace, the door's stained-glass "fanlight," and the imperious "widow's walk" that overlooks "[s]alt winds that ruffle the surrounding firs" (notice how the fricative *f* in "ruffle" and "firs" arouses a soughing among the evergreens). Wilbur's next question goes beyond the merely rhetorical: "Is she now there, wherever there may be?" His final answer is to venture forth into an eternal unknown: "Night after night, my love, I put to sea."

At the time it first appeared in *Things of This World*, Randall Jarrell declared "A Baroque Wall-Fountain in the Villa Sciarra" without the least hesitation "one of the most marvelously beautiful, one of the most nearly perfect poems any American has ever written." Considering other masterpieces such as Frost's "Stopping by Woods on a Snowy Evening," Stevens's "Sunday Morning," Lowell's "The Quaker Graveyard in Nantucket," and Plath's "Candles," one is compelled to assent. To be sure, Richard Wilbur never authored an epic length poem—James Merrill's *The Changing Light at Sandover* comes most immediately to mind—but he indisputably penned a half-dozen or so lyrics not likely to be shaken loose from the canon anytime soon. His sacramental vision and masterful idiom set him apart as one of finest poets of his era.

Forms Open and Closed:
The Poetry of W. S. Merwin

The poetry of open form written in America during the past thirty-five years can be more readily described, as Samuel Johnson once described poetry in general, by saying what it is not rather than what it is. Most scholars agree that it began as a reaction against a perception of the New Critical concept of "closure," the supposed desire of theorists and practitioners such as Cleanth Brooks and John Crowe Ransom to convert the poem into a self-contained object, a language artifact as polished and perfected as an urn. By taking "the poem out of competition with scientific, historical, and philosophic propositions," Brooks clearly intends to emphasize its separateness from mere discourse; a poem for him is a discrete object of art and not a commentary on the life that surrounds us. And while few critics, myself included, would join chronic naysayers such as Terry Eagleton in labeling the New Criticism "the ideology of an uprooted, defensive intelligentsia who reinvented in literature what they could not locate in reality," these proponents of the formalist tradition in modern American poetry did most certainly emphasize correct grammar, logic, regular meter, rhyme, stanzaic form, structural coherence, compression, and control. While laudable in themselves, these conventions became increasingly associated, in the minds of young poets such as W. S. Merwin, with a rigorous ethos wherein expression was seldom valid unless concise, subtle, and complex. Intellect held sway over impulse: the formalist tradition of the fifties was exemplified by the laconic humor of Philip Larkin in England and the choleric wit of Howard Nemerov in America.

Revolt against the perceived values of the New Criticism was inevitable. Ginsberg's *Howl and Other Poems* (1956) made an early assault against the New Critical way of writing, moving away from the poetic wit of writers such as John Donne and T. S. Eliot and toward the visionary mode of Blake and Whitman. Other poets born during the third decade of this century gravitated to the open forms of Ezra Pound and William Carlos Williams, and many critics considered Merwin the foremost of these. In *Crowell's Handbook of Contemporary American Poetry* (1973), Karl Malkoff called Merwin "the representative poet of his time, having gone through a process that is not only common to many of his contemporaries, but a microcosm of the history of modern verse as well." That same year, in an essay that also considers the poetry of John Ashbery and A. R. Ammons, Harold Bloom referred to Merwin as "the indubitably representative poet of my generation."

Whether Merwin is any more representative a poet than Sylvia Plath, James Wright, or Galway Kinnell is debatable, but the poetry he wrote beginning in the early sixties does indeed seem antithetical to the New Critical desire for artifice, formality, and compression. From "Lemuel's Blessing" on, his poems have aimed at spontaneous utterance, or at least the illusion of it, and his method of composition has emphasized the poem as an ongoing process of the mind rather than a closed and finished product of language. In lieu of humanist values, Merwin increasingly has opted for what David Perkins defines as "creatural realism"—"emphasis on man's vulnerable and suffering body and mortality as these unite all human beings"—while extending the idea to include all living species.

The two volumes under consideration in this essay, *The Second Four Books of Poems* (1975) and *Travels* (1993), reveal how Merwin first ventured onto the cleared path of open forms, then lost his way in an unfortunate detour, and finally has begun to move in a new direction that is already leading to some of the most substantial work he has written. *The Second Four Books of Poems* gathers under one cover the books Merwin published during the sixties and early seventies—*The Moving Target* (1963), *The Lice* (1967), *The Carrier of Ladders* (1970), and *Writings to an Unfinished Accompaniment* (1973). In *The Moving Target,* Merwin evolves a world view that opposes both the aesthetic and ideological principles of the New Criticism. Resorting to various methods of defamiliarization, including an animism that often declines to distinguish between subject and object, Merwin develops a disjunctive and associational style that privileges intuition over intellect. *The Lice* carries the experiment still further in an effort to create a self-sufficient open form, one that provides for its own metamorphosis. However, Merwin's arrangements become increasingly obscure and elliptical; they acquire a phantasmic tonality that corresponds, for example, to the chaos of the Vietnam War. By the time *The Carrier of Ladders* and *Writings to an Unfinished Accompaniment,* appeared, however, Merwin has retreated into a private vision that relies on a generic vocabulary and a minimalist style; the intertextual resonances that had been awakened in *The Moving Target* and *The Lice* now lapse into an obsessive metalanguage, a system of signs and counters that seldom refers beyond itself. Fortunately, in *Travels,* his most recent book of poems, Merwin breaks free of this linguistic trap and turns to a communal spirit that is almost entirely lacking in his previous thirteen volumes. In his "Cover Note" to the volume, he offers us "words that I hope might seem / as though they had occurred / to you and you would take / them with you as your own." In doing so, he modifies both his vision and aesthetic so that they might include a larger audience than ever before.

II

W. S. Merwin's career had perhaps the most auspicious beginning of any poet in his generation. Having studied under R. P. Blackmur at Princeton, he graduated with a degree in Romance languages in 1948 and spent 1950 tutoring Robert Graves's son on the island of Majorca. When W. H. Auden proclaimed Merwin's first book-length manuscript, *A Mask for Janus,* the winner of the Yale Younger Poets Award for 1952, Merwin was launched in earnest at the age of twenty-five. By the time Atheneum issued *The First Four Books of Poems* in 1975, he had been the recipient of both the P.E.N. Translation Prize (1969) and the Pulitzer Prize (1971). Merwin's poetry not only exhibits intelligence and industry, but also savors that "Muse of fire" so ardently invoked by Shakespeare in the opening lines of *Henry V*. Still in his forties, Merwin seemed a poet whose enterprise could not fail to prosper.

However, any recapitulation of the official laurels that Merwin plucked en route to our rapidly approaching fin de siècle can be somewhat misleading. He began as a traditionalist, and proponents of the New Criticism welcomed with zeal his precocious gift for manipulating various forms. *A Mask for Janus* included carols, ballads, sestinas, sonnets, and several adaptations of the Provençal canso. However, in his second book, *The Dancing Bears* (1954), Merwin expresses a profound dissatisfaction with ornate and symmetrical patterns employed for their own sakes. The key poem is "East of the Sun and West of the Moon"; reminiscent of Keats's "Eve of St. Agnes" and the knight's quest recounted by Chaucer's Wife of Bath, this long narrative unfolds in regular stanzas of thirteen lines each and derives from a Norwegian folk tale about a peasant girl who marries a werebeast. Oddly enough, it is by proxy of his nubile protagonist that the poet descants on

> a hall they entered
> That blazed between mirrors, between pilasters
> Of yellow chrysolite; on walls of brass
> Gold branches of dead genealogies
> Clutched candles and wild torches whence the flames
> Rose still as brilliants. Under a fiery
> Garnet tree with leaves of glass, sunken
> In a pool of sea-green beryl as in still water
> A gold salmon hung. And no sound came

Hung with rhyming mirrors, lit by flames cold and scintillant as frost, the palace is bereft of life. Except in the eye, the gorgeous decor strikes no spark of Heraclitean fire: "What shall I say, / How chiseled the tongue soever, and how schooled / In sharp diphthongs and suasive rhetorics, / To the echoless air of this sufficiency?" The cloying aesthetics of perfection no longer engage the author's creative impulse. Indeed, the surfeit of artifice deadens the spirit as well as the senses: the beryl in which the "gold salmon" is suspended pathetically mocks "That dolphin-torn, that gong-tormented sea" of Yeats's "Byzantium." Accordingly, Merwin roughens his diction and syntax in *Green With Beasts* (1956), especially in poems such as "Leviathan": "This is the black sea-brute bulling through wave-wrack, / Ancient as ocean's shifting hills." Here the alliterative rhythms of Old English answer to the buffeting motion of the "sea-brute" rolling up a swath of foam. Linguistic vigor builds to a new pitch in subsequent volumes. Unlike the enchanted lovers of "East of the Sun and West of the Moon," the mock-Orphic figure portrayed in the title poem of *The Drunk in the Furnace* (1960) revels in his "bad castle," often "hammer-and-anvilling with poker and bottle." Although

Merwin retains the dense musicality characteristic of his earlier verse, his voice is now more relaxed and colloquial, his language less arcane.

Only in *The Moving Target*, the first of the second four books, does Merwin finally break decisively from the formal qualities he thought were urged and exemplified by the New Critical mode. An alien sensibility begins to emerge, a cosmology inimical to the strictures of regular meter, rhyme, traditional stanzaic patterns, structural coherence, and logic. Whether or not this seemingly abrupt shift resulted, as Merwin's detractors claim, from his having translated such South American and European surrealists as Pablo Neruda and Jean Follain, the various personae and landscapes depicted in *The Moving Target* are difficult to fix in time and space. "Lemuel's Blessing," a watershed poem, takes its epigraph from Christopher Smart's *Jubilate Agno*: "*Let Lemuel bless with the wolf, which is a / dog without a master, but the Lord hears his / cries and feeds him in the desert.*" Merwin embraces both Smart's conception of the wolf as a dog that refuses to acknowledge the sovereignty of human beings and the indeterminacy inherent in this vision. Dusk, the hour between dog and wolf, is a place of perpetual twilight; "Lemuel's Blessing" therefore invokes one of the dark gods of the earth: "You that know the way, / Spirit, / I bless your ears which are like cypresses on a mountain / With their roots in wisdom. Let me approach." The petitioner implores deliverance

> From the ruth of approval, with its nets, kennels, and taxidermists;
> It would use my guts for its own rackets and instruments, to play its
>   own games and music;
> Teach me to recognize its platforms, which are constructed like
>   scaffolds;
> From the ruth of known paths, which would use my feet, tail, and
>   ears as curios.
> My head as a nest for tame ants,
> My fate as a warning.

Merwin's satiric counter-thrust to Frost's remark that writing free verse is like "playing tennis with the net down" suggests that the nets "of approval" lead first to the kennel, then to the taxidermist. Here Merwin plays on the polytropic potential of language: "guts" may be literally interpreted as viscera, or it may also allude to emotions stripped bare, the poet's untrammeled *cri de coeur*. The conflation of rackets with instruments and of games with music suggests that the Orphic impulse must bow to the constraints of society. Even the ants who knit their way into the decapitated head are tame.

The speaker of this poem is both a domestic exile and an expatriate. He wishes to remain marginalized, aloof from the encroachments of civilization. His most poignant appeal to the lupine "Spirit" comes in the eighth verse paragraph: "But lead me at times beside the still waters; / There when I crouch to drink let me catch a glimpse of your image / Before it is obscured with my own."

The speaker longs for nothing less than a momentary effacement of his own presence; he appeals not to the angelic orders of the universe, but downward to an animal unknowing that will allow him to live in the eternity of the moment: "Let fatigue, weather, habitation, the old bones, finally / Be nothing to me, / Let all lights but yours be nothing to me." "Lemuel's Blessing" repudiates the formal orthodoxy that made Merwin a "faithful custodian of fat sheep."

Unlike the New Critics, Merwin refuses to privilege strictly humanist concerns. In "Dead Hand," the emblems of power taint existence far more than the frailty of the flesh: "Temptations still nest in it like basilisks. / Hang it up till the rings fall." The medieval tone conjures the right hand of Thomas à Becket: on his index finger he wears the Chancellor's ring embossed with the golden lions of State; on his third finger, the Archbishop's purple stone, richer than the blood of the Plantagenets. In a similar poem, "The Saint of the Uplands," the persona laments from beyond the grave the misplaced devotion of his adherents: "Their prayers still swarm on me like lost bees. / I have no sweetness. I am dust / Twice over." The implied metaphor is a telling one; the saint has returned to the dust that the world is, and yet his followers mistake him for the grainy yellow pollen promising renewal. As does Eliot in *The Wasteland*, (1922) Merwin goes on to describe spiritual malaise in terms of a dry landscape, but his protagonist never has recourse to the received wisdom of the Church:

> I took a single twig from the tree of my ignorance
> And divined the living streams under
> Their very houses. I showed them
> The same tree growing in their dooryards.
> You have ignorance of your own, I said
> They have ignorance of their own.

Enlightenment emanates from subterranean sources; it stems from the "tree of my ignorance," the wand that multiplies "the living streams" with a single gesture. Moreover, the saint's vatic wisdom extends no further than the spiritual insight of each disciple. Compassion, the rare water of the eye, rises from the depths and should not be squandered in ceremonial grief: "Over my feet they waste their few tears." After the followers have erected the supreme monolith, the church with its far-flung vaults and marble font, the saint must acknowledge failure: "I taught them nothing. / Everywhere / The eyes are returning under the stones. And over / My dry bones they build their churches, like wells."

Merwin's initial venturing beyond the aesthetic precepts and ideological principles of the New Criticism met with scant approbation. Reviewers in the early sixties found little to praise and much to blame in *The Moving Target*. Ralph J. Mills alluded to a "willful and cryptic privacy," while James Dickey accused Merwin of indulging in "fortuitous" imagery and pursuing "the fetchingly precious, the *different*." Among those who admonished Merwin, perhaps Joseph

Bennett was most direct: "One cannot find five ordinary lines without coming on something extraordinary; but it is all dispersed, nothing connects; all the good stuff is scattered there impartially, inexplicably." However, the assumption of cultural stability that informed critiques such as theirs was rapidly eroding. Merwin succinctly expresses the psychological and social fragmentation of his milieu in the closing lines of "Standards": "Up until now the pulse / Of a stone was my flag / And the stone's in pieces." The disembodied voice of *The Moving Target*, Merwin's frequent recourse to animism ("the wheat is camped / Under its dead crow"), his tendency to blur the distinction between words that evoke an image and words that evoke an object ("A playing on veins a lark in a lantern"): these are methods of defamiliarization that far transcend stylistic eccentricity.

III

In the frequently anthologized "For the Anniversary of My Death," an elegy that epitomizes the tone of *The Lice* as a whole, Merwin speaks of his own eventual demise: "Then I will no longer / find myself in life as in a strange garment." The metaphor conveys a sense of intimacy exhilarating in its strangeness, as if the poet felt the heart of a great ram beating beneath the fleecy lining of his coat. But he also hears a portent stirring in the frost, and he knows the hour will come when he must shed the garment. Only then will he learn whether or not the stars twinkle in a void: "the silence will set out / Tireless traveler / Like the beam of a lightless star." The star's muted ray travels at light speed across untold eons, bringing home to us what an infinitesimal niche human beings occupy in the cosmic scheme.

Throughout *The Lice*, Merwin nurtures silence, a mood of hushed expectation. The lock-step metric deriving from the English tradition seems now as unthinkable to him as the parade drill "walkovers" attempted on the Somme in July 1916. Indeed, Merwin eradicates all traces of punctuation and truncates and fractures lines, so that his speakers often appear to be brooding among the shattered capitals and toppled columns of an ancient ruin. Here is "December Night" entire:

> The cold slope is standing in darkness
> But the south of the trees is dry to the touch
>
> The heavy limbs climb into the moonlight bearing feathers
> I came to watch these
> White plants older at night
> The oldest
> Come first to the ruins
>
> And I hear magpies kept awake by the moon
> The water flows through its
> Own fingers without end

> Tonight once more
> I find a single prayer and it is not for men

To those critics who would apply the locution "surreal" to this landscape, it should be pointed out that the stream evoked with delicate felicity in stanza three is emphatically not playing a sonata. Moreover, the throaty cacophony of the magpies spares us the duel between nightingales typical of nocturnal scenes. The ineffable nature of prayer in this place is actually a disclaimer, Merwin's refusal to extrapolate beyond the numinous simplicity of sensory experience.

From beginning to end, Merwin in *The Lice* is devoted to following necessities that are his own, searching relentlessly for a poetry capable of sustaining its own form. "How We Are Spared" is a tersely humorous three-line dramatization of how self-conscious artifice sometimes fails to achieve its desired effect: "At midsummer before dawn an orange light returns to the mountains / Like a great weight and the small birds cry out / And bear it up." The creaking of a thousand tiny pulleys hoists the orange sun above the mountain rim, a singular parody of the *deus ex machina*, the tendency of literature to point smugly at its own devices. "Provision," on the other hand, eschews the grandiose intonations of "How We Are Spared," opting instead for what Cary Nelson describes as "a stark lexical modesty":

> All morning with dry instruments
> The field repeats the sound
> Of rain
> From memory
> And in the wall
> The dead increase their invisible honey
> It is August
> The flocks are beginning to form
> I will take with me the emptiness of my hands
> What you do not have you find everywhere

The percussing of laden wheat stalks in the days before harvest reminds the speaker of spring rain. In medieval lore, a bee among the flowers is a symbol of death, a concept Merwin treats more directly in "News of the Assassin"; here a somnolent swarm actually increases the honey of generation in the wall's cracked masonry. Everything flows toward a season of quiescent fullness, a place where words seem to be appropriated by things rather than things by words. In his interview with Nelson, Merwin indicated the centrality of this philosophy to his writing:

> Arrogance comes from saying that that world [of silence] doesn't exist or is of no importance, when of course in my view, it's that world that gives

words their real life. It also allows them to be luminous, transparent, and to illuminate the world, which in itself is transparent and luminous. Arrogance and an attempt to possess that world as something which is absolutely solid and can belong to somebody, completely nullifies that whole dimension of existence, and deprives existence of any kind of sense, and it deprives it of its senses. It deprives us of our own senses.

In "Provision," Merwin hearkens to a primal music, an unrehearsed harmony in the cycle of birth, growth, death, and renewal. Unencumbered by stylistic conventions, his voice moves with the lyric grace of the Psalms. Although its more buoyant interludes are almost invariably ignored, *The Lice* is not an endless series of gentle epiphanies. Silence acquires a spectral aspect in many of the poems; indeed, it becomes "a stillness such as attends death" ("The Room"), a planetary calm wherein Death exchanges its republic for a kingdom, final and absolute. "The Widow" is perhaps the bleakest of such poems, an elliptical meditation on the arrogance of humankind:

> How easily the ripe grain
> Leaves the husk
> At the simple turning of the planet
>
> There is no season
> That requires us
>
> Masters of forgetting
> Threading the eyeless rocks with
> A narrow light
>
> In which ciphers wake and evil
> Gets itself the face of the norm
> And contrives cities

Though the seed has already been sown, the need for reaping and threshing is past: the grain swells each husk to bursting, but not for the turning of any millstone. The celebratory mood of the Psalms gives way to the somber intonations of Ecclesiastes: "To every thing there is a season, and a time to every purpose under the heavens." The earth itself is the "Widow," and we are her feckless progeny, born out of season. As for the cryptic phrase in stanza three, "Threading the eyeless rocks with / A narrow light," how can any plausible reading be brought to it? We may glean the remote eye gazing through the apex of the pyramid on the back of the one-dollar bill, and remember the motto beneath, *novus ordo seclorum*: "a new cycle of the ages." This interpretation is in keeping with other references to Mammon in *The Lice*: "they [the prophets] had not stayed in spite of the assurances proceeding from the mouths of the presidents in the money pinned thick as tobacco fish over the eyes of the saints" ("Unfinished Book of Kings"). In fact, Merwin often avoids the strong closure advocated by the New Critics, for the very purpose of creating intertextual resonances among individual poems. However, we approach the third stanza, "narrow light" connotes a lack of vision that gives birth to the myriad "evils" of the great metropolis.

The Widow's domain is the world of nature and seasonal rebirth; the world of the city—from the Cyclopean stone of Mycenae, with its carved heraldic lions and beehive tombs, to the glass and steel towers of Manhattan—lies outside the province of the poem:

> The Widow rises under our fingernails
> In this sky we were born we are born
>
> And you weep wishing you were numbers
> You multiply you cannot be found
> You grieve
> Not that heaven does not exist but
> That it exists without us

The humanist principle naming man the paragon of animals and lord of the Creation is denied: "Everything that does not need you is real." Merwin's insistent fracturing of structure in "The Widow," his elliptical phrasing and cryptographic style, intimates the ultimate ruin of civilization: "This is the waking landscape / Dream after dream after dream walking away through it / Invisible invisible invisible."

Originally, the nightmarish tableau enacted in "The Widow" provoked a few critics to employ such adjectives as "obscure," "nihilistic," and "misanthropic," with some justification. On the other hand, the phantasmic tonalities evoked in "The Widow" prove altogether appropriate in poems such as "The Asians Dying" and "For a Coming Extinction." The landscape of "The Asians Dying," a direct treatment of the Vietnam War, rises eerie and insubstantial as an opium dream piped through the *o* and *r* sounds of the first strophe:

> When the forests have been destroyed their darkness remains
> The ash the great walker follows the possessors
> Forever
> Nothing they will come to is real
> Nor for long
> Over the watercourses
> Like ducks in the time of the ducks
> The ghosts of the village trail in the sky
> Making a new twilight

Everything slumbers in the wake of "the ash the great walker," until the last wisp vanishes in the aspirate of "twilight," revealing the aftermath: "Rain falls into the open eyes of the dead / Again again with its pointless sound / When the moon finds them they are the color of everything." The lifeless Asians stare into the first "pointless" drops of the monsoon. They are as unreal as the images dialed up in a rifle scope. When moonlight strikes a dead guerrilla wearing tiger-stripes, he is gone in a ripple: "The nights disappear like bruises but nothing is healed / The dead go away like bruises." Blood percolates "into the poisoned farmlands," as the occupying forces glide like phantoms over the countryside:

> The possessors move everywhere under Death their star
> Like columns of smoke they advance into the shadows
> Like thin flames with no light
> They with no past
> And fire their only future

The "possessors" linger only in fricatives—"flames," "fire," "future"—the ghoulish whisper of corpses rotting in the field. One suspects "the ash the great walker" could never be contained in the urn so exquisitely wrought by Cleanth Brooks and the New Critics. As Merwin states in his preface to *The Second Four Books of Poems*, "by the time *The Lice* appeared in 1967. . . formal changes and even some of the changes in tone and content that went with them, seemed less surprising to those who remarked on them in print, and it was possible for the new book to be considered as a reflection of its historical context, the world of the sixties."

However, the best poetry in *The Lice* defies contextualization, historical or otherwise. The whale in "For a Coming Extinction," for example—no longer the sea-brute shouldering foam in the heroic Old English cadences of "Leviathan"— is the subject of a valedictory address fraught with jubilant derision:

> Gray whale
> Now that we are sending you to The End
> That great god
> Tell him
> That we who follow you invented forgiveness
> And forgive nothing
>
> I write as though you could understand
> And I could say it
> One must always pretend something
> Among the dying

"The End" remains the starkest signifier in our language. As the deity of those who traffic in the extinction of other species, it will always justify the means of those who serve it. An additional ludicrous dichotomy attaches to naming the genius of extinction a "great god." This apparent contradiction, coupled with the lofty and condescending tone of the second stanza, posits a fathomless *contemptus mundi* in the speaker: "Tell him that we were made / On another day." The gray whale—notwithstanding its capacity for experiencing the mysterious grandeur of the marine world on a scale that dwarfs our own—embodies an alien intelligence that is perforce inferior: "The bewilderment will diminish like an echo / Winding along your inner mountains / Unheard by us." Thus we refuse to hear the haunting strains of whalesong, the mountain ranges repeated along the corridors of the Leviathan's inner ear. It scarcely matters if a portion of the knowable universe perishes each time a harpoon takes its own soundings in the whale's massive heart. Naturally, the speaker goes on fueling his harangue with murderous bliss:

> When you will not see again
> The whale calves trying the light
> Consider what you will find in the black garden
> And its court
> The sea cows the Great Auks the gorillas
> The irreplaceable hosts ranged countless
> And foreordaining as stars
> Our sacrifices
>
> Join your word to theirs
> Tell him
> That it is we who are important

The whale, whose precious oil once anointed the heads of Saxon kings and later lit the lamps of the New World, ends as a memorial exhibit in a municipal museum. The cornerstone of this edifice is laid not in the realm of projected fantasy, but in the domain of scientific fact.

IV

The Lice was the summit of Merwin's poetic achievement for twenty-five years. Even when he received a Pulitzer Prize for *The Carrier of Ladders*, he was already beginning to refine his mode of expostulation and reply out of existence. However, to defy a formalist program that tended to minimize the dialogue between poetry and scientific, historical, and philosophical propositions was one thing; to succumb eventually to his own rhetorical excesses was quite another: "To succeed consider what is as though it were past / Deem yourself inevitable and take credit for it / If you find you no longer believe enlarge the temple" ("A Scale in May"). Perhaps a wry ambiguity informs these lines from *The Lice*, but some witticisms conceal more than one barb. *The Carrier of Ladders* was too far enlarged, and "The Dead Hive" serves as an emblem of the aesthetic disappointment inherent in such attenuated structures: "I knock / from the arcade of your portal / a fly steps out." The sophisticated syntactical surface characteristic of Merwin's poetry in both traditional and open forms loses its density:

> I open the roof
> I and the light
> this is how it looks later
> the city the dance the care
> the darkness
> the moment
> one at a time
> that is each one alone

This is not "gold to airy thinness beat," but a breaking down of the tissue of language itself, a reduction of the fine to the diaphanous. Moreover, in an attempt to extend a private mythos beyond the visionary to the oracular, Merwin relies too often on a generic vocabulary based sometimes on visual association ("eyes," "mirror," "dew," "lamp," "mist") and other times on aural resonances ("lark," "key," "song," "heaven," "gate"). Patterns of imagery from *The Moving Target* that evince an almost pristine clarity ("How many times have I heard the locks close / And the lark take the keys / And hang them in heaven"), become dull and formulaic in "Lark":

> Fire by day
> with no country
> where and at what height
> can it begin
> I the shadow
> singing I
> the light

Each spare line in this stanza contains at least one term from Merwin's now obsessive lexicon. Words no longer have any anchoring in a physical or temporal presence, but are instead an interchangeable set of counters tirelessly manipulated in an increasingly narrow variety of arrangements. White space encroaches relentlessly on the innate potential of speech: brick, mortar, and trowel, the virtuoso of open form seals the poem like a tomb.

And yet, *The Carrier of Ladders* does not invariably disappoint. In "The Judgment of Paris," a ninety-one line recitation of events from the *Cypria*, Merwin brings his incomparable lyric gift to bear on a narrative over three thousand years old:

> it was only when he reached out to the voice
> as though he could take the speaker

> herself
> that his hand filled with
> something to give
> but to give to only one of the three
> an apple as it is told
> discord itself in a single fruit its skin
> already carved
> *To the fairest*

The mellifluous interplay of vowels and consonants, especially in the last four lines of this passage, revives the empathic urge found throughout *The Moving Target* and *The Lice*. The barrier of language erected between poet and reader slowly crumbles: "then a mason working above the gates of Troy / in the sunlight thought he felt the stone / shiver." Syntactical richness and sensual imagery supplant a belabored austerity:

> in the quiver on Paris's back the head
> of the arrow for Achilles' heel
> smiled in its sleep
> and Helen stepped from the palace to gather
> as she would do every day in that season
> from the grove the yellow ray flowers tall
> as herself
>
> whose roots are said to dispel pain

Merwin engages a larger myth than he has been able to construct on his own, and the result is a poem perhaps comparable to Auden's "The Shield of Achilles."

Writings to an Unfinished Accompaniment concludes the tetralogy of books written between 1960 and 1973. With the possible exception of *Finding the Islands* (1982), it is the weakest production of a career spanning four and a half decades, a volume in which Merwin reduces the definitive style of his middle phase to its lowest common denominator. In "Exercise," the poet exhorts us to "forget how to count," a process "starting with even numbers / starting with Roman numerals / starting with fractions of Roman numerals." Here Merwin pulverizes the few remaining pillars within a limited system of signs. Indeed, deliberate self-parody becomes the distinguishing feature of a poetry bent on self-erasure:

> go on to forgetting elements
> starting with water
> proceeding to earth
> rising in fire
>
> forget fire

Utter vacuity follows from instructions such as these, in a poem more "hermetically sealed" than any language artifact fashioned by the New Critics. The book's few ripe kernels of meaning are gnomic and aphoristic utterances, as when Merwin parodies the Orphic mode in "The Old Boast": "Listen natives of a dry place / from the harpist's fingers / rain." A work-chant derived from the anonymous oral tradition, "Song of Man Chipping an Arrowhead" is perhaps the finest piece in this volume: "Little children you will all go/ but the one you are hiding / will fly." Sparks leap as Neolithic man perceives the core of a new ballistics slumbering in igneous rock.

It seems pointless to bludgeon Merwin further with the fact that in *Writings to an Unfinished Accompaniment* he had momentarily exhausted what Wallace Stevens called "the poem of the act of the mind." The vision forged with patience and skill in *The Lice* has lapsed into a repertoire of convenient effects, as Merwin himself insinuates in "Old Flag":

> When I want to tell of the laughing throne
> and of how all the straw in the world
> records the sounds of dancing
> the man called Old Flag is there
> in the doorway
> and my words might be his dogs

The wolf invoked in "Lemuel's Blessing" has been led to "sniff baited fingers" once too often.

V

After listening almost a quarter-century to inner voices singing out of empty cisterns and exhausted wells, Merwin once again taps the true source of imaginative plenitude in *Travels* (1993), his fourteenth volume of poetry. For one thing, he moves from marginalization to community, forsaking the sense of spiritual isolation so pervasive in every book since *The Moving Target*. Death and mutability remain dominant concerns, but for the first time in years, one perceives a genuine authorial presence behind each poem, an inspired connection to both the things of this world and to whatever lies beyond. Several biographical narratives such as "Rimbaud's Piano" and "Marnini" rehearse the events of actual lives, sure tellings in which Merwin refuses to treat people as mere archetypes or cultural avatars, as has been his tendency in the past. However, the most salient aspect of *Travels* is his re-engagement with and reconciliation to the innate power of language to embody and enlighten. In poem after poem, Merwin sunders the links that have shackled him to an outworn mode of perception.

"The Hill of Evening," a lengthy meditation on aging and the encroachment of time on our ambitions, consists of fourteen five-line stanzas over which the ghost of a meter occasionally hovers. The setting appears to be the rural uplands of the Dordogne region in southwest France, and the poet writes directly to an absent friend:

> You will remember I think through the crowd
> of events there how quietly the days
> pass here on this hill where the two houses
> most of the year seem to be the whole
> of the inhabited world

In spite of a certain rough-hewn symmetry, the subtle enjambment coupled with fluid diction and phrasing sends each stanza brimming over into the next, a movement inevitable as a mountain stream braiding from ledge to ledge. This is still open form, and the lush imagery and felt cadences lend impetus to a voice once trapped in the dwindling echoes of *Writings to an Unfinished Accompaniment*. The speaker recalls how "the fine single stroke / of the new moon" presided over their last parting, and then recounts the events of the present day: a birthday gathering for an elderly woman, a party likened to "a wedding flowers everywhere / long tables covered with white cloths under / the lime trees and the meal went on for hours / with the toasts the speeches." There is also music, not the ominous conrinuo of Merwin's earlier poems, but "the roofer's accordion / and two violins with songs the old woman / asked for." We can almost see the pearlescent beads of the roofer's accordion squint like raindrops as the violins carve out the ancient air of feasting and celebration. Only when the speaker describes his reluctant leavetaking from this communion and the subsequent journey home do we chance on the reason he is writing his friend:

> [I] looked up to see the thin moon now this evening
> there was no moon but in the long summer
> grass to the right of the lane as I came
> I saw a shining crescent a new sickle
> bright as water and the blade
>
> glittering with the dew and I stood there
> as startled as the faces of the dancers
> not knowing whose it could be how it had
> come to be there what I was to do
> with it now that I had seen it

The sickle not only intimates the presence of the Reaper, but also betokens the earth's bounty, and the two emblems fuse in one numinous gleam of recognition. Cool and lustrous as the new moon, the harvest blade becomes the catalyst for past and present:

> I reached down
> and picked it up cool as the dripping grass
> to carry home and lay on the table
> here in front of me and tomorrow I must
> try to find who it belongs to

Merwin resolves his inner conflict through images as unsettlingly lovely as any found in James Joyce's "The Dead" without once retreating into his former hermeticism.

The subversive spirit that first compelled Merwin to embrace open form resurfaces in "Rimbaud's Piano," a long narrative depicting an incident extraordinarily singular even in the life of a youthful poete maudit. When the poem begins, Rimbaud is already intensely, even absurdly twenty-one, "his manuscripts fed to the flames two years / since and his final hope / in the alchemy of the word buried," his poverty so keen that he can no longer afford the trappings of a buffoonish decadence: "his shoes even then no / longer laced with lyre strings and his fingers / penniless once more." If we listen carefully to the alliterative *l* sounds braced by vowels, *o, a, y,* and *i*, we perceive the doomed poet's fingers rummaging the banked keys for the elusive harmonies of Pythagoras. Returned from Brussels and the ill-fated liaison with Verlaine to the aegis of his domineering mother in Charleville, Rimbaud conceives a passion for the piano. Denied because of his mother's parsimony,

> he carved
> a keyboard on the dining room table
> for practicing scales on while he listened
> to his pupil's untuned
> German and hearkened beyond them both
> to the true sound until his mother
>
> out of concern for the
> furniture hired a piano which came
> on a cart like part of a funeral

Rimbaud scores the wood not with music, but with a mute, soulless facsimile of tuned ivories. Still, the spirit of improvisation lingers, a melody opening into the days after his departure and eventual death:

> stellar harmonies the drummed
> notes of that winter continued to ring
> in the heads that heard them they rose through
> the oilcloth and the fringed
> embroidery that hid the carved keyboard
> they echoed the closing of the door

Even when the oak and lead coffin slides like a long drawer into the family vault, an unforeseen joy continues to swell "the choir of eight / with five principal singers and twenty / orphans who bore candles / at his funeral."

"Another Place" provides a verse intertext for certain passages in *Unframed Originals* (1982), Merwin's series of autobiographical sketches. Another extended narrative, the poem relates several incidents from the life of his father, a Presbyterian minister then nearing his fortieth year. Caught up in the pursuit of his vocation, he follows his professional ardors into various intrigues: "the side street and his car / and late haunts a running sore / in his marriage." The evidence of a fall from grace is unmistakable; however, in this last metaphor, Merwin anticipates and simultaneously disarms James Dickey's contention that Confessional poetry seems to be the idle pleasure of a lot of "scab-pickers." Moreover, the dichotomy suggested by his father's austere yet passionate nature may explain in part Merwin's revolt against his notion of the orthodox values of the New Criticism. Apparently, it was seldom pleasant to be one of the children

> who were
> also his although never
> had he seemed to be able
>
> really to touch them or
> address them except in anger

The rigors of a formal oratory were repugnant to the speaker: "every Sunday the order / of service giving the scripture / verses hymn numbers psalter." Still, elements of a filial devotion and grudging admiration permeate the poem at every turn. The pastor's words, like Rimbaud's, are dutifully consigned to flame: "his last instructions were / carried out and the white pyre / of all his preaching built high."

Other poems deal with ecological concerns, addressing not only the survival of animals, such as the gray whale in "For a Coming Extinction," but also the preservation of the South American rain forests and the red bark of the cinchona, a tree whose medicinal properties spared white men the lancet and innumerable bloodlettings when malaria raged in the capitals of Europe. In "Cinchona," the poet describes how the wife of the Viceroy, "Countess // of Chinchon lay stricken" with the fever. Merwin's invective on ensuing events is as bitter as the quinine extracted from the cinchona's bark:

> so when it had given
> back her life the tree all at once was seen
> as something of value
> like gold and with her name it was christened
> and though bitter its taste it was sought stripped shipped
> to be sold in Spain carried by

missionaries defended fought over
killed for

On a less harsh note, "Inheritance" speaks to the scarcity of an "opulent pear" once abundant "in fields and gardens of France" and treasured for "all the preserves liqueurs / pies and perries contrived to prolong it." In both poems, Merwin's parallel structures and skillfully enjambed stanzas are an inspired tactic, a form open enough to convey the genuine breadth of emotion without lapsing into blatant didacticism.

Travels is Merwin's finest book of poems since *The Lice*. Having once depleted the resources of an arduously evolved, albeit eccentric modality, he has had the courage and vision to begin anew in "the foul rag and bone shop of the heart." Perhaps "Left Open," the second in a suite of six poems set on the limestone plateau in southern France where Merwin completed *The Lice* in the mid-sixties, captures most memorably a moment of what he has called the "unrepeatable world":

The shutters are rusted open on the north
kitchen window ivy has grown over
the fastenings the casements are hooked open
in the stone frame high above the river
looking out across the tops of plum trees
tangled on their steep slope branches furred
with green moss gray lichens the plums falling
through them and beyond them the ancient
walnut trees standing each alone on its
own shadow in the plowed red field full
of amber September light.

Derek Walcott: Caribbean Nobel Laureate

The Bounty is Derek Walcott's first volume to appear since he received the Nobel Prize for Literature in 1992. Because the purveyors of culture in his native region refuse to relinquish the stereotype of the West Indian artist as exemplified by Walcott in "What the Twilight Says" ("the old colonial grimace of the laughing nigger, steelbandsman, carnival masker, calypsonian limbo-dancer"), transcendence becomes all the more necessary to his poetry. Notwithstanding the influence of Robert Lowell on his early work, Walcott typically foregoes the solipsistic maundering and private tropes of Confessionalism. His magnum opus, *Omeros*, marked the first successful attempt since James Joyce's *Ulysses* to fuse ancient impulse and present reality. By casting local fishermen, prostitutes, and colonial landlords in such classical roles as Achilles, Helen, and Hector, Walcott managed to affirm mythic and historical parallels between the Caribbean and Homer's Aegean. Indeed, the island of St. Lucia earned the epithet "Helen of the West," as French and British galleons warred relentlessly for her throughout the eighteen and nineteenth centuries.

Although "awe in the ordinary" is the ostensible subject of *The Bounty*, a certain epic splendor emerges from Walcott's dazzling blend of world and word. In poem "36," one of many untitled lyrics in the volume, the poet revives the colors of a fading day:

> In late-afternoon light the tops of the breadfruit leaves
> are lemon and the lower leaves a waxen viridian
> with the shaped shadows greenish black over the eaves
> of the shops of the rust-crusted fences that are Indian
> red, sepia, and often orange; but by then the light has
> ripened and grass and the sides of the houses and even a
> rooster crossing a yard blazes like a satrap.

The properties of light that translate objects beyond the ordinary are crucial to Walcott's vision. He reinforces the polychromatic effects of the first two lines with rolling *l* sounds. The corrosive hues of "rust-crusted fences" bleed from "Indian / red" to "sepia" to "orange." The light then "ripens" turning the common rooster to "a satrap" in one broad stroke. If Walcott's avocation of painter shows through, he also deems this surfeit of natural beauty unpalatable at times: "the lighthouse / is already on, and bulbs, and they are saying the novena / in the cathedral and the fisherman consciously become / silhouettes in the postcard sunset." The slick, two dimensional "postcard sunset" makes a gaudy frame for fishermen who brazen out the Antillean heat in dugout canoes. Walcott deliberately invokes the Tourist Board image of a Caribbean twilight, then counters it with vivid sensory details: "this is when / a powerful smell of baked bread drifts and when the hum / of mosquitoes becomes tangible." Drawn from clay ovens with an oar, the bread of the island poor breathes new life into the failing light. The locution "tangible" puts a keen edge on the mosquito's insistent note; Walcott restores a gusto to everyday sensations omitted from the travel brochures. He thus transcends the elegiac pathos that Claude Levi-Strauss dubbed *Tristes Tropiques*, the spiritual enervation supposedly endemic to a land "where stars and fireflies breed."

Like W. S. Merwin and Charles Wright, Walcott foregrounds a concern with death and mutability—as we see in the title poem of *The Bounty*, an elegy for his mother consisting of 220 lines divided into seven sections. The desire to transcend grief and come to terms with the transient quality of life lies at the heart of the elegiac tradition. Indeed, Walcott's incantatory lament often approaches a mood of celebration. Here are the first six stanzas:

> Between the vision of the Tourist Board and the true
> Paradise lies the desert where Isaiah's elations
> force a rose from the sand. The thirty-third canto
>
> cores the dawn clouds with concentric radiance,
> the breadfruit opens its palms in praise of the bounty,
> *Bois-pain*, tree of bread, slave food, the bliss of John Clare,
>
> torn, wandering Tom, stoat-stroker in his country
> of reeds and stalk-crickets, fiddling the dank air,
> lacing his boots with vines, steering glazed beetles
>
> with the tenderest prods, knight of the cockchafer,
> wrapped in the mist of shires, their snail-horned steeples
> palms opening to the cupped pool—but his soul safer
>
> than ours, though iron streams fetter his ankles.
> Frost whitening the stubble, he stands in the ford
> of a brook like the Baptist lifting his branches to bless
>
> cathedrals and snails, the breaking of this new day
> and the shadows of the beach road near which my mother lies,
> with the traffic of insects going to work anyway.

Walcott taps into the Judeo-Christian mythos, placing himself between the realms of the spirit and the flesh. His loose terza rima prepares us for the Dantesque resonance of lines three and four, but the juxtaposition of "bread-fruit" and "bounty" in the fifth line proves bitterly ironic. Introduced to the

West Indies by British imperial interests in the eighteenth century, the bread-fruit was meant to be a cheap source of plenty for the slaves needed to harvest sugar cane. Baked until the rind blackened, the core remained "soft, tender, and white like the crumb of a penny-loaf," a phenomenon that launched the infamous voyage of the *H. M. S. Bounty*. In the first two tercets, Walcott summons the forces of history that conspired to produce him, the self-proclaimed "mulatto of style." Such a panoramic view ostensibly enables the poet to transcend personal bereavement; however, his identification with "mad John Clare" reveals the depth of his passion. Walcott shares not only Clare's abiding love for the flora and fauna of his native landscape, but also the loss of a mother who encouraged his intrinsic gifts. By proxy of Clare, he delights in the lacquered shell of a beetle, and subtly likens a snail to a twin-spired cathedral. Celebration of nature becomes a subliminal exaltation of Walcott's mother, who is now the *genius loci* or presiding spirit of the earth's bounty.

Throughout *The Bounty* Walcott's allusions to the Western canon—the Bible, Dante, Shakespeare, and even Clare—endow his elegy with a Modernist complexity. Of British, Dutch, and African ancestry, he transcends any one nationality or culture in the range and diversity of his tropes. His tone mingles anger and tenderness in section two:

> There on the beach, the desert, lies the dark well
> where the rose of my life was lowered, near the shaken plants,
> near a pool of fresh tears, tolled by the golden bell
>
> of allamanda, thorns of the bougainvillea, and that is
> their bounty! They shine with defiance from weed and flower
> even those that flourish elsewhere, vetch, ivy, clematis.

Ultimately, Clare's presence serves as a buffer between Walcott and extremity of emotion: "there is grief, there always will be, but it must not madden / / like Clare who wept for a beetle's loss, for the weight / of the world in a bead of dew." The dewdrop refuses to melt, fired to opal hardness by these "tinder-dry lines." The pun on *tender* belies Walcott's inclination to yield to sorrow. In section three, he transcends personal loss by extolling the fullness of the earth wherein his mother lies buried: "Bounty! / In the bells of the tree-frogs with their steady clamour / in the indigo dark before dawn, the fading morse / of fireflies and crickets." Nevertheless, he is moved to descant once again regarding the encroachments of empire in section four: "Sails move into the harbour, the breadfruit plants on *The Bounty* / will be heaved aboard, and the white God is Captain Bligh."

In section five, Walcott effaces the boundaries between world and word, comparing the lines of his poem to waves that "crepitate from the culture of Ovid / its sibilants and consonants." He assuages anger, if not grief, as he traces history, literature, and his mixed racial heritage back to a common source:

> No soul was ever invented
> yet every presence is transparent; if I met her
> (in her nightdress ankling barefoot, crooning to the shallows),
>
> should I call her shadow that of a pattern invented
> by Graeco-Roman design, columns of shadows
> cast by the Forum. Augustan perspectives?

Something ominous, a ringing of ghostly fetters, still attaches to the image of the poet's mother "ankling barefoot" through the cold shallows. In sections six and seven, Walcott seeks transcendence through a vision of spring renewal in the cold North European climate from whence his paternal grandfather hailed: "glaciers shelve and thaw, / frozen ponds crack into maps, green lances spring / from the melting fields, flags of rooks rise and tatter / the pierced light." But he remembers that the only two seasons in St. Lucia are heat and rain: "There is no change now, no cycles of spring, autumn, winter, / nor an island's perpetual summer; she took time with her; / no climate, no calendar except for this bountiful day." Genuine transcendence emerges only from contemplating nature's abundance, now permeated with the spirit of the poet's mother:

> As poor Tom fed his last crust to trembling birds,
> as by reeds and cold pools John Clare blest these thin musicians,
> let the ants teach me again with long lines of words,
>
> my business and duty, the lesson you taught your sons
> to write of the light's bounty on familiar things
> that stand on the verge of translating themselves into news:
>
> the crab, the frigate that floats on cruciform wings,
> and that nailed and thorn-riddled tree that opens its pews
> for the blackbird that hasn't forgotten her because it sings.

The closing benediction affirms his ongoing devotion to a visionary aesthetic, "the light's bounty on familiar things." Walcott reveals an extraordinary talent for assimilation; like Whitman, he contains multitudes yet retains a unique poetic identity. However, the elliptical style of *The Bounty*—its multiple allusions, rich metaphors, and lush imagery—owes more to techniques developed by T.S. Eliot and Hart Crane than the white-bearded emissary of the barbaric yawp.

Some critics would argue that Walcott arrives at Eliot's visionary sadness by way of French Symbolists such as Jules Laforgue. On the other hand, this passage from a ten-part sequence titled "Homecoming" blithely echoes Eliot's

"The Love Song of J. Alfred Prufrock" in the second line:

> This is Gros-Ilet,
>
> with a Sunday stretched out on its bed, to the sadness
> of an ice-cream van whirring its mechanical tune
> over and over, and all your sins in that noise,
>
> your childhood, and now your grandchildren in turn,
> like a shepherdess slowly turning on a music box,
> silvery and sparkling like a drizzle in the sun.

Unlike Prufrock, Walcott's speaker has transcended the loneliness and isolation that sunder the individual from his immediate culture. Still, he conveys a certain urban malaise: as the "ice cream van" registers its anapests and trochees, the accented monosyllables "sins" and "spin" ring like loose change. The music-box figurine implies a pastoral yearning, its tinsel melody glinting like "drizzle in the sun." Evoking the rainbow flavors in the refrigerated van, smacks of frozen confectionery. Here Walcott's facile eloquence and linguistic extravagance enchant too readily. Nostalgia for the youthful enthusiasm that transcends the process of aging is expressed far more succinctly by these lines from poem "9": "All I require is an acre of sunlight and salt wind. One acre / only, and nothing beyond that, with my own version / of the world beyond. I was here anyway, a maker / from boyhood." For Walcott, personal utterance tends to obviate the preening melancholy of the Confessional poets, embracing instead the grace and plenitude of the natural world: "the running stream's bliss / contradicts the self-importance of despair / by these glittering simplicities, water, leaves, and air / the elate dissolution which goes beyond happiness."

Walcott's unerring vision of the West Indies constantly demands that he transcend the bleaker aspects of an ostensibly idyllic landscape. Indeed, even its beauty can beguile for the worse on occasion. St Lucia's craggy profile leaves the airborne traveler so dear to the Tourist Board with an innate fear that something solid exists in that liquid world as a cloud wall on the horizon abruptly shifts into a mountain peak. Crystalline waters, coral reefs, quayside markets hung with gossamer fishing nets, the tin-enameled roofs of the wooden shacks: all these images conspire to make the poverty of the Lesser Antilles a subject for poetry. As Walcott has said, "poverty is poetry without a V, un vie, a condition of life as well as of the imagination." Sometimes transcendence derives from the ability to perceive squalor beneath the veneer of loveliness: "the rusted enamel tin / of the moon stuck in the silt at the depth of the ochre river / the choked canals were part of an imperial decay, / parliament and poor plumbing." Fortunately, Walcott engages both the physical and spiritual elements of his domain: "My country heart. I am not home until Sesenne sings, / a voice with woodsmoke and ground-doves in it, that cracks / like clay on a road whose tints are the dry season's." For Derek Walcott, world and word converge in a poetry that inculcates wonder: "Bounty in the ant's waking fury, // in the snail's chapel stirring under wild yams, / praise in decay and process, awe in the ordinary."

Tiepolo's Hound is Derek Walcott's second volume to appear since he was awarded the Nobel Prize for Literature in 1992. Composed in couplets rhyming alternately—*ab ab cd cd* /—the long poem consists of 164 pages divided into four books of varying lengths. The poet's multilayered narrative defies strict chronology, as he manipulates a continuous parallel between his own artistic development and that of Impressionist painter Camille Pissarro, a Sephardic Jew born on the island of St. Thomas in 1830. Because he first saw the light of day one hundred years later in St. Lucia—another provincial backwater in the Caribbean archipelago—Walcott identifies with the painter compelled by aesthetic zeal to embark eventually for France. Indeed, the poet speaks more intimately than ever before of his desire to excel in the plastic arts. A scant five pages into the poem, he remembers with startling clarity his first and only encounter with the wolfhound of his title:

> I remember the stairs in couplets. The Metropolitan's
> marble authority, I remember being
>
> stunned as I studied the exact expanse
> of a Renaissance feast, the art of seeing.
>
> Then I caught a slash of pink on the inner thigh
> of a white hound entering the cave of a table,
>
> so exact in its lucency at *The Feast of Levi*,
> I felt my heart halt. Nothing, not the babble
>
> of the unheard roar that rose from the rich
> pearl-lights embroidered on ballooning sleeves
>
> sharp beards, and gaping goblets, matched the bitch
> nosing a forest of hose. So a miracle leaves
>
> its frame, and one epiphanic detail
> illuminates an entire epoch:
>
> a medal by Holbein, a Vermeer earring, every scale
> of a walking mackerel by Bosch, their sacred shock.
>
> Between me and Venice the thigh of a hound;
> my awe of the ordinary, because even as I write,
>
> paused on a step of this couplet, I have never found
> its image again, a hound in astounding light.

The power of introspection—primed by a British colonial education at the University of the West Indies that included canonical authors from Homer to Keats proves the defining element in this crucial passage. Despite the spontaneous nature of his encounter, Walcott's elevated diction echoes the marmoreal splendor of the museum staircase. His couplets enriched by assonance, alliteration, and interior rhyme, the poet presents an allegory of seeing. He studies the High Baroque feast of Giovani Batista Tiepolo's contriving, the bloat surfeit of "ballooning sleeves" and the iridescent tints struck from seed pearls delicately stitched into fabric. "Gaping goblets" brim with red wine. But the lucid stroke of an inner thigh—"a slash of pink—" arrests the heart, awakening Walcott to "awe of the ordinary." He appropriates the white hound as his muse, an incarnation of the numinous, a trope for imaginative dexterity that redounds on the polished marble: "a hound in astounding light."

Relentless scrutiny yields to empathy as Walcott traces the affinities between his life and Camille Pissarro's in Book One. He begins in *medias res*: an aspiring artist recently returned from the Lycée Savary in Paris, Pissarro must now pore over the ledgers in his father's hardware store. Strolling the docks in the rustic West Indies colony of St. Thomas, he yearns for another seven years abroad. Indeed, the tropical seascape conspires to hasten his flight: "like commas / in a shop ledger gulls tick the lined waves. // Sealight on the cod barrels he writes: *St. Thomas* / the salt breeze brings the sound of Mission slaves// chanting deliverance." With the fluency of a brush dipped in cerulean, the reflected sun illuminates the lettering on the barrels. The youth sees the tribesmen of the African diaspora shackled to a common destiny, a reminder of his family's tacit complicity in the nightmare of history: "Before the family warehouse, near the Customs, / his uncle jerks the locks, rattling their chains." Juxtaposing his development as a painter with Pissarro's, Walcott imposes on his long poem a structure both dialectical and hauntingly introspective. Pissarro's father expects his son to pursue the family's lucrative concerns and thus mire his art in an environment that refuses to nurture it: "The Saint Thomas drawings have it, the taint / of complicit time, the torpor of ex-slaves // and benign planters, suffering made quaint/ as a Danish harbor with its wooden waves." On the other hand, young Walcott must scrimp to buy pigment, scroll each tube until a dollop oozes out like a snail. Crushed oils and distilled resins make every vessel sacred, and for years to come the finished canvas embalms the air: "Precious, expensive in its metal cruse / and poured like secular, sacramental wine, / I still smell linseed oil in the wild views / of villages and the tang of turpentine." But Walcott exchanges his brush for a pen nib's stroke and the glittering spires of New York. Pissarro discovers how the Caribbean's excess of natural beauty cloys the senses and induces a spiritual malaise called *Tristes Tropiques*. Consequently, he books passage on a steamship for Paris:

Shadows and shanties, shade-crossed bamboo paths,
its fragrant forests never penetrated,

and narrow falls with white, cascading baths,
and parrots screaming betrayal overhead

from saffron ceilings over Santa Cruz,
and flame trees fading indigo

over brown, rumorous brooks? They had their use.
The new had gotten old. He had to go.

In Book Two, Walcott focuses primarily on Pissarro's assimilation of Impressionist theory: a canvas is no longer a window, but a material surface covered with pigments—we must look at it, not through it. More than ever before, the poet emphasizes the rich surfaces and textures of language: "Courbet and Cézanne made a solid / architecture of quarries and cathedral oaks // hardening the wisps of Corot, so paint was laid/ thick as plasterer's or bricklayer's strokes." Introspection becomes a corollary of style as Walcott seeks the confluence of deft brush strokes and rapt inflections: "both fictions sharing a single eye, that of the pen." He offers aural delectations in addition to ravishments of the eye in his description of Pissarro waiting out the autumn rain in a snug retreat: "Black downpours on a clouded, dripping day, / tinkle of rain like cutlery in the leaves, // pencil thin drizzle. Deep in the brown café / he watches ropes of water twisting from the eaves." In Paris, Pissarro participates fully in Walcott's "awe in the ordinary," his primary subjects rural labor and vibrant landscapes, regardless of season or weather. But he remains frustrated in his desire for recognition beyond his circle of contemporaries, as the Academy rejects canvas after canvas. Here Walcott's tendency to identify his own career with the expatriated painter's lapses into an acerbic diatribe: "Success at home meant nothing, this was the center / of opinion; for a Danish colonial Jew // from a dirty backward island to enter / the museum's bronzed doors." Like his protagonist, Walcott prospers in the vast empire of light. His vowel clusters radiate harmonies and scintillant discords on a field of white: "The Pointillist surface darts like sardines/ in the shallow of the Oise; they shoot like mullet // from the reader's approaching shadow, their darting lines / splinter in bits." As he closes the second book of *Tiepolo's Hound*, Walcott concedes that both he and the Impressionists treat images as conscious fictions: "I shift this biography as he shifted houses / in his landscapes; not walled facts their essence; // neither the strict topography that was Pontoise's / nor the charted contours that were Seine's." His poem, too, is a partial fabrication; although grounded in personal history and the empirical realm, it is a product of introspection: an amalgam that includes imaginative depth, scrupulous revision, and a durable aesthetic philosophy.

In Book Three, Walcott chronicles the vicissitudes of a Pissarro driven to England by the Franco-Prussian War. Far from the raillery of musket fire and the thunder of big guns on the continent, he must endure patiently as the obscene carnival festers in his imagination: "the tubes of red like disembowelled entrails, // the gamboge pus of wounds." He knows penury and its attendant sorrows: "A sick child screaming. Counting every cent / with a wife as fertile as she was morose." After the death of his daughter, he begins to doubt his former vision, but a return to France brings renewed vitality and extends his grasp of the sublime through a prolonged contemplation of nature:

> He sensed no other world than what he saw,
> he caught no glimpse of some celestial river
>
> other than the chimneys of the humbling Oise
> and the soft fog that scarved the hills at morning,
>
> though, inexplicably, aspens with one noise
> silvered her name, a joy without a warning.
>
> Death claims more lives than one; it claims
> others by sharing its exacting grief,
>
> as when the aspens' tongues repeated names
> that shared her passing, loud in their belief.
>
> The dusk over Louveciennes was not a heaven
> of Tiepolo's cherubs; every stroke he made
>
> absorbed her absence; with calm, even
> paint he built its blue. This was the way he prayed.

Here Walcott consolidates and enhances his narrative through subtle modulations of rhythm, syntax, and diction. He relinquishes polychromatic tonalities, muting color motifs to silver and blue. Aspirates and fricatives slow the measure of each line. But he never recants his former exuberance, offering an apologia by proxy of Pissarro: "If I pitch my tints to rhetorical excess, / it was not from ambition but to touch the sublime, to heighten the commonplace into sacredness/ of objects made radiant by the slow glaze of time."

In Book Four, Walcott foregrounds his ongoing search for the white hound, its gorgeous flesh tone and white sinew laid bare by a single brush stroke. Memory and imagination have so beguiled the passing years that he can no longer ascertain the source of his inspiration: "Research / could prove the hound Tiepolo's or Veronese's." Here introspection takes the form of an inner dialogue, whether Walcott churns the canals of Venice in a vaporetto or haunts "my skull's rotunda in his quest for the 'spectral hound." But he never finds the pictured lineaments that kindled his own creative spark. Neither divine communion nor bacchanalian revel, The *Feast of Levi* symbolizes both imaginative plenitude and the heart's bounty. A cynical reader might contend that Walcott longs for the proverbial place at the table, the one claimed by William Butler Yeats in his admonition "To a Young Beauty": "There is not a fool can call me friend/ And I may dine at journey's end/ With Landor and with Donne." But this is not the case. For all his extravagance with language, Walcott seemingly disdains what he perceives to be Yeatsian bombast. Veneration of the image, both visual and aural, prompted the Caribbean laureate to choose the white hound as the elusive genius of his poetry. But the gift requires nurturing:

> Then one noon where acacias shade the beach
> I saw the parody of Tiepolo's hound
>
> in the short salt grass, requiring no research,
> but something still unpainted, on its own ground.
>
> I had seen wolfhounds straining on the leash,
> their haunches taut on tapestries of Spring;
>
> now I had found, whose azure was a beach,
> this tottering, abandoned, houseless thing.

The moment of recognition—"The hound was here"—derives from introspection and needs "no research" to confirm it. To fulfill his promise as either poet or painter, Walcott must continue to refine his skills and trust the mystery to abide in the commonplace: "St. Thomas hazing as it rains / And love, the mist-bow bent on paradise." He invokes the guidance of his fellow Caribbean in his ongoing quest for beauty:

> Camille Pissarro, on our beaches the breezy
> light over our bays, help me to begin
> when I set out again, at sixty-nine,
> for the sacred villages. Dole out in each tin,
> clear linseed and redemptive turpentine.

After a half-century of devotion to his craft, Walcott asks only a modest benefice and a sustaining grace to achieve the sovereignty of spirit necessary for complete mastery.

White Egrets (2010) is Derek Walcott's fourteenth volume of poetry, undeniably his best since *Tiepolo' s Hound* (2000). His language derives from Jacobean drama and the King James Bible; its richness of surface and texture owes much to his training as painter. Memory acts as both touchstone and catalyst for passion in his writing, a circumstance provoking the occasional *cri de coeur* regarding its tentative nature, understandable in a poet over eighty. Of mixed Dutch and African ancestry, Walcott is no stranger to London, New York, Barcelona, Amsterdam, Venice, or Stockholm, but is perhaps best known for his love of the place he was raised, tiny St. Lucia in the Caribbean archipelago.

The first poem in *White Egrets* displays Walcott's phenomenal skill with language to rare advantage. Like many other entries in the volume, the piece is untitled, and curiously restrained for a poet who typically qualifies as a voluptuary of style. Here are the first ten lines:

> The chessmen are rigid on their chessboard
> as those life-sized terra-cotta warriors whose vows
> to their emperor with bridle, shield and sword
> were sworn by a chorus who has lost its voice;
> no echo in that astonishing excavation.
> Each soldier gave an oath, each gave his word
> to die for his emperor, his clan, his nation,
> to become a chess piece, breathlessly erect
> in shade or crossing sunlight, without hours—
> from clay to clay and odourlessly strict.

Walcott opts for the contemplative mood, likening his chessmen on their board to the funeral statuary unearthed in the Shaanxi province of China in 1974. Eight thousand "life-sized sculptures of kiln-fired clay, varying in stature according to rank, were excavated from an underground necropolis containing all that was mortal of Q'in Shi Huang, the first emperor of China. Walcott's analogy proves unnervingly apt, evoking a recognition of both strangeness and familiarity. The warriors remain rigid as Walcott manipulates the background to the strict rhythms of a nearly flawless metric with a few substitutions and inversions. Moreover, the repetition of *o* and *r* sounds in "chessboard," "warriors," "emperor," "sword," "sworn," and "chorus" imbues these lines with an incantatory stupor in keeping with its mute subject. The red clay, kneaded dumb and oven-baked, is free even of the grave's cloying stench. Walcott minces few words when he conjures "crossing sunlight, without hours." Thus, one passes from death's republic to its empire, infinite and absolute. The poet astonishes his reader in his closing passage, wherein he reveals that this is a love poem of direct address:

> If vows were physical they might see ours
> as changeless chessmen in the changing light
> on the lawn outside where hammered breakers toss
> and palms gust with music that is time's
> above the chessmen's silence. Motion brings loss.
> A sable blackbird twitters in the limes.

Walcott extends his controlling metaphor as he compares the "vows" exchanged between two lovers to the "changeless chessmen" in a world of flux. However, nature will not stay for a seemingly benign stasis that nevertheless amounts to *spiritus mortuum*. Mutability insists on the "music that is time's." One hearkens, therefore to the "sable blackbirds" singing in the lime grove.

Walcott's linguistic dexterity—coupled with a memory that seldom falters, despite his claims to the contrary—pervades line after line of *White Egrets*. In a five-part segment titled "Sixty Years After," he tempers the grandeur of his ubiquitous seascapes with an affinity for visual details that disdains the fetchingly precious: "away from the road / a frog shoots its tongue at the stars." Even the croaking denizens of the marsh aspire heavenward. As Samuel Johnson once observed: "*Grand* nonsense is insupportable," so it follows that Walcott takes many risks, but he usually succeeds admirably.

Most engaging in this section are the people and places from the poet's past. In a passage numbered twenty-seven, the poet remembers a meeting in a "lounge at Vieuxfort" with an unrequited love from his youth. Both the speaker and his old companion are now wheelchair-bound, doubtless sipping gin and tonic with bitters: "She was treble-chinned, old, her devastating smile was netted in wrinkles, but I felt the fever / briefly returning as we sat there, crippled, hating / time and the lie of general pleasantries." Perhaps what the poet really misses is some idea of himself that went into loving her: "the one whom I thought / as the fire of my young life would do her duty / to be golden and young forever / even as I aged." Walcott almost invariably converts his women into some semblance of the Petrarchan "Cruel Fair," but here he must confront the ravages wrought by time and chance. Even so, he manages to evoke a scene of breathtaking beauty:

> Small waves still break against the small stone pier
> where a boatman left me in the orange peace
> of dusk, a half-century ago, maybe happier
> being erect, she like a deer in her shyness, I stalking
> an impossible consummation; those who knew us
> knew we would never be together, at least not walking.
> Now the silent knives from the intercom went through us.

Perhaps "being erect" is an unfortunate turn of phrase in this context, but it scarcely blurs the voluptuous hues of the sun-touched water at dusk. Walcott's use of alternating rhyme, both exact and approximate, evolves as a subtle and unobtrusive strategy. Yet his last line dissolves the reverie in the most painful manner imaginable: "Now the silent knives from the intercom went through us."

In passage twenty-eight, Walcott prepares us for another of his gorgeous seascapes, this one set in the "crescent miles of Rodney Bay" in St. Lucia: "The gulls settle like standards on the piles / while pluming waves march past them in their legions." His ingenuity for concocting martial metaphors out of foaming breakers appears inexhaustible, although another oblique reminder of the British Empire's former occupation of the West Indies seems a shopworn trope at this point. However, Walcott abruptly shifts his stance, calling on his powers of recollection:

> . . . memory revisits two regions:
> one, liquid Venice, then the indigo weight
> of solid Stockholm. In both a cherub smiles
> at gurgitating, lion-headed fountains, their basins bright
> with chattering water, repetitious questions;
> one region consonantal, obdurate,
> the other vowelled.

The participle "gurgitating" is a masterstroke. Here Walcott borrows a page from his fellow Nobel laureate Seamus Heaney, contrasting the iron consonants of Stockholm with the lucent vowels of rheumy-stoned Venice on the Adriatic. His depiction of the Italian city proves particularly beguiling: "the freight of bobbing gondolas and the unknown domes / of palaces and chapels, Santa Maria della Salute." Unlike many poets nowadays, Walcott refuses to shy away from the purely belletristic: "On a day like this, all blaze with same beauty."

In a poem numbered thirty-seven, Walcott brings his aptitude for language to bear on a remembrance of the Trinidad Theatre Workshop he founded in 1959 with his twin brother, Roderick, to promote art and culture in the West Indies. The opening lines call to mind a neglected actor named Arthur Jacobs:

> Quick, quick, before they all die, the hard ebony
> head of Arthur Jacobs, the bare pate, the broken teeth
> that make his grin more powerful, a man with no money
> despite his tremendous presence, light as a leaf
> and as delicate dancing, coal-black and like coal
> packed with inspiring fire, a diamond with its memory fading;

The poet portrays his protagonist as a man of luminous joy and untrammeled spirit, one who exudes a Falstaffian exuberance and subversive wit despite his obscurity as a professional player. On the contrary, his bald pate and marred grin mark him as a veritable Lord of Misrule. Walcott's unstinting use of *l* sounds—"light," "leaf," "delicate," "coal black," and "coal—" rolls trippingly off the tongue, unimpeded by dental stops in "delicate," "dancing," and "diamond." Indeed, his description of Jacobs acquires the dimensions of a paean: "Jesus, the beauty he contains, a beauty of soul / no less than that, a wit, an intelligence, the degrading / indifference he has had to endure." Like Yeats, Walcott is all too familiar with the arduous task of establishing nothing less than a national theater, as he recalls other actors already vanished from the footlights: "some of the best already/ gone, Wilbert Holbert, Claude Reid, Ermine Wright." All the poet can offer by way of homage are the electric stroke of a firefly and the muted ray of a fairly good star: "I must make room / for a shrine before they all die, with fireflies and starlight."

One is grateful for *White Egrets*, perhaps Walcott's final book, especially when one considers his age and failing health. Since his previous collection, *The Prodigal* (2004), was wildly uneven and offhand in tone, it would have been a shame to see an illustrious career end on such a false note. His abiding knack for both the aural and visual nuances of English—a mastery of rhythm, syntax, and diction, together with a profusion of rich and various imagery—remains unmatched by any poet save Richard Wilbur. Moreover, when it comes to sheer cognitive power (a gift for figurative language that at once startles and illuminates) he is without peer. In fact, at the time of his death, Walcott was the New World's greatest living poet. Nevertheless, a hint of soul-weariness emerges in *White Egrets*:

> If it is true
> that my gift has withered, that there's little left of it,
> if this man is right, then there's nothing left to do
> but abandon poetry like a woman because you love it
> and would not see her hurt, least of all by me.

A passion for language and memory has served Derek Walcott's career to decided advantage. Indeed, he can scarcely bid the craft or sullen art farewell, even in a poem: "be grateful that you wrote well in this place, / let the torn poems sail from you like a flock / of white egrets in a long last sigh of relief."

Metamorphosis Within the Poetry of Charles Wright

I

Charles Wright's new collection, *The World of the Ten Thousand Things*, gathers his four most recent individual volumes—*The Southern Cross* (1981), *The Other Side of the River* (1984), *Zone Journals* (1988), and *Xionia* (1990), inside a single cover jacketed by Cézanne's *Bend in the Road* (1900-06). Consequently, readers will register no surprise at finding the first poem titled "Homage to Paul Cézanne." We may be surprised, however, that Wright's ghostly paean seems entirely concerned with the metaphysical implications of death; not even the obliquest allusion to Cézanne occurs in the first three parts of the poem. Only in what Wright himself terms the fourth "overlay" does it become apparent that he is seeking entrance to Cézanne's creative genius through a fusion of the master's technique with his own:

> The dead are a cadmium blue.
> We spread them with palette knives in broad blocks and planes.
>
> We layer them stroke by stroke
> In steps and ascending mass, in verticals raised from the earth.
>
> We choose, and layer them in,
> Blue and a blue and a breath,
>
> Circle and smudge, cross-beak and buttonhook,
> We layer them in. We squint hard and terrace them line by line.

The modulating of tone through the use of color motifs, specifically "cadmium blue," is reminiscent of Cézanne, though Wright does not lose sight of the fact that plane and space relationships in Cézanne's paintings are fundamentally linear. In "Blue and a blue and a breath," one may glean the rasp of trowel on mortar—the inexorable bricking of the dead into the blue vault of heaven. Thus, "we are come between, and cry out," in a subsequent line.

Of particular interest is the repetition of the verb "layer" no less than three times in this segment of "Homage to Paul Cézanne." Wright's accretive method of composition has been noticed by Helen Vendler: "Because Wright's poems, on the whole, are unanchored to incident, they resist description; because they are not narrative, they defy exposition. They cluster, aggregate, radiate, add layers like pearls." Despite the fact that *The Princeton Encyclopedia of Poetry and Poetics* no longer deems tenable the traditional association of "baroque" with the Portuguese *barrôco* ("irregular pearl"), Vendler's metaphor resonates with what Peter Stitt in a chapter of his forthcoming study on contemporary American poetry identifies as "Imagism Gone Baroque." While distinguishing between the baroque in art and architecture, music, and poetry, Stitt designates Wright as the contemporary whose work best exemplifies the baroque mode in poetry: "Not only does he write—musically, imagistically, and metaphorically—in the strikingly lush style that we call baroque, but he does so with real substance, habitually searching for signs of the spiritual within the physical, the unseen within the seen." Of course, Wright did not arrive at the fullest expression of this unique coupling of style and content overnight. His vision has always provided for its own metamorphosis with each successive volume. A brief study of the growth and development of Wright's early work will allow a more comprehensive view of this metamorphosis as it occurs within *The World of the Ten Thousand Things*.

II

Of the four books that make up *Country Music: Selected Early Poems* (1982), the first two—*The Grave of the Right Hand* (1970) and *Hard Freight* (1973)—demonstrate most vividly Wright's initial obsession with technique, with the surfaces and textures of language, sometimes at the expense of meaning. Wright reprinted in his selected volume only five prose pieces from the original text of *The Grave of the Right Hand*. Although "Homage to Ezra Pound," the first poem in *Hard Freight*, suggests an earnest development of the theme of place within his poetry, it was in "Dog Creek Mainline," set in the western North Carolina of his first youth, that Wright began to develop a sense of a poem undeniably his own. During an interview with William Heyen and Stan Sanvel Rubin, Wright described "Dog Creek Mainline" as "a poem about memory and how we change memory, how memory changes and memory becomes imagination. And imagination becomes language." The poem's sixth stanza illustrates Wright's concise conjoining of theme and methodology:

> The lake in its cradle hums
> The old songs: out of its ooze, their heads
> Like tomahawks, the turtles ascend
> And settle back, leaving their chill breath
> In blisters along the bank;
> Locked in their wide drawer, the pike lie still as knives.

Even as it empties itself into the lake, Dog Creek becomes the tributary of primordial song. Turtles nudge the surface, peer and poke, briefly metamorphosed by the poet's imagination into Neolithic stone. And before the image can settle again beneath the waters of memory, the onomatopoeia of "breath" and "blisters" seals it forever in language. Underscoring the whole experience—glittering, enigmatic, predatory—the pike abide in the twilight of 1941, Wright's sixth year.

In his third book, *Bloodlines* (1975), Wright continues his search for the numinous quality of experience in language while also undertaking a conventional exploration of childhood epiphanies. Each of the twenty fifteen-line sections of the autobiographical poem "Tattoos," for example, is a highly poetic, highly imagistic rendering of the event or detail explained in that section's note. Placing "Notes to Tattoos" at the end of the twenty-part sequence allows Wright to avoid the narrative contract implicit in a series of separate titles. In section twelve, the poet remembers the process of learning to write, and presents it as a firsthand experience: "Oval oval oval oval push pull push pull . . . / Words unroll from our fingers." Thus Wright conjures, as the note would have it, "words as 'things' ": "The words, like bees in a sweet ink, cluster and drone, / Indifferent, indelible, / A hum and a hum." The paper drinks each stroke of the pen, vowels and trochees like stingers in a drowse.

China Trace (1977), Wright's fourth individual volume, marks his first attempt at a book-length poem—"an ongoing story about a character who went from childhood to his demise and inscription in the heaven of fixed stars," as Wright explained to J.D. McClatchy in their then-recent *Paris Review* interview. While the book's gnomic tone may be traced to Pound's *Cathay*, the persona's desire in "Clear Night" to achieve transcendence through divinely imposed suffering also echoes Old English visionary poems such as "A Dream of the Rood":

> I want to be bruised by God.
> I want to be strung up in a strong light and singled out.
> I want to be stretched, like music wrung from a dropped seed.
> I want to be entered and picked clean.

Even Wright's spectral, back-lit nightscapes express a pervasive longing for regeneration: "Behind me an animal breaks down, / One ear to the moon's brass sigh. / / The earth ticks open like a ripe fruit" ("12 Lines at Midnight"). A spiritual yearning linked to nature, "a metaphysics of the quotidian," becomes an integral part of Wright's poetry at mid-career.

III

The title of Charles Wright's fifth book, *The Southern Cross*, the first of the four that comprise *The World of the Ten Thousand Things*, cannot appear to us as other than enigmatic, especially in light of his persona's final destination in *China Trace*. Now Wright unveils yet another constellation, hoisted clear when the sky of the northern tropics is popped with stars: "Things that divine us we never touch: / / The black sounds of the night music, / The Southern Cross, like a kite at the end of its string." The image hints at a momentary stasis buoyed up by secular mysticism, an odd conflation of astronomy and Christian iconography. The title poem continues: "And now this sunrise, and empty sleeve of a day, / The rain just starting to fall, and then not fall,

/ / No trace of a storyline." Actually, this crucial passage signals Wright's arrival at a methodology honed, refined, and prepared for throughout his first four collections; in his prose collection, *Halflife: Improvisations and Interviews, 1977-87* (1988), Wright explained that "My plots do not run narratively or linearly, but synaptically, from one nerve spark to another, from one imagistic spark to another." Now memory and imagination converge as never before. Wright's images illuminate; his metaphors transmute the myriad accidents of experience into essences:

> River of sighs and forgetfulness
>   (and the secret light Campana saw),
> River of bloom-bursts from the moon,
>   of slivers and broken blades from the moon
> In an always-going-away of glints . . .
>
> Dante and Can Grande once stood here,
> Next to the cool breath of S. Anastasia,
>   watching the cypress candles
> Flare in their deep green across the Adige
> In the Giusti Gardens.
>   Before that, in his marble tier,
> Catullus once sat through the afternoons.
> Before that, God spoke in the rocks . . .
>
> And now, it's my turn to stand
> Watching a different light do the same things on a different water,
> The Adige bearing its gifts
>   through the April twilight of 1961.

The Adige is not Dog Creek, and the Adriatic Sea is more than a far cry from the lake in North Carolina, where the six-year-old Wright saw pike burn like knives in the shallows. The poet's companions are no longer "Rosendale, Perry and Smith"—now Campana, Dante, and Catullus inhabit those "silhouettes / Against the American twilight." The language is more lush and sensual, the lines terraced. White space builds against the left-hand margin, reminiscent of Cézanne's excavations in his later landscapes.

The spiritual province of "The Southern Cross" is Italy, its presiding genius, Dante. At times, Wright seems to evoke the medieval world of Christian synthesis that enabled Alighieri to write his immortal *Commedia*:

> Thinking of Dante, I think of La Pia,
>   and Charles Martel
> And Cacciaguida inside the great flower of Paradise,

And the thin stem of Purgatory
>rooted in Hell.

On the other hand, he is not about to kick off the traces of his upbringing in the southeastern United States:

The Big Dipper has followed me all the days of my life.
Under its tin stars my past has come and gone.
Tonight, in the April glaze
>and scrimshaw of the sky,

It blesses me once again
With its black water, and sends me on.

The allusion to the Twenty-third Psalm implies a ritual anointing, but we must remember that the Big Dipper is also known as Charles's Wain *(wain* being a heavy wagon for farm use). In a playful manner, Wright thus reminds us of his roots in the agrarian South, a theme clearly articulated in the anecdotal "Virginia Reel":

In Clarke County, the story goes, the family name
Was saved by a single crop of wheat,
The houses and land kept in a clear receipt for the subsequent suicides,
The hard times and non-believers to qualify and disperse:
Woodburn and Cedar Hall, Smithfield, Auburn and North Hill:
Names like white moths kicked up from the tall grass,
Spreading across the countryside
From the Shenandoah to Charles Town and the Blue Ridge.

The poet crumbles the depleted soil through his hands, musing on those ancestors who are dust twice over: "this is the dirt their lives were made of, the dirt the world is, / Immeasurable emptiness of all things." Even among the carved headstones of "limestone and marble and locust wood," Wright expresses a desire for communion through a nature which is itself passing into eternity: "Just down the road, at Smithfield, the last of the apple blossoms / Fishtails to earth through the shot twilight, / A little vowel for the future, a signal from us to them."

Memory and desire, the twin agencies of renewal in Eliot's *The Wasteland*, endow Wright's landscapes with a poignancy no less keen for all their sensuality, and beauty: "There's always a time for the grass, teeming / Its little four-cornered purple flowers, / tricked out in an oozy shine" ("Holy Thursday"). Although nature seems to share with the poet a gift for artifice in these lines, it is useful to note how both light and dark shades of vowel sounds serve as pigmentation. The overall tone is brooding, the Sunday morning resurrection anything but guaranteed: "*ooo ooo* of a mourning dove / In the pepper tree, crack / Of blue and a flayed light on the hills."

If visual images strike the synaptic sparks that drive the lyric chronology of most poems in *The Southern Cross* ("the dragonfly, hanging like lapis lazuli in the sun"), a surprising portion of the book is devoted to experimentation with the plastic arts. The painterly techniques applied with only marginal success in "Homage to Paul Cézanne" are brought to full fruition in "Dog Day Vespers":

> Everything drips and spins
> In the pepper trees, the pastel glide of the evening
> Slowing to mother-of-pearl and the night sky.
> Venus breaks clear in the third heaven.

Here the horizon fades like a Renaissance mural into the opalescent tints of dusk. Even Wright's titles, "Composition in Grey and Pink," "Landscape with Seated Figure and Olive Trees," suggest textures more palpable than the written word.

Indeed, Wright betrays a vague dissatisfaction with the self-reflexive aspects of writing in "Childhood's Body": "It isn't enough to transform the curlicues." Words, as they unroll from his fingers—like "cluster and drone" in section twelve of "Tattoos"—no longer embody "things." For Charles Wright, poetry has transcended the sacred technology so lovingly acquired in *Bloodlines*. Hence, his search for identity in *The Southern Cross* becomes more than mere fancy or fidelity to autobiographical fact: "My poems in a language now / I finally understand, / Little tablets of salt rubbed smooth by the wind." Salt is the essence of the quotidian; as a metaphor for language it is at once infinite and irreducible.

At the time of its publication, critics were almost unanimous in designating *The Southern Cross* as Wright's finest book to date. While many of the poems, because of their slow cumulative growth and ornate language, retain a certain nacreous quality, they are anything but the discrete *objets d'art* that Pound once descried as representative of his own verse. Always a poet of landscape, Wright becomes a genuine poet of place, perhaps for the first time in his career. Almost invariably the locale is south: southern California, the southeastern United States, and the Italian peninsula, from the cemetery plot in Rome that hoards the petaled ivory of Keats's bones to the "lime, electric green of the April sea / off Ischia." Gradually the haunts and habitats of Wright's past begin to provide him with a unity of vision commensurate to his gift for image and metaphor. The old themes of death, loss, and salvation acquire a personal dimension largely absent from his earlier collections. "The Southern Cross," which began with the constellation buffeted like a kite in the night heavens, ends with a desire to reinhabit the vanished region of the poet's birth:

> Pickwick was never the wind . . .
>
> It's what we forget that defines us, and stays in the same place,
> And waits to be rediscovered.
> Somewhere in all that network of rivers and roads and silt hills,

A city I'll never remember,

> its walls the color of pure light,

Lies in the August heat of 1935,
In Tennessee, the bottomland slowly becoming a lake.
It lies in a landscape that keeps my imprint
Forever,

> and stays unchanged, and waits to be filled back in.

Someday I'll find it out
And enter my old outline as though for the first time,

And lie down, and tell no one.

The Other Side of the River extends the sense of a personal signature that Wright sought so arduously for years and took full possession of only in *The Southern Cross*. In his interview with J. D. McClatchy, he explains the importance of acquiring a definitive style: "I want people to be able to look at a poem of mine on the page, read it, and to say, as though they had seen a painting on the wall, 'This is Charles Wright.' " Once poets are linked to the formal and structural elements of a particular style, they become free to reshape their identity, to begin writing public poems in a private language as opposed to private poems in a public language. Wright's self-portraitures in *The Other Side of the River* increasingly depict incident and anecdote within the context of place—the present belonging to California, the past to Italy and the American South, the future to that mysterious river with one shore in the temporal world, the other in eternity.

"Lost Souls," an elegiac piece about the death of the poet's father in 1972, offers a sharp contrast to similar poems in *China Trace*, such as "Where Moth and Rust Doth Corrupt." Although the first of its seven sections amounts to an invocation and responsorial, the poem as a whole avoids the sort of arid bliss characteristic of Wright's previous elegies:

From the bad eye and early morning

> you raise me

Unshuttered from the body of ashes

> you raise me

Out of the dust and moth light

> memory

Into the undertow of my own life

> you make me remember.

In "Lost Souls," memory betokens for him "the residue / Of all our illuminations and unnamed lives." It enables Wright to speak beyond the hermetic contours of an *in memoriam* to the finite yet hauntingly numinous moments that denote both grief and joy:

The last time I saw George Vaughan,
He was standing in front of my father's casket at the laying out,
One of the kindest men I've ever known.

When I was sixteen, he taught me the way to use a jackhammer,
                                        putting the handgrip

Into my stomach and clinching down,
Riding it out till the jarring became a straight line.

He taught me the way a shovel breathes,
And how the red clay gives away nothing.
He took my hand when my hand needed taking.

While every section save the first is a self-contained narrative, a series of layers through which the poet rises to some cherished recollection of himself and others, the piece is chronologically circular. In section four, Wright remembers siphoning gin with a straw from the chilled cask of a watermelon:

One evening in 1957, I found myself outside of Nashville,
                                        face down on the ground,
A straw in my mouth, the straw stuck deep
In the ginned heart of a watermelon,
                        the faces of five friends
Almost touching my face
As we sucked the sweet gin as fast as we could.
Over the green hinge of the Cumberland Plateau
The eyelash dusk of July was coming down
                                effortlessly, smooth as an oiled joint,
Agnes rolled over and looked up at the sky.
Her cousin, our host, rolled over and looked up at the sky.

What a life, he said. Jesus, he said, what a life.

The heart of the watermelon is red fruit; like Persephone's pomegranate, it was considered by the ancients to have been exclusively the food of the dead. However, sensual and evocative this passage, the youthful poet and his friends partake of both worlds simultaneously. The host's beguiled utterance is fraught with a wonderful irony that no one present comprehends.

Wright reminisces in the fifth section about the reporting assignment he held with the Kingsport *Times-News* the summer of his seventeenth year. An interlude he elaborated on during the Southern Autobiography Conference at the University of Central Arkansas in April 1991, his job consisted of checking the police blotter for "the drunks, the suicides, midnight's minions," remembered as "the desperate grey faces / Of dirt farmers caught in the wrong dark at the wrong time" in "Lost Souls." The year was 1953, before the days of air conditioning in newsrooms, when Wright weathered "many a six-Coke night."

Despite the vividness of these reflections, he recognizes the past as inevitably transformed by memory and imagination in section six: "Nothing you write down is ever as true as you think it was." The last section of "Lost Souls" alludes to his mother's funeral and the sepulchral existence his father endured until his own death:

> It was June again, and 1964 again,
>   and I still wasn't there
> As they laid her down and my father turned away,
> I still imagine, precisely, into the cave of cold air
> He lived in for eight more years, the cars
> Below my window in Rome honking maniacally
>   *O still small voice of calm . . .*

A glimmer of expatriatism, rare in the poetry of Charles Wright, is embedded in the penultimate line. However, his nostalgia for the American South as it existed during the decade of the fifties, that post-war cultural ambience of "no sweat" clearly delineated in sections four and five, undercuts the poet's sense of personal isolation. Moreover, the bustle of modern traffic in the streets of the Eternal City lends assurance that he is not alone.

"Lonesome Pine Special" is structurally similar to "Lost Souls," the argument of each section a highway that scatters its kudzu-hung narrows throughout Kentucky, Tennessee, Virginia, and the Carolinas: "In Kingsport, when I was growing up, / Everyone seemed to go to Big Stone Gap, Virginia, up U. S. 23, / All the time." Whether the business at hand was a liquor run or a clandestine wedding, the landscape with its mud-chinked cabins and wind-raked jack pines is what always rises like a relief map from the page. On the other hand, "Arkansas Traveller" delves into the personal history of Wright's great-grandfather, who "took a Minie ball in his palate / At Chickamauga he carried there till his death / Almost half a century afterward." The Minie, perhaps smaller than grapeshot, nevertheless punningly calls to mind Keats's "Ode on Melancholy" ("none save him whose strenuous tongue / Can burst Joy's grape against his palate fine") as Wright's forebear, immediately after his convalescence, resorts to verse:

> And wrote a poem back
> To the widow of one of his men about a sure return
> "Where life is not a breath
> Nor life's affections, transient fire. . . in heaven's light."

Surprisingly, the evanescent beauty of the grandsire's fragment reveals that he is a spiritual forefather as well. Wright later remembers the childhood idylls of late evening in Little Rock, where he counted fireflies "Like miniature jellyfish / off the reefs of the sleeping porch / Whose jasmine-and-rose-scented air broke over me back and forth."

At least one of the poems in *The Other Side of the River* seems as abstract as the "Tattoos" sequence in *Bloodlines*. Like "Tattoos," "Cryopexy" has an appended note at the end of the collected volume: "An operation to repair, by freezing with liquid Freon gas, a tear on the eye's retina." But even this piece, consisting of twelve short sections of latticed lines, is grounded in personal experience. When the poem was first submitted for journal publication *(Raccoon 14)* on October 18, 1982, a short note from Wright was included: "I had such a thing [cryopexy] this past June, and for 2½ weeks could do nothing but stare straight ahead—no reading, no writing, no nothing. Hence the resultant poem about light and the eye." The piece begins with a question that is apparently more than rhetorical for the poet: "Looming and phosphorescent against the dark, / Words, always words. / What language does light speak?" The imagery is decidedly baroque, as the speaker seeks elaborate correspondences in the outer world for his own necessarily subjective experience:

> Blood clots, like numb houseflies, hang
> In the alabaster and tracery,
>   icy detritus
> Rocked in the swish and tug
>   of the eye's twice-turned and moonless tides.

Suspended by the primary verb "hang," the fiercely somatic simile for coagulated blood, "numb houseflies," loses its aural nuance when it is effaced by the metaphor "icy detritus" in line three. Lines four and five consist of an extended participial phrase expanding this image into a conceit that strands the speaker, as it were, amid floes in the Arctic. The overall tone is one of isolation and pain, reminding us that Wright is engaged in more than dissecting sunbeams with a prism. For him, light means radiance, something beyond the circumference of the eye:

> What are the colors of true splendor,
>   yellow and white,
> Carnation and ivory, petal and bone?
> Everything comes from fire.

However, Wright's metaphysic refuses to buy into the Renaissance doctrine of hierarchies that locates humankind somewhere between the angels and base minerals. Instead, he continually celebrates the aura of spirit that clings to the universe of matter: "What other anagoge in this life but the self? / What other ladder to Paradise / but the smooth handholds of the rib cage?" ("California Dreaming").

IV

Zone Journals, the third volume collected in *The World of the Ten Thou-sand Things,* posits a subtle variation on Wright's tripartite formula—memo-ry, imagination, language—for artistic growth. By presenting the poem as a conscious record, he implies that any language artifact eventually serves the purpose of memory and hence returns to its point of origin. "Yard Journal," the book's first entry, articulates the notion that poetry is a sacred encoding:

> the more luminous anything is,
> The more it subtracts what's around it,
> Peeling away the burned skin of the world
> > making the unseen seen.

Ultimately, what the poet burns into memory should break from the carbon of the page with a diamond luster. Of course, Wright continues to derive his sense of identity from place, adding England to the more southerly en-virons of California, Italy, and Virginia.

"A Journal of English Days" continues the longer, more expansive and inclu-sive poem that Wright began to pursue earnestly in *The Other Side of the River.* Set in London, 1983, this verse journal accumulates over a period of several months, September through December. The dominant motif amounts to a catalog of poets and artists, those "towering dead" whose works have made an indelible im-pression on Wright. Making his way along the Kensington Church walk, the first poet he recalls is Ezra Pound, "fresh up from Italy" in 1908: "A couple of books of his own poems in one hand / and a dead galaxy / Set to go off in crystal inside his head." Naturally, the flora of the landscape in late September is irresistible:

> . . . the fire-knots of late roses
> Still pumping their petals of flame
> > up from the English loam,
> And I suddenly recognize
> The difference between the spirit and flesh
> > is finite, and slowly transgressable. . . .

Although the image of the rose alludes to the *carpe diem* theme so prominent in the sixteenth-century lyric, it also suggests the spiritual hierarchy represented by the tiers of the great Rose in Dante's *Paradiso.* Wright seems unwilling to accept the blatantly corporeal values of the first, but neither can he embrace completely the spiritual values of the second.

Death emerges as a dominant concern in "A Journal of English Days." In the October section, Wright contemplates Fulke Greville's sarcophagus in a Warwickshire crypt. Later, on All Hallow's Eve, he conjures the "arterial drop of blood" which Keats once coughed into the bed linen, pronouncing it a "Little black light magnet," an absurd image which turns chillingly plausible when we remember the iron component of blood, and how the one drop eventually drew others by the cupful from Keats's lungs. Nor can he be, any more than Keats was, deceived in that color. Here black represents the negation not only of light, but also of life. Interestingly enough, Wright has previously hinted at the presence of the daemonic through color motifs. His inversion of Stevens's solar imagery in the earlier homage to Giacomo Leopardi (another poet whose life was cut short by consumption) is equally arresting: "When the moon's like a golden tick on the summer sky / Gorged with light." The sun's life-giving benefice is negated when the moon fills up with a light not its own. In "Night Journal II," Wright refers to the moon as a "stamped horn of fool's gold." The metaphor is Dionysian, echoing Yeats's "On a Picture of a Black Centaur by Edmund Dulac."

The inscription, which begins the November section, *"—A Traveler between life and death,"* keynotes the prevailing mood of the London entries. By resorting to personification, Wright intimates that we ourselves are stripped bare even as the planet begins to move toward the winter solstice: "November pares us like green apples, / circling under our skins / In long, unbroken spirals." The image of the apple, shedding its green continents of skin, scoured clean by the wind's chill blade, implies that each of us is a world in little. However, in the December section, Wright seems deliberately to dismantle Dryden's definition of the metaphysical poet as one "who sees nature as the key to a transcendent truth alive in the entire universe." The disclaimer is at once abrupt and sobering:

> How sweet to think that Nature is solvency,
> > that something empirically true
> Lies just under the dead leaves
> That will make us anchorites in the dark
> Chambers of some celestial perpetuity—
> > nice to think that,
> Given the bleak alternative,
> Though it hasn't proved so before,
> > and won't now
> No matter what things we scrape aside—
> > God is an abstract noun.

"A Journal of the Year of the Ox" is the centerpiece of *Zone Journals*. A long meditation spanning the year of Wright's fiftieth birthday, its entries are dated chronologically, January through December, though the narration is typically circular. The poet begins by describing himself as "the poor pilgrim, the setter forth," and goes on to disclose that memory, his primary vehicle for creation, occasionally tends to falter: "How shall we hold on, when everything bright falls away? / How shall we know what calls us / when what's past remains what's past?" He is intent on setting down the removal, by treaty, of the Cherokee from the Long Island of the Holston, a river in east Tennessee. As always, the actual narrative is put in motion by an image: "A lone squirrel running the power line / neck bowed like a tiny buffalo." The simile, which transforms the squirrel into a microcosm for bison hunted to the brink of extinction, strikes a familiar synaptic spark, allowing Wright's creative juices to crackle and flow. Recalling the history of the Cherokee's banishment from their sacred ground also enables him to journey back to Italy, the crucible of his artistic birth.

The whole of "A Journal of the Year of the Ox" involves a search for redemption through the "one word / For each of us," at a time when words "hang like bats in the throat, / their wings closed, their eyes shut." Just when the power of language to illuminate seems destined to fail, Wright receives guidance from Dante, the great poet of light:

> *Brother, remember the way it was*
> *In my time: nothing has changed:*
> *Penitents terrace the mountainside, the stars hang in their*
> *   bright courses*
> *And darkness is still the dark:*
> *   Concentrate, listen hard,*
> *Look to the nature of all things.*

Only with the help of his mentor can Wright approach the incarnation, the word made flesh, as in *The Gospel According to St. John:* "The heart is a spondee." This line cannot be read as a simple subject-verb-substantive complement, but must be read as a metaphor, an expression of divine symbiosis. By referring to the heart not only as a word but also as the embodiment of prosodic measure, he insists that poetry transcends the purely rational principles of language. Although Wright denies in what he calls his "darker moments" a belief in the Judeo-Christian mythos, his concluding statement on the art of poetry in *The Paris Review* is worth quoting:

> Language is the element of definition, the defining and descriptive incantation. It puts the coin between our teeth. It whistles the boat up. It shows us the city of light across the water. Without language, there is no poetry, without poetry, there's just talk. Talk is cheap and proves nothing. Poetry is dear and difficult to come by. But it poles us across the river and puts music in our ears. It moves us to contemplation. And what we contemplate, what we sing our hymns to and offer our prayers to, is what will reincarnate us in the natural world, and what will be our one hope for salvation in the What's-To-Come.

In the December 5 entry, Wright returns to the Long Island of the Holston to ponder the names of various Cherokee clans cut into a commemorative slab of marble: *"Wolf Clan, Blue Clan, Deer Clan, Paint Clan, Wild Potato Clan, / Long Hair Clan, Bird Clan."* The catalog of vanished tribes is itself a journal inscription, a manifestation of the dwelling in absence that words betoken. Despite the existential tone of this, perhaps Wright's finest poem, he continues to look for the writing in the void: "I seek out, unsuccessfully, / In Luke's spyglass Halley's comet and its train of ice." The last entry is dated Christmas Day, 1985—the poet still nurtures one precious syllable as the year hastens to its close:

> The afternoon shuts its doors.
> The heart tightens its valves,
>   the dragon maple sunk in its bones,
> The grass asleep in its wheel.
> The year squeezes to this point, the cold
> Hung like a lantern against the dark
>   burn of a syllable:
> I roll it around on my tongue, I warm its edges. . . .

Xionia, the fourth and final gathering in *The World of the Ten Thousand Things*, represents Wright's attempt to synthesize and compress the multiple gleanings of *Zone Journals*. Language, and its ability to crystallize toward an uncertain future, is the central theme of these fifteen comparatively brief entries. The first poem, "Silent Journal," indicates Wright's unwillingness to view words as abstractions existing apart from the natural world: "Inaudible consonant inaudible vowel / The word continues to fall / in splendor around us." Here snow becomes a metaphor for silence, for what remains unspoken, the landscape a psalter untouched by grackle or crow as far as the eye can reach:

> Window half shadow window half moon
>   back yard like a book of snow
> That holds nothing and that nothing holds
> Immaculate text
>   not too prescient not too true

Thus the poet confronts an incandescence prior to and beyond the subtle articulations of hand or heart.

A number of the poems in *Xionia* have an aphoristic flavor, perhaps an indication that Wright is currently about naming a few intrinsic truths. However, to proceed too rapidly on this assumption would be risky, especially when we consider his predilection for Pound's borrowed concept: "Poetry consists of gists and piths." Nowhere is this more evident than in the first section of "China Journal":

North wind like a fine drill
                    sky Ming porcelain for a thousand miles
The danger of what's-to-come is not in its distance
Two inches can break the heart.

However, if we look to longer, more discursive poems, such as "Language Journal," we discern an attempt to establish a dialogue between language as a self-contained reality and nature as a transient yet transcendent truth. Wright begins with a concession of sorts: "Maybe the theorists are right: / everything comes from language." Although the argument is rhetorically convincing, "Nothing means anything, the slip of phrase against phrase / Contains the real way our lives / Are graphed out and understood," we are being set up for an abrupt counterstroke:

But I don't think so today,
                    unless the landscape is language
Itself, which it isn't.
The water beads necklaced across the bare branch of this oak tree
Have something to say now
                    but not about syllables,
For water they are, and to water they shall return.

Despite his austere pronouncement in *Zone Journals* ("God is an abstract noun"), Wright repudiates the idea that all experience is foregrounded in a language that ultimately refers back to itself. In "A Journal of Southern Rivers," he asserts the primacy of the individual personality, the vital creative energy radiated by those first tentative strokes on the page: "What lasts is what you start with. / *What hast thou, O my soul, with Paradise,* for instance, / Is where I began, in March 1959." For him, poetry is the numen, "the black angel asleep on my lips," which can only be awakened through memory and imagination. Words thus formed are more than the simulacre of everything real; they exude a presence, glowing and pungent long after we abandon them: "How can we trust the sure, true words / written in blue ink? / Does the amber remember the pine?"

The extraordinarily simple formulation of memory, imagination, and language which began to serve Wright so well in the seventies comes full circle in *Xionia*. Hence, *The World of the Ten Thousand Things* rounds out a vision two decades in the making, one that combines the complex structure of the later poems with the imagistic and lyric richness of the early ones. What began as a concern with technique or pure form gradually evolves into an engagement with larger themes. In 1927 Ezra Pound wrote to his father, announcing as part of his design for *The Cantos* "the 'magic moment' or moment of metamorphosis, burst thru from quotidian into 'divine or permanent world.' Gods, etc." For Charles Wright, metamorphosis consists not of a sudden break with the things of this world, but an awareness that the magical realms of the spirit and flesh are finally one, as we see in "December Journal":

> From somewhere we never see comes everything that we do see.
> What is important devolves
> > from the immanence of infinitude
> In whatever our hands touch—
> The other world is here, just under our fingertips.

Stanley Plumly: An Appreciation

When Stanley Plumly succumbed to cancer at his home in Frederick, Maryland, on April 11, 2019, it marked the passing of the most versatile and accomplished man of letters since death of Donald Hall the previous year. Born in Barnesville, Ohio, in 1939, Plumly grew up in the lumber and farming regions of Ohio and Virginia. His father plied the hardscrabble trades of lumberjack and welder, and his fatal heart attack at fifty-six was linked to overwork and alcoholism. His mother was a homemaker. Plumly's relationships with both parents, as well as his blue-collar origins, figure prominently in his poetry, especially the later volumes. A graduate of Wilmington College, he took a master's degree in creative writing at Ohio University, and after a brief stint as a visiting poet at Louisiana State University, he returned to Athens with his first book, *In the Outer Dark* (1970), winner of the Delmore Schwartz Memorial Award, already in hand. After Ohio University hired him as a tenure-track assistant professor, Plumly also enrolled in the university's PhD program with the idea of teaching and doing coursework toward an advanced degree. There, he helped Wayne Dodd and Stanley Lindberg found *The Ohio Review* and its renowned interview series, which included American poets such as W. S. Merwin, Galway Kinnell, William Matthews, and Louise Glück. Although he did not complete his doctorate, he subsequently taught at Iowa, Columbia, Princeton, and Houston before finally settling in and establishing the creative writing program at the University of Maryland, College Park, where he eventually retired, having attained the rank of Distinguished University Professor.

During the course of a career that spanned five decades, Plumly garnered an impressive array of accolades. His third book-length collection, *Out-of-the-Body Travel* (1977), took the William Carlos Williams Award and was nominated for the National Book Critics Circle Award. *Old Heart* (2007) won the *Los Angeles Times* Book Prize and was a finalist for the coveted National Book Award. Other honors included fellowships from the Guggenheim, Ingram Merrill, and the National Endowment for the Arts. Plumly was generous when it came to his devotion to the craft, taking time away from poetry to write and gather essays on what Wallace Stevens so memorably called "the supreme fiction" into *Argument & Song: Sources & Silences in Poetry* (2003), the most perspicacious and engaging collection about poetry and poetics since Donald Hall's *Goatfoot Milktongue Twinbird* (1978). Moreover, his *Posthumous Keats: A Personal Biography* (2008) compares favorably with Walter Jackson Bate's canonical assessment of the sublimely gifted young English poet. Perhaps Plumly's own working-class background was a source of identification with Keats, who was once relegated to the "Cockney School" by hostile Tory critics, but as he observes in a *Kenyon Review* conversation with fellow poet David Baker regarding the chapter titled "This Mortal Body," "Mortality, ironically, is Keats's ultimate subject—

mortality placed in tension with its corollary, immortality." Like his English precursor, who died of what was then termed consumption in a small second-floor apartment overlooking the Piazza di Spagna in Rome on the evening of February 23, 1821, Plumly too shared an interest in these themes, which recur throughout his numerous collections.

While Plumly's passion for those poets who ultimately dwell on the upper slopes of Parnassus would ultimately center on John Keats, he was also extravagantly fond of others who belonged to the Era of the Romantic Triumph (though he preferred the designation Regency Period), and William Wordsworth was foremost among these. The myriad wonders of nature (limestone formations fretted with cataracts, evergreen forests carpeted with fragrant needles, dense thickets teeming with redwings and thrashers) and the larger cosmos (the night heavens glittering with "stars of the sixth and seventh magnitude") are omnipresent in Plumly's oeuvre. In his fourth full-length collection, *Boy on the Step* (1989), the opening poem, "Hedgerows," amounts to a Wordsworthian celebration of the phenomenal world's flora and fauna:

> How many names. Some trouble
> or other would take me outside
> up the town's small hill, into the country,
> on the road between them.
> The haw, the interlocking bramble, the thorn
> head-high, higher, a corridor, black windows.

Having chosen to quit the enervating confines of the town for the more agreeable environs of the countryside, Plumly conjures the pleasantry of being lost in the tangle of his sensory experience with the red fruit of the hawthorn and its "interlocking bramble," a self-reflexive analogue for the poem. In the rolling *o* and *r* sounds of "thorn" and "corridor," readers sense the poet savoring vowels and consonants like ripe berries. If one has any reason to doubt this interpretation, he dispels the misgivings in the ensuing lines: "the taste / of the judas elder, and somewhere / the weaver thrush that here they call mistle, / as in evergreen, because of the berries." The poet deems these walks bracing and proceeds with his richly synesthetic recitatives: "the blue air almost cold, / wind like traffic, the paper flowering of the ox-eye / and the campion still white, still / lit like spring." Nevertheless, in spite of the "clarity of morning" gained from these sojourns into nature, the poem's closure is fraught with ineffable sorrow rooted in an irretrievable past: "one more day of the harvest counted, / yellowing, winnowing, / the boy lost in thought / of the turning of the year and the dead father." The title poem of Plumly's fourth collection, *Out-of-the-Body Travel*, offers rare insight into this recurrent subject: the complex and ambivalent relationship with his father. It opens *in medias res* with the enthralled youth's progenitor readying to play a violin, to carve out a classical or Celtic air, but it is the lucid and almost loving attention with which his father plays that holds the speaker and company spellbound:

> And then he would lift this finest
> of furniture to his big left shoulder
> and tuck it in and draw the bow
> so carefully as to make music
>
> almost visible on the air. And play
> and play until a whole roomful of the sad
> relatives mourned.

This gathering is a wake; the elder Plumly's feverish tune is not the fierce music of an instrumental solo, but instead the solemn strains that attend this saddest of occasions: "They knew this was / drawing of blood, threading and rethreading / the needle." As the family listens to his slides and glissandos and watch his bowing, they are stitched with blood, the substance that binds the dead and the survivors, like thread through a needle. Moreover, the speaker sees the impression his father makes on his auditors: "They saw even in my father's / face how well he understood the pain / he put them to—his raw, red cheek / pressed against the cheek of the wood." But in the second part of "Out-of-the-Body Travel," Plumly reveals a darker side of his father's personality when he speaks of his present vocation: "and in one stroke he brings the hammer / down, like mercy, so the young bull's / legs suddenly fly out from under it."

His slaughterhouse endeavors have necessarily inured the man to the murderous and soul-numbing stroke of the eighteen-pound sledge that shatters the cranial bones of cattle and spatters his apron, leaving son and readers alike to contemplate the deadly man wielding a brain-clotted hammer alongside the tender one nuzzling the canted fiddle to his "raw red cheek." Beyond question the vessel of consciousness in the next three lines belongs to the poet: "While in the dream he is the good angel // in Chagall, the great ghost of his body / like light over the town." Marc Chagall was a painter justly famous for his ethereal blue canvases that often feature angels hovering over landscapes populated with fiddlers, lovers, and cattle. Plumly's closure juxtaposed with his dream is decidedly knotted:

> The violin
> sustains him. It is pain remembered.
> Either way, I know if I wake up cold,
> and go out into the clear spring night,
> still dark and precise with stars,
> I will feel the wind coming down hard
> like his hand, in fever, on my forehead.

Critics who insist that Theodore Roethke's "My Papa's Waltz" is a thinly veiled allegory about child abuse will have a veritable field day with this pivotal turn in "Out-of-the-Body Travel." But first, the readers must note the subtle and complex tonal modulation of Plumly's vignette wherein he wanders into a spring night assuredly chill and smelling of damp verdure, "still dark and precise with stars." (One can't help but marvel at the internal half-chime of "dark" and "stars," as well as the *mot juste* "precise.") What follows proves ambiguous, inasmuch as readers must decide whether the hand "coming down hard" on the speaker's forehead is merely callused with toil and now ministering to a sick child or connotes a feckless ire and spontaneous brutality visited "in fever" on the hapless speaker. Does the earlier apparition of "the good angel" bespeak wish fulfillment born of fear? Or does the father contain aspects of both angel and demon?

Further insight into Plumly's various portraits of his father can be gained by looking closely at a poem written later in his career, "For My Father Dead at Fifty-Six on My Fifty-Sixth Birthday," which first appeared in *The Marriage in the Trees* (1997). In it, Plumly recounts an incident from his youth that probably smacked of heroism at the time but avoids the solipsism so prevalent in the Confessional mode by mythologizing the brooding masculinity of his alcoholic father: "I watched you humble a man in a fight once....He went down like an animal whose spirit / world has suddenly collapsed and all that's left / in the wounded moment after is not quite / animal or man." The brutal encounter transforms his father's burly antagonist, the description of which eerily echoes the dispatching of the bull in "Out-of-the-Body Travel." While doubtlessly frightened, the speaker remains entranced by his father's strength, a grip so terrible it could subdue a large man without seriously hurting him: "You had his right / arm at the wrist in your right hand and simply / turned him down onto the floor, which stank of wear / and sawdust." But Plumly also recalls a time when the same hand fell like a thunderbolt on the heads of diseased farm animals: "you hammered home the forelocked skulls of steers / whose sickness wouldn't cure—they were yours to kill / against the slaughterhousing autopsies of / medicine." In a masterstroke of aural mimesis—abrupt glottal stops and fractured *k* sounds—the massive cranial bones of livestock erupt. Yet, in a closure at once poignant and decidedly bitter, Plumly foregoes all family pities:

> you the dire sentimentalist
> who wouldn't let the dead hands of the doctor
>   inside you, while all four chambers of your heart
> filled with the effluvium of both our lifetimes.
>   The man at the bar had the option at least
> of rising and turning back into a man.

For the son, the ultimate defeat derives from his father's overreaching pride, his adamant refusal to submit to the care of a physician. At least the opponent in the bar had the courage and dignity to resume the posture of a man. Indeed, Pumly's own *agon* with the shade of his father proves a sustaining leitmotif throughout his career. In an arresting prose poem titled "Drunks," he voices an ambivalence toward the quixotic individual who labored eighteen hours a day, building a house for his family in the hours after work: "my father was drunk everyday of his life, except for a few Sundays. It's not surprising that he couldn't quite complete the house; or, that as he aged past forty, get to his job on time. He was kind of a failed house himself—large, complicated, incomplete."

During an interview, Plumly once discussed how his mother—invariably a source of compassion and comfort—enabled him to cope with his father's disturbing presence, yet she remains a marginal figure throughout his poetry. In "Naps," however, the poet offers us a glimpse of this nurturing albeit firm matriarch: "In a dream or fantasy I see my mother, / having put me down, leaning over me, / pulling the door shut twice, and if I rise / again, locking it." Apparently an irrepressible child, the boy often threw off his patchwork counterpane and roamed about the house unless his mother turned a brass key. Even in grammar school, his teacher—that archetypal mother surrogate—learns that the future poet has already acquired a listing imagination, that he is prone to "cogitate the tree / within the cloud, the long sunlit fingers / of the crow, and how to hold an object / in the mind and let it turn." Plumly's vivid imagination invites reader participation in the most emphatic way; one sees the shapeshifting cumulonimbus formations turn into oaks that rain leaves and acorns in the fall, as well as the viridescent sheen of a crow's "sunlit" wing. Indeed, the whole of "Naps" is an extended metaphor: "the way / a doorknob with its facet-gaze of glass / becomes a diamond or a crystal / and as you fall asleep, disintegrates, / snow in a paperweight." Plumly's closure is both poignant and hauntingly numinous:

> Then wait the voice outside calling our return,
> the same voice as the moment of instruction:
> to lie down in the middle of the day,
> dream fragmentary, dusk-enhancing dreams,
> to be the body-of-the-one looked-upon,
> come back to life, O startled, distant child.

The vocative "O" is an earnest imploration, nothing less than a fervent desire to return to those miraculous hours of childhood lived under the aegis of the good mother.

In this critic's opinion, *Orphan Hours* (2012) and *Boy on the Step* (1989) emerge as Plumly's finest volumes, one confronting the remorseless specter of his mortality, and the other lending the fullest expression to his personal origins, especially the often tragic circumstances of his parents. Indeed, the poems in *Boy on the Step* are among the finest written by any American poet during the eighties. In the meditative "Above Barnesville"—an elliptical narrative divided into a half-dozen sections, each running sixteen lines—Plumly devises a personal creation myth, starting with the heavens and earth: "In the body the night sky in ascension— / the starry campion, the mallow rose, the wild potato vine. / You could pick them, though they'd die in your hand." Here, Plumly's vision of the phenomenal world is both corporeal and spiritual, the lush vegetation failing ethereally in plundering hands. In his birthplace, time takes on familial, geological, and historical implications. The terrain once held the dubious allure of easy riches, precious nuggets of yellow metal scattered in the wake of a retreating glacier: "It's here, in the thirties, that the fathers panned for gold, / pick-and-shovel, five-to-a-dollar-a-day—you could survive / panning the glacial drift, the spilt rock, the old alluvial scar." But the landscape soon dwindles to a legacy of poverty and bootless toil: "The rock-soil thinning out, coal breaking ground like ice."

In the poem's second part, the speaker juxtaposes his biological origins against the vast myth of the land and magnifies his parents like a constellation:

> Deep autumnal nights, I imagine my parents lying side
> by side on the good grass looking up at the coal-and-diamond dark,
> as they will lie together for the rest of their lives.
> The star lanes scatter, and disappear. I will be born
> under the sign of the twins less than a mile from here,
> with too much blood on the floor. My father, right now
> is turning toward my mother. In the doctrine of signatures
> the body is divisible, the heart the leaf of a red bud
> or the blue ash in a fire, the genitalia
> the various and soft centers of the shell
> the long spathe and cleft, the pink pouch of the flower.

Even as Plumly's future parents lie in a nocturnal embrace in the "good grass," gazing at the configuration of stars overhead, "the coal-and-diamond dark" intimates the hazards and privations of an environment being robbed of its mineral resources. Moreover, the curious double-adjective combination "coal-and-diamond" promises little hope for immediate metamorphosis, in that carbon ticks but once in a thousand years. Although the poet is born amid natal fires—one envisions the big, bloody clinker of a rose—and likens "genitalia" to the "spathe and cleft" of the region's flora, the overall tone of this passage is decidedly ambiguous. The heart itself is divided between "the leaf of a redbud" and "the blue ash in a fire."

In the third section of "Above Barnesville," the poet remembers his father's mercurial temperament in a more favorable light, as the older man becomes enraged at the sight of a tree "gouged and rendered useless and cut down." The poet is still a youth, but already he has a sense of the vatic and living history recorded in his environment: "The word for wood is xylem, which is the living tissue, / and by a kind of poetry graduates inward / from summer to winter to sapwood to the heart." In the poem's fourth section though, the speaker's musings yield to the realities of a diminishing landscape:

> At night, sometimes, you could hear the second shift,
> and fantasize the train's elliptical passage through town
> or the mythical ocean pulling moonlight from your windows.
> You could hear the celestial traffic taking off.
> But in the morning crack-white and plain it would be nothing
> but the earth made new again, a little less each time.

Sections five and six eulogize the death of the poet's father, who gets "down on his knees" but refuses to "climb the ladder so loved by believers." The earlier image of the "fathers" panning "the old alluvial scar" comes to rest in one man whose body will drift forever in "the black and crystalline light of coal and rock, / through the flake and mica leaves, layer upon layer." Soon the poet's mother is swept away in endless snowdrifts: "She'd watch it for hours, letting it fall." Eventually the natural landscape, with its "wildflowers, corn-blues and golden rod," will be consumed by the demand for fossil fuels. Plumly's final assertion is so fraught with the inevitable that it takes on the force of an axiom: "if water rises, stones will burn." The valedictory tone of its last two sections notwithstanding, the extraordinary range and scope of "Above Barnesville" enable Plumly to achieve a rectitude and solace unprecedented in his earlier reminiscences, making it one of the most vital poems in his oeuvre.

With regard to Plumly's nuclear family, in particular his vexed relationship with his father, one is obliged to look closely at yet another poem in *Boy on the Step*. Oddly enough, Plumly often cited Emily Dickinson's influence as more personally meaningful than Walt Whitman's; however, in "The Foundry Garden," his recourse to anaphora, balance, antithesis, and a profusion of participles functioning as adjectives very clearly echoes "Out of the Cradle Endlessly Rocking":

> Myths of the landscape—
> the sun going down in the mouths of the furnaces,
> the fires banked and cooling, ticking into the dark, here and there
>   the sudden flaring into roses,
> then the light across the long factory of the field, the split and rusted
>   castings,
> across the low slant tin of the buildings, across fallow and tar and burnt
>   potato ground....

. . . .
then the milling back to earth, rich earth, the silica of ash.

In a passage at once sonorous and expansive, resonant with the onomatopoeia of "slant tin roofs," Plumy conjures an interlude when poverty obliged his family to eke out a bare subsistence from potato rows planted in a field flanked by a pasture and a foundry. As usual, his father combines a relentless resilience with the urge to imbibe: "Arable fields, waste and stony places, waysides— / the day he got the job at the Wellbaum and Company Foundry he wept, / and later pulled the plug on a bottle." The more typical turn of phrase would be "pulled the cork," but the locution "plug" implies that the elder Plumly's thirst for hard liquor had no bottom. Like Whitman, the poet relishes the act of naming: "I remember the fencerow, the white campion, / the calyx and coronal scales, the hawthorns, cut to the size of a hedge, / the haws so deep in the blood of the season they bled." Thus, he counters the previous image of the industrial slag heaps ticking down with a mellifluous incantation of wildflowers sprung from fencerow and hedge. But the memory of digging for coarse brown tubers with his father supplants all other recollections:

> The year we were poor enough to dig potatoes we had to drive there,
> then wait for the men to leave who let fires go out.
> There'd be one good hour of daylight, the rough straight rows running
>   into shade.
> . . . .
> I can see my father now, cut in half by the horizon, coming toward
>   me, both arms weighted down.

This crepuscular delving seems an almost transgressive activity, yet the father once more becomes a transcendent figure "weighted" with the earth's bounty. Young Plumly will eventually paint the foundry's exterior, a gesture that both renews and replenishes. "Later, in the summer, I'd have painted the dead rust undulant sides of all the buildings aluminum, / which in the morning threw a glare like water on the garden." The poet locates the nexus between flesh and spirit in the daily striving to nourish the body; for the mature Plumly, the foundry represents what William Butler Yeats so aptly called "the foul rag and bone shop of the heart." Redemption lies in the garden paced off in its shadow.

Plumly's musings on his personal history and parents' mortality are matched by a keen, all-pervasive historical sense, which encompasses the broad sweep of human history as well as his own confrontation with inevitability. He is ever mindful of the eternal verities indelibly expressed in myth and lore, which he deploys to stunning effect in his poem "In the Old Jewish Cemetery in Prague," set in the Prague ghetto, one of the oldest in Europe: "Winter riot of waves the way these stones / pile up, as if the dead, twelve deep in places, / had risen cold and left in anger." The frequent aspirates—especially *w* sounds—whistle up bone-chilling gusts that seem to buffet the slanted headstones. Plumly intuits a burgeoning groundswell in the weathered necropolis that accreted, layer by layer, over the course of four centuries: "Something / threatening in their supernatural overlap / and angle, too alive, awkward, accidental, / some pushed from under, like roots." A melancholy so profound he cannot lend it utterance overtakes the poet as the season's first flakes break into crystal high above the quarried markers—"under the limes and brooding maples— limestone, sandstone, rose Silvenec marble ruined"—but Plumly effects an abrupt shift of scene and tone in his second stanza:

> At *The Watering of the Horses of the Sun*
> Apollo holds the water in a shell from
> which one blazing stallion drinks, while
> holding off three others breathing fire
> with a hand and the pure power of his body—
> this in bas-relief above the double stable
> doors of the eighteenth-century Hotel de Rohan.

Here, Plumly extends his elegiac mood and achieves apotheosis through the medium of stone, describing a bas-relief sculpture carved into the pediment of the stables adjoining the Paris residence of Cardinal Armand Gaston Maximilien de Rohan. The French artist, Robert Le Lorrain, surely had no thought for the Prague cemetery, choosing a scenario from Hellenic mythology to fulfill his commission. Plumly combines visual and aural effects, intimating through cumulative long *o* and glyptic *t* sounds how skillfully Le Lorraine blended the contour of muscular flanks and roiling clouds in his tableau; moreover, fricatives in "holding off" and "breathing fire" evoke the dilated nostrils and proud mettle of the sun-god's plunging stallions. The poet marvels at the evanescent beauty chipped free from such an obdurate substance:

> Le Lorraine has built his story,
> at the source, both rain and horses coming
> out of the clouds, with the sun-god almost casual
> between, in pockmarked pearl, sepulchral stone
> but full of the life of the sky.

In the delicate plosives of "pockmarked pearl," readers glean the lapidary stroke of a chisel tracing out the lineaments of fractious, powerful beasts. The breathing plasticity and rare translucence of Le Lorraine's sculpture contrast sharply with the names of the dead cut deep into the cold slabs uprooted and tossed about the Jewish cemetery. However, Plumly locates the life principle in the dialectical opposition between pagan myth and historical fact:

> When you
> stand in the middle of the ghetto graves
> and look straight up you can see why the dead
> hate weather, why blue is the color of the
> spirit rising, light the weightless moment.

Here, the poet enunciates an ontological rather than an optical truth; moreover, he recognizes that stone itself proves all too mutable: "Stone is the shade of memory, / snowfall, dust, the piling and the drift." It is also important to remember Chagall, the compelling contrast between the Jewish painter's nimbus-lit seraphs and Le Lorrain's rampant studs hewn from *le pietra de luce* ("the stone of light"); all are destined to perish.

By the time *Orphan Hours* (2012) was released, Plumly had written extensively about the relationship with his parents, their mortality, and mortality in general, subjects he continued to explore in this collection while also working to come to terms with his cancer diagnosis and his own impending demise. Throughout this volume he embodies Samuel Johnson's remark to his young protégé, James Boswell, when the latter expressed trepidation regarding the idea that, from the moment of conception, we hasten inexorably toward our end: "Sir, a man knows it must be so and submits. It will do him no good to whine." Although its conclusion is somewhat bleak, the poem "Lost Key," rather than a maudlin plaint about the certainty of death, expresses a firm resolve while contemplating the inevitable. As he explores cultural attitudes toward mortality and the afterlife, the poet recalls various tableaux in rich dictions reminiscent of Wordsworthian "spots of time": "Signs and wonders. / My mother would sit for hours inside silence, / who also loved windows and the picture of the world inside of them." In another scenario, he meditates on parables from Arabian and Muslim mythology:

> In the story
> of the Jinnee, the soul is a sparrow hidden
> in a box hidden in another, diminishing to seven,
> diminished further in seven smaller chests
> hidden in "a coffer of marble," with the captive
> placed in covenant, to be hidden in a cave
> "within the verge of the circumambient ocean,"
> only to be discovered, the sparrow strangled.

The marmoreal "coffer"—a chest carved from that most valued stone—contains the avian "soul" hidden in ever smaller boxes and eventually secreted away in a cavern surrounded by an ocean of unfathomable beryl. Rather than submit to the fatalism of the Arabian parable—"the sparrow strangled"—he ponders other prospects: "Or is the soul the raindrop as it falls back / to the sea or the single star stationed in Orion?" The poet prefers to locate intimations of the divine in nature and the larger cosmos, but he dismisses even this notion as too facile and reductive: "Rhetorical compared to the thrush's evensong, / the beauty of the redwing, and the living soul / about to leave the mouth, moth then butterfly." Most affecting are the segments wherein Plumly recollects his mother's dying. "The night my mother died she held onto me // in order to keep her upright over the depths / above which lying down means falling." Such moments are at once austere and heartbreakingly lovely:

> Air, she said, was the angel
> outside the white constructions of snow,
> building at different speeds, falling from different
> heights, replaced by the shapes of things with ghosts:
> her snow-covered hands holding fast to the fear
> that she was alone and without death would end
> as one of those women on the street
> who in weather sleep wrapped up in cars.
> My mother's poverty, her soft hand on a forehead
> still prone to fever and a childhood fear of ceilings.

His mother's nurturing hand will soon lie inert on the cold sheets, and the poet's legacy will be one of loss later than he can dream now. Plumy pines for the comfort of the sacred rituals once prominent in European culture but to little avail:

> Water and its wine
> turned into blood, bread of the body.
> Who can trust in these except to love the dead?
> Flesh back into the word, like the spirit into dried wood
> rising from the fire, channeling the airy brightness.

Each successive layer of "Lost Key" forms a palimpsest that in some measure subsumes and supplants previous speculations: "I break bread seasoned with rosemary. These, / in themselves miracles." Lest we imagine that this is the bread of transubstantiation rather than affliction, the poet leaves us with this grim coda: "No wonder death / is stone, sealed lips, and beyond recognition. / No wonder words are wasted breath."

Elsewhere, Plumly adopts an attitude of seeming resignation, as in "Deciding Not to Be Buried but Burned," ultimately abjuring Judeo-Christian beliefs about death and the afterlife. Initially, he meets with an attorney to arrange the disposal of his earthly remains: "When the lawyer asked I thought the options through, / not that there are many, then decided, like the majority, / to end up underground in order to assume my throne in heaven." On the surface, it would appear that Plumly has capitulated to "the majority" concerning the disposition of his remains. The poet's tone is actually a bit acerbic here, in that he dismisses *sotto voce* the Christian doctrine that "the dead shall be raised incorruptible" only if the body is interred whole in sanctified ground. He deliberately plays on the verb "assume," ever mindful of the church liturgy that consigns the corpse to the earth "in sure and certain *hope* of the resurrection." In short, he suggests, nothing is to be "assumed."

> But later, and in love, the truth about the body bothered me,
> the way gravity, another word for *grave*, had taken over—
> pull of the earth, moon tides, reformation of the stars,
> leaf by leaf, the dying heart alive inside its bell,
> my parents lying side by side beside their parents.

The speaker, now "in love"—clearly a reference to Keats's "Ode to a Nightingale" ("I have been half in love with easeful Death")—deliberately plays on the etymology of "*grave,*" which is rooted in the Old English *græf* and sounds like "grief" when spoken aloud. Tying it also to the force of gravity, he evokes the folding and falling of the ocean, its tides governed by the meteor-pocked satellite that orbits our planet. He then resorts to a pun on the locution "reformation" apropos of the stars. It could also be read as a noun—the sixteenth-century movement to purge the Roman Catholic Church of abuses that led to the various Protestant sects—or perhaps a verb that denotes the realignment of the constellations. Inevitably, as he considers "the truth about [his] body," the pull of gravity manifest in his aging, he envisions his parents asleep with their own forebears under the satin-lined rafters of the tomb, something he intimates is less than appealing. Plumly then contemplates what "the mind" wants, equating it with the psyche or soul:

> The mind wanted nothing more than early mornings,
> early evenings of the doves in the live oaks they sing in
> and fly from, lifting, turning, circling back to home:
> it wanted clarity, stone, the bright air water blue,
> to see the mile of the animal still moving on the hill,
> to lie down in the grass and rest and wake up free
> from tasks, especially remembering.

In expressing the mind's desire for an eternal now, the poet's voice is given unfettered scope. There is an urge toward Whitmanian cataloging in this passage, and structurally it mimics the "lifting, turning, circling back"—in this instance, the mourning birds—that defines poetry as a return upon an orbit already traced. The mood is celebratory, but the desire "to lie down in the grass" echoes unmistakably the Twenty-third Psalm's "he maketh me to lie down in green pastures," dampening the celebration with more dogma. The poem waxes lachrymose as Plumly subsequently meditates on the tiny, eloquent objects of daily life destined to become grave goods: "things they place in pockets / or in your hands—letters, wedding rings, photographs so dated / no one knows where or from whom." The poet knows that these mementos are for the living, for posterity, that such things await the inevitable hour "when someone finds them, / hopes they matter in the afterlife, along with the pyx and cups / and golden bread and Lacrima Christi." Do the accoutrements of the Eucharist, or any ritualized act, ensure immortality? Plumly, in his desire for an obliterating dispersal via smoke and heat-flaked bone that closes the poem, doesn't think so. Thus, he opts instead for incineration, the refining fires of the crematorium: "That's / when I knew that when the time came that what was left of me, / especially memory, had to be purged, forgotten in fire."

Thus far this appreciation has dealt for the most part with the influence that Plumy's parents had on his personal and artistic development and how both served as subjects for some of his most compelling verse. But I must shift here to note more deeply those literary precursors who were seminal in his refinement as a poet, particularly John Keats, and that entails acknowledgement of his *Posthumous Keats: A Personal Biography* and a close look at a few of the poems Plumly wrote about his most cherished of Romantic poets. The biography runs almost four hundred pages, and if it does not add significantly to previous biographical assessments written by W. Jackson Bate and Robert Gittings, it offers the unique perspective of one who was a master practitioner of the craft and whose lyrical prose style is the epitome of what Alexander Pope intended by his line, "What oft was thought but ne're so well expressed." Jack Salinger said of *Posthumous Keats*, "It's certainly the best book ever written about Keats (and I've read all the others) and may well be the best book anyone has ever written on any writer." Indeed, Plumly was no armchair chronicler of Keats's brief and somewhat ill-starred sojourn on this planet. He was himself acquainted with Hampstead Heath and lived for a time in an apartment one floor above the tiny bedroom, overlooking the Piazza di Spagna in Rome, where the twenty-five-year-old poet coughed his life out during the winter of 1821. In *Posthumous Keats,* Plumly makes this telling observation: "He feared he had failed, his body brought down by disease, his poems belittled by Tory critics. But he also knew something: 'Trust the writing.'" In short, the author of "The Eve of St. Agnes" and the great odes brought a witness to his achievement that could not lie—the poems themselves. Moreover, Plumly hints that if Keats's accomplishments did not equal Shakespeare's, his inherent genius did.

Plumly's biography of Keats evolved over the course of twenty years, and its narrative structure is concentric, comparable to his own description of a tree's growth in "Above Barnesville," which merits repeating here: "The word for wood is xylem, which is the living tissue, / and by a kind of poetry graduates inward / from summer to winter to sapwood to the heart." One is immediately reminded of Keats's axiom from a letter to John Taylor dated February 27, 1818: "If poetry comes not as naturally as leaves to a tree, it had better not come at all." Both Plumly's poetry and prose have deep taproots in the fertile soil of the imagination, but they are firmly anchored in the empirical world. He stated in an interview that "for me it is impossible to live in the enclosure—and what I consider the claustrophobia—of a completely imagined world." Indeed, *Posthumous Keats* had its inception in Plumly's poem of the same title. Thus, "Posthumous Keats" now serves as a vital intertext for his biographical work. It opens not on "faery lands forlorn" but with a vivid description of the carriage ride the young English poet took with Joseph Severn, who would soon sit vigil at his deathbed. As the pair move over rough terrain sprung and teeming with wildflowers, the Eternal City looms some six or seven days distant:

> The road is so rough Severn is walking,
> and every once in a while, since the season is
> beautiful and there are flowers on both sides,
> as if this path had just been plowed,
> he picks up by the handful what he can
>
> and still keep up. Keats is in the carriage
> swallowing blood and the best of the bad food.
> It is early November, like summer,
> honey and wheat in the last of the
> daylight, and above the mountains a clear
>
> carnelian heart line.

Keats had already composed his Horatian ode "To Autumn" on that cold island in the North Atlantic when he embarked for the Italian Peninsula, and, despite the fact that he is coughing up arterial blood and swallowing what bad provisions could be purchased with the pittance his publisher advanced him, Severn piles the coach with fresh-plucked flowers as if it were a hearse. Plumly's measured syntax and diction provide an interesting counterpoint to the lurching progress Keats endures over wagon-rutted roads. Equally adroit is the facility with which the vessel of consciousness shifts from Severn to Keats. It is through the lens of the painter Severn that readers take in the languorous "honey and wheat in the last of the / daylight" and the horizon burning the color of red jasper, "a clear / carnelian heartline." Severn continues to heap the wobbling conveyance with blossoms of various hues: "rust, magenta, / marigold and the china white of cups." Meanwhile, "Keats is floating, his whole face luminous," and the reader can almost discern the translucent skull beneath the skin, as in the poet's death mask, attributed to Gheradi. Here, Plumly interjects with a biographer's apparent detachment, probably unaware that his own prose account would in the fullness of time flow mellifluously through a pen nib's eye: "The biographer sees no glory in this, / how the living, by increments, are dead / how they celebrate their passing, half in love." The poet's "Posthumous Keats" is no mere transcriptive retelling: at every turn readers are aware of an impassioned albeit ordering intelligence. Plumly, adhering scrupulously to a decasyllabic line, compresses the pathos of Keats's predicament into one stanza:

> In his head he is writing a letter
> about failure and money and the ten-
> thousand lines that could not save his brother.
> But he might as well be back at Gravesend
> with the smell of sea and the cold sea rain.

Unlike Severn, who rapturously plunders the countryside's polychromatic flora, Keats's mood is introspective as he ponders the harsh realities that led him to this bleak pass. He is acutely aware of sums unwisely lent and borrowed as well as the "ten- / thousand lines" of *Endymion,* subjected to a vitriolic review by John Gibson Lockhart at *Blackwood's Magazine.* Inasmuch as Keats's combined volumes sold only two hundred copies in his lifetime, he could not hope to afford his younger brother Tom (who died of tuberculosis) optimum medical help. Ironically, Keats threw over his own training as an apothecary for a literary career and no doubt, as he watched his sibling's emaciated shadow cast upon the wall by a guttering candle, he reflected bitterly on Lockhart's opprobrium: "We venture to make one small prophecy, that this publisher will not a second time venture 50 quid upon anything he can write. It is better and a wiser thing to be a starved apothecary than a starved poet; so back to the shop Mr. John, back to the plasters, and pills and ointment boxes, & etc."

Plumly can be startlingly adept with regard to word choice. Note his subtle play on "Gravesend," Keats's point of departure for Italy and a foreshadowing that his destination will mark "grave's end." Plumly's ensuing lines are eerily prescient: "he might as well be lying in a room, / in Rome, staring at a ceiling stylized / with roses." The roses portend the violets growing over Keats's plot in Rome's Cimitero Accatolico. With "the taste in the air of apples," he depicts Keats relishing the cider-tart odor as the doomed young poet's ruminations turn back to England's "meadows near / St. Cross." Plumly then recollects the days prior to composing the ode "To Autumn": "In the poem it is Sunday, the middle // of September, the light a gold conglomerate / of detail." He cites one of the letters from that interlude, how Keats renounced "the chilly green of spring," observing how a fall stubble field looked warm "in the way some pictures / look warm." As Keats evokes painting, he and Severn become one vessel of consciousness:

He has closed his eyes.
And he is going to let the day close down.
He is thinking he must learn Italian.
By the time they reach Campagna the wind
will be blowing, the kind that begins at sea.
Severn will have climbed back in, finally a
passenger, with one more handful to add
to what is already overwhelming.

The two pilgrims are already well into the 140-mile overland journey from the port town of Naples, but only Keats seems aware of how perilous his condition is at the time. Plumly, who typically composes in long sentences complete with internal phrases and clauses broken across several lines, introduces three terse periods into his penultimate stanza. Implicit in the tonal and structural shift is a sense of how exquisitely weary and perhaps resigned his protagonist is at the moment. But Keats's resolve to learn the Tuscan dialect indicates that some semblance of hope remains. In Plumly's final stanza, Severn resumes his place in the carriage; however, the flowers he's gathered prove more overwhelming than heartening. Nevertheless, he is on board both figuratively and literally. He will tend Keats through the hemorrhages, bloodlettings, and prescribed starvation diet (one anchovy and a crust of bread), and abide Keats's bitter reproaches when he withholds the lethal dose of laudanum intended to end the poet's mental and physical anguish. Severn will endure days without sleep, sketching the countenance drenched with feverish night sweats more to keep himself awake than for posterity. He eventually follows the tiny predawn processional to Keats's pit, gouged out of raw clay in Rome's Cimitero degli Inglesi.

In "Keats in Burns Country," which first appeared in *The Marriage in the Trees*, Plumly adopts an innovative tripartite structure consisting of interlocking blank-verse sonnets. It is written in decasyllabics, and Plumly employs substitutions and inversions to approximate colloquial speech. The dramatic situation is a walking tour of the countryside around Scotland, Ireland, and the English Lake District undertaken by Keats and Charles Brown during the summer of 1818. Plumly's highly evocative language amply demonstrates his willingness to grow and develop as an artist; indeed, he made this arduous pilgrimage himself: "I've climbed Ben Nevis; I've trailed along much of the journey north that Keats and Brown made that fateful summer. There is no substitute, whatever the subject, for being there." In short, Plumly deliberately sought, as Keats did in the previous century, new imaginative perspectives that the breathtaking vista from Scotland's lofty Ben Nevis, the highest peak in the British Isles, still provides. This firsthand experience enables Plumly to adopt the second-person point of view in "Keats in Burns Country," and hence his mode is one of direct address, deepening the historical ironies and lending the poem a genuine sense of urgency that is earned in line after line.

Plumly conveys emphatically as the piece unfolds that Keats's visit to the Burns Cottage at Alloway—birthplace of the Scots tenet farmer who penned "Highland Mary," "My Love Is Like a Red, Red Rose," "Banks o' Doon," and "Auld Lang Syne"—occasions disillusionment and even dismay: "It wasn't so much that Burns, like the best, / dies young, nor that he's buried among / Lowlanders at the Borders." Although this is a narrative poem, Plumly's narrative bent is hardly prosaic. Notice the alliterative *b* cadences and internally rhyming voiced velar stops—"young" and "among"—in these first three lines. Plumly draws attention early to the ways that Burn's life prefigures Keats's, then proceeds to reconfigure Burn's dismal life circumstances through Keats's eyes:

> nor that in
> eighteen eighteen, Scotland, in spite of its
> beauty, is black granite country, nor that
> the Kirk is presbyterian stone
> over the soul, nor that the poverty
> of the dirt farmer, which Burns was and was
> poorly, is medieval, nor even that
> his widow survives and haunts the churchyard—

By proxy of his young protagonist, Plumly confirms, then paradoxically refutes—note the repetition of the coordinating conjunction "nor"—the desolate existence of Scotland's national bard. Through the plosive *b* in "beauty" and "black," Plumly intimates the austere yet unsettling loveliness of the border terrain. His contention that the "Kirk" or church is "presbyterian stone / over the soul" presents readers with a felicitous conflation of geology and theology, a subtle trope indicating the oppressive nature of religious institutions. The grueling days that Burns spent behind the double yoke of oxen pulling the long furrow toward sundown, Plumly's Keats now deems medieval, at once feudal and futile. (Recall the potato rows gleaned by Plumly and his father in "The Foundry Garden," indicating that he too has transcended his roots, both literally and aesthetically). His next assertion stems almost wholly from Keats's perspective and proves chillingly portentous: "his widow survives and haunts the churchyard." For years after his death, Keats's secretly betrothed Fanny Brawne would dress in widow's weeds and walk the woods of Hampstead Heath long after nightfall. The closure to Plumly's first stanza is equally ominous, suggesting that his Keats sees in Burns's predicament the very portraiture of his own: "It isn't these hostilities nor those / you can imagine so much as the fact / of Burns alive in failure, with only words on paper to compensate his death."

The second stanza of "Keats in Burns Country" ostensibly betrays even more gloom than the first: "Tom's alive in Hampstead hanging on, / younger than both of you will ever be / again." His description of Keats's journey to Burns country is also bitingly evocative: "mostly it's a ragtag walk

/ between the town's consumptive rain and chill- / blain wind." The Scottish poet's monument seems appropriate to young Keats—"you think his white marble tomb's on scale"—but its chiseled legend is not commensurate to the Highlander's indominable spirit and searing lyric acumen: "nothing of the spirit of the man / or the half-perfect heartbreak of his poems." For Plumly's youthful but doomed Keats this is a heady moment—Plumly's repetition of fricative *f* in the turn of phrase "half-perfect heartbreak" deftly emblazons these lines on readers' minds. Huddled that night beneath a thatched roof, Keats assays his first dram of potations: "This is your first warm taste of whiskey, / your first real taste of the barley-bree of fame"—underscoring the tragedy of Keats's fate and his stunning triumph. Plumly's closure to this splendid poem is deeply affecting:

> Burns worked here and walked here you are thinking
> and talked with Bitches and drank with Blackguards,
> the ultimate sublime of what he wrote.
> You're failing too and by the time you climb
> the snow cloud of Ben Nevis you'll be dead.

Keats refuses to be daunted when confronted by the stark reality of Burn's life, and this is in some measure evident in Plumly's flawless accents. The alliterative sounds in "worked" and "walked" as well as the internal rhymes of "walked" and "talked" tread nimbly as the cleft hooves of a mountain goat along the auditory canal. But Plumly comes down hard on the metrical register in the locutions "Bitches," "drank," and "Blackguards," conjuring the table-pounding cadences of a drunken rout. Thus, Plumly imparts, through the pitch and timbre of his rhythms, that Keats was aware of Scotland's Ploughman Poet having consorted with "Bitches" and caroused with "Blackguards," but this dissolute behavior did not mitigate "the intimate sublime of what he wrote." Nevertheless, Plumly deems Keats the better poet by implying that Ben Nevis, shrouded in altostratus clouds, is not quire Parnassus. The observation "you're failing too" proves doubly, even triply, ironic since both Keats and Burns have secured their foothold in the Western canon, which perhaps Plumly will do also in the fullness of time.

Another of Plumly's exquisite meditations on Keats and the artists of the Romantic Triumph is "Constable's Clouds for Keats," which splits its focus between Keats and the British landscape painter John Constable, whose naturalistic oil canvases would eventually earn him a place in the Royal Academy. Plumly manipulates a continuous parallel between the lives of Constable, who survived well into middle age, and Keats, remaining acutely aware of the similarities and differences between the two aesthetic virtuosos. Comprised of six quatrains executed in flawless iambic pentameter, the poem opens with an account of Constable's subject and methodology: "They come in off the sea peaceable masters / and hold the sea in the sky as long as they can. / And you write them down in oils because of their / brilliance, and to remember, in turn, each one." The "they" here are the titular clouds, and Constable wants to record these massed formations before the rain pours down, reducing each one to a distillate mist. The liquid nasal "oils" is wonderfully evocative, almost onomatopoeic, of Constable's brush strokes and each raindrop as it falls. In the ensuing lines, the lives of Constable and Keats intersect:

> It's eighteen twenty-two after the Regency,
> and it would be right in the year after his death
> to think of these—domed above the Heath
> in their isolated chronicle—as elegies
>
> of the spirit; right to see the forms
> as melancholy hosts, even at this distance.
> Yet dead Keats is amorphous, a shapelessness
> reforming in the ground, and no one you can know enough
>
> to remember. He lies in the artist's paradise
> in Rome, among the pagan souls of sheep at pasture.

Naturally, Plumly refers to Keats, whose special province—like Plumly's—was the "vale of soul making," when he suggests Constable's cloud are "elegies of / the spirit." But for Constable he is "no one you know enough / to remember": in fact, the recently deceased poet is "amorphous, a shaplessness / reforming in the ground." Blood to mold, heart to mineral, he lies with the lock of hair and unopened letter from Fanny Brawne in the pocket of his wine-colored waistcoat. Near Keats in the Cimitero Accatolico are the mortal remains of Percy Bysshe Shelley, another in "the artist's paradise / in Rome," and now, Plumly poignantly reminds readers, sheep crop the grass and defecate on the graves of two poets who never lived to celebrate their thirtieth birthdays but are now numbered among the master spirits of the age.

Plumly goes on to note that both Constable and Keats mused and sought inspiration in the same locale: "You'll lie in Hampstead where he should have stayed / to meet you in your walks up Lower Terrace / or along the crowning High Street heading home." Constable will be interred in the Hampstead Parish Church, and Keats wrote "Ode to a Nightingale," arguably the finest ode in the English language, beneath a plum tree near his residence at Wentworth, also in Hampstead. Although the two artists crossed paths, they never met and thus were unable to discuss technique with regard to brush strokes or anapests, a missed opportunity that intrigues Plumly: "Keats could have met you—you must have seen him once / against the light, at least. He could be / crossing on Christchurch Hill Road now." Only Plumy's knack for syntax or formal elegance could capture Keats in chiaroscuro so memorably. As auspicious as a meeting between these two luminaries would have been, it is not surprising that the myriad what-ifs Plumy evokes ultimately alight more on the poet than the painter, even when Constable is the one imagined as the seer:

> He could be looking at the clouds blooming between
> buildings, watching the phantoms levitating stones.

> He was there your first summer writing odes,
> feeling the weather change from warm to chill,
> focused no less than you, on daylight's last detail,
> wondering what our feelings are without us.

Plumy effaces the boundary between heaven and earth as Constable luxuriates in the foliate shapes the cloud masses assume, lending each a breathing sentience. A valedictory tone creeps in as Plumly alludes to Keats's great odes, especially "To Autumn," the last poem he wrote before boarding the *Maria Crowther*, which bore him to Italy and his "posthumous existence." Plumly, through Constable's perspective, yearns to seize "daylight's last detail" and wonders "what our feelings are without us," obliged as both he and his poetic father John Keats are to stake all on the dwelling in absence that words betoken.

Against Sunset (2017), Plumly's last volume to be published during his lifetime, shows the Ohio poet entering into an intimate dialogic relationship with those poets of the Romantic pantheon whose lives and aesthetic sensibilities shaped his own. "Shelley's Arrogance" begins as he watches a thunderstorm building above Lecco, a town of fifty thousand inhabitants in Lombard, North Italy: "it woke me, the lighting arcing / the water between the tops of the lake's green hills / below the ghostly snow-capped Alps." This passage crackles with kinetic energy, as chain blue lighting links trees like green finials to "ghostly snow-capped Alps." Thunder breaks and rolls in long *o* sounds, and the repetition of plosives snap like a whiplash above the Lago di Lecco. He then segues into the warning a ship's captain cried out to Shelley on the day the poet's schooner, the *Don Juan*, foundered in a sudden storm on the Gulf of Spezia ("For God's sake reef your sails or you are lost") and follows this with a diminuendo from *Adonais*, Shelley's elegy for Keats: "I am borne darkly, fearfully afar." Plumly then interposes a tableau of his own:

> I think I know
> what Shelley means by fate, which is to say what looks
> like life invented in a painting or a story or a poem
> is actually a life planned right up to the end after which
> a highly well-wrought "piece of art" thought out
> in a boat ahead of a thunderstorm the year before
> he sails from Leghorn / but is, as Mary says, an elegy

> for Shelley / foreshadowing that long day of "dead
> calm—the atmosphere…oppressive…the sun excessive
> until it all suddenly changes into a sky of "smoke and rags."

Here, Plumly dispenses with any semblance of metrical regularity, and "Shelley's Arrogance" becomes a densely allusive palimpsest perhaps inaccessible to any save those well acquainted with the various interactions among the second generation of Romantic poets. Moreover, he introduces slashes, normally indicating line breaks, into his own text, a device that endows the piece with a structural singularity. He contemplates Shelley's theory about life imitating art but dismisses this naïve assumption and contends that what passes for "fate" is actually a self-fulfilling prophecy. He posits that Shelley conceived of *Adonais*—a lament modeled on Milton's pastoral elegy "Lycidas" about his close friend Edward King who drowned at sea—in "a boat ahead of a thunderstorm the year / before he sails for Leghorn." Plumly then concedes "how perfect/his poem for Keats may well be/a well-wrought 'piece of art.'" Doubtless these two lines refer to a self-congratulatory letter dated June 5, 1821, that Shelley wrote regarding *Adonais*: "It is a highly wrought 'piece of art' perhaps better in point of composition than anything I have written." Possibly, in this telling intertextuality lies the source of Plumly's title. Indeed, he quotes Shelly's young widow, Mary, who harbored forebodings even before the squall that swamped her husband's seagoing craft.

Plumy's subsequent rendering of the outcome is understated compared with nineteenth-century accounts of Shelley's death: "so little of him left / from falling through the sea into the mouth inside the sea/ / ten days and Keats's book of poems to help say who he is / in pieces washed ashore." The Keats volume eventually discovered in Shelley's pocket, its spine broken, turned out to be *Lamia, Isabella, The Eve of Saint Agnes, and other poems* (1820), including the six great odes upon which Keats's reputation as the greatest lyric poet since Shakespeare rests.

Stanley Plumly's enthusiasm for the Romantic poets, in particular John Keats, continued unabated throughout his own career, as is evident in the poems in *Against Sunset*. Although recognition of the kind conferred by the Pulitzer Prize or the National Book Award eluded him, unlike Keats, Plumly has been celebrated in his lifetime as the author of some of the finest poetry written by any American poet born in the fourth decade of the twentieth century. He was an indefatigable scholar and an able editor, as well as a dedicated and nurturing teacher. Perhaps it is fitting to conclude this appreciation by quoting the last section of his poem "Early Nineteenth-Century English Poet Walks": "He is only before us on the road, as he was in / everything else, and that we are coming after him. And have."

Pattiann Rogers: Motives for Metaphor

Of all the poets considered in this study, Pattiann Rogers is perhaps the most gifted in the use of figurative language or what is more commonly called metaphor. Metaphor is the richest element of poetic composition and almost certainly the most elusive. In his *Poetics*, Aristotle declared it "the one thing that cannot be learnt from others," and hence a token of genius. More pragmatic in his views, Samuel Johnson referred to metaphorical expression as "a great excellence in style when used with propriety, for it gives you two ideas for one." Coleridge, in his turn, defined all art as an interaction or "coalescence" of mind and nature. Ezra Pound's "In a Station of the Metro," the consummate Imagist poem, is almost pure metaphor: "The apparition of these faces in a crowd: / Petals on a wet, black bough." Indeed, our language abounds with figures of speech that have been consigned by overuse to mere abstraction, and poets have always enlivened their work by breathing new meaning into these locutions. For example, the turn of phrase "piping hot" acquires renewed intensity when Robert Lowell's persona, Jonathan Edwards, hears a black widow "whistle on a brick" in the Eternal Kiln of his devising. Thus, in "Mr. Edwards and the Spider," Lowell resurrects a dead metaphor, even as the little spinner scrambles up a strand of smoke and disappears.

According to *The New Princeton Encyclopedia of Poetry and Poetics*, the word *metaphor* derives from the Greek *metapherein*, "to transfer." Whether employed for the purpose of "adornment, liveliness, elucidation, or agreeable mystification," it is most commonly understood to involve a comparison of two essentially disparate things so as to arrive at a meaning inexpressible in any other context. Sylvia Plath's "Metaphors" enacts the transition between tenor, the literal, and vehicle, the figurative, with unparalleled exuberance:

> I'm a riddle in nine syllables,
> An elephant, a ponderous house,
> A melon strolling on two tendrils.
> O red fruit, ivory, fine timbers!
> This loaf's big with its yeasty rising.
> Money's new-minted is this fat purse.
> I'm a means, a stage, a cow in calf.
> I've eaten a bag of green apples,
> I've boarded the train there's no getting off.

For Plath, all metaphor is pregnant with meaning, a dynamic coupling of x and y. Doubtless her multiple tropes would have dismayed Dr. Johnson, but nowadays, we are delighted with Plath's ingenuity, especially in the last line. Many critics assign to metaphor the more general rubric *imagery*; however, the striking resonances that derive from phrases such as "the round / Zion of the water bead" are actually metaphorical in nature and comprise a vital component of the poetry written since the Second World War. In the words of Dylan Thomas, "I learnt the verbs of will and had my secret; / The code of night tapped on my tongue; / what had been one was many sounding mind-ed." In *Firekeeper: New and Selected Poems,* Pattiann Rogers views metaphor as far more than a literary stratagem calculated to enlighten and amuse. For her, metaphor represents the shaping force of an entire cosmos; for example, in "The Rites of Passage" she stresses a correlation between the plasticity of language and the physical world by comparing the division of cells to a "crossing," a transfer. She emphasizes resemblances, recurring patterns in nature—from the hexagons that converge to form a turtle's shell to the "sil-vered curve" of the moon's "brilliant hip." Rogers's knowledge of science is unparalleled among contemporary poets, and she celebrates the natural world with a verve reminiscent of Ovid's *Metamorphoses.*

In her essay, "Twentieth-Century Cosmology and the Soul's Habitation," Pattiann Rogers quotes a brief but salient passage from Jacob Bronowski's *Science and Human Values*: "Every act of imagination is the discovery of like-ness between two things that were thought unalike." Although Bronowski speaks of scientific matters and the relationship of humankind to the natural universe, his belief in resemblances is the same belief that forms the aesthetic bedrock of Rogers's *Firekeeper: New and Selected Poems.* The poet endows her cosmos with an alien beauty, adopting a vision that often exalts the so-called lower forms: she celebrates the horned lizard's thorny hide, the stick bug's swagger, and the snail's frosted track no less than "the comet Biela speeding in its rocks and ices." For Rogers, metaphor is more than a literary device; her poems focus on an ever-evolving universe, one in which natural metamor-phoses rival the wonders of Ovidian myth.

In the selections from *The Expectations of Light* (1981), her first volume, Rogers asserts a parallel between language and the physical world in an idiom that likens both to an organic process. "The Rites of Passage" begins with a description of frog spawn laid in open water and surrounded "By melanin pigment, by a jelly capsule / Acting as a cushion to the falling of the surf." The syllables' rhythmic pitch and roll bears the gelatinous mass ever nearer the doubling and quadrupling of cells: "At 77° the single-cell cleaves in 90 minutes, / Then cleaves again and in five hours forms the hollow / Ball of the blastula." The plosive *b* of "blastula" hints at a creative potential even before the embryo "turns itself / Inside out unassisted and becomes a gut." In the stanza immediately following, one word provides the vital infusion:

> What is the source of the tension instigating next
> The rudimentary tail and gills, the cobwebs of the veins?
> What is the impetus slowly directing the hard-core
> Current right up the scale to that one definite moment

When a fold of cells quivers suddenly for the first time
And someone says loudly "heart," born, beating steadily
Bearing now in the white water of the moon
The instantaneous distinction of being liable to death.

We sense life stirring in the aspirate qualities of "heart." Spoken loudly, the word anticipates a surge in the tenuous "cobweb of veins." Beating two ways, diastole and systole, this minute bulb of muscle is the incarnation of metaphor's transfer. To dispel any doubts, we need only peruse the closing stanza:

Think of that part of me wishing tonight to remember
The spilt-second edge before the beginning
To remember by a sudden white involution of sight
By a vision of tension folding itself
Inside clear open waters, by imitating a manipulation
Of cells in a moment of distinction, wishing to remember
The entire language made during that crossing.

The final line sets the transition from egg to living tadpole in metaphorical relation to language. By describing the process as a "crossing," Rogers dramatizes the very concept of metaphor, placing it at the heart of "The Rites of Passage." In a similar poem, "The Brain Creates Itself," she lends imaginative depth to Aristotle's theory that the mind or soul grows only through its succession of cognitive actualizations, a development that depends on contact with the physical world: "A thread of tissues takes shape / As I first comprehend the red rock crossed twice / By the fringe-toed lizard at dusk." In "Concepts and Their Bodies (The Boy in the Field Alone)," Rogers underscores the contention of contemporary anthropologists that all language is metaphor: "Staring at the mud turtle's eye / Long enough he sees *concentricity* there / For the first time, as if it possessed / Pupil and iris and oracular lid." Cynical readers might claim mutually exclusive realms for poetry and scientific thought, but they would do well to recall W. H. Auden's maxim: "Without art we should have no notion of the sacred; without science we should always worship false gods."

Rogers continues her celebration of nature in the poems culled from *The Tattooed Lady in the Garden* (1986), her second volume. Like a benign Faustus, she takes as her province "All things that move between the quiet poles," her intricate catalogs embracing the marvels of creation. In "The Verification of Vulnerability: The Bog Turtle," metaphor functions as the keystone of the poem's linguistic structure. In densely textured rhythms, Rogers tells how the armored reptile's disparate parts converge in a beautifully patterned symmetry:

Guarded by the horned beak and nails, surrounded
By mahogany carapace and molded in tiles

> Like beveled wood, hidden within the hingeless
> Plastron, beneath twelve, yellow-splotched
> Black scutes, buried below the inner lungs
> And breast, harbored in the far reaches
> As it must, that particle of vulnerability.

Ensconced between decks of horn and plate, the bog turtle hoards its mortality "like a pinpoint / Of diamond in a dark pouch." Rogers extends and subsumes this simile with yet another, comparing the brilliant particle to "a crystal of salt-light locked in a case / Of night." Both minerals, the precious and the quotidian, connote the essence of life: "I can understand / How the body has taken form solely / Around the possibility of its own death." Oddly, such terms as "Plastron" or "scutes" introduce an air of mystery without embedding the poem too deeply in zoological argot.

"Finding the Tattooed Lady in the Garden" proves metaphorical in its very conception. "Tattooed from head to toe in yellow / Petals and grape buds," the lady is a living hieroglyph of sylvan loveliness run away from a circus: "Sometimes the gold flesh of the butterfly, / Quiet and needled in the spot of sun on her shoulder, / Can be seen and sometimes the wide blue wing / Of her raised hand." Did the artist's needle indelibly pinion the butterfly or will a spasm of sunlight release it? Who can mediate between the "blue wing" and "raised hand?" In any case, Rogers's tattooed lady embodies metaphor in her shifting figurations:

> Some call her searched-for presence the being
> Of being, the essential garden of the garden.
> And some call the continuing postulation
> Of her location the only underlying structure
> The single form of flux, the final proof
> And the presence of crafted synonymy.

Even "the bronze / Lizard basking at her navel" could be a chameleon crept into flesh tones. Closure consists of a simple, albeit extraordinary, turn: "the moon rising by its own shape / From the silvered curve of her brilliant hip."

Poems selected from *Legendary Performance* (1987) and *Splitting and Binding* (1989), Rogers's third and fourth volumes, tend to represent extremes in her working philosophy. A coterie of five characters—Sonia, Cecil, Albert, Gordon, Felicia—dominates the earlier collection. Any one of these aesthetes would have been at home in Oscar Wild's *The Importance of Being Earnest* (1895), especially Felicia, who enjoys holding an afternoon salon for the "Gentlemen of Leisure":

> Felicia thinks the Gentlemen of Leisure
> Are magnificently regal in their lavender

Lamb's wool suits and pearl buttons. She adores
Their subtle aromas of unsmoked tobacco, crushed marjoram
And black cinnamon stem.

Even if someone were to produce a silver hip flask and lace everyone's coffee with absinthe, such an assemblage of aromatic dandies would remain facile and perhaps a tad dull: "Sonia must pray for all true Gentlemen of Leisure / who lend such glorious affirmation / To passivity." Only a Native American zany named Kioka offers any respite from the waxwork effigies that people *Legendary Performance*. In "One in Three," he intuits the true identity of a visitor by using his abilities to perceive resemblances in nature: "he can put his hand on the trunk / Of the tree and feel how it shudders / In exactly the same way the sea trembles / Beneath a quivering figurehead." His knack for metaphor invests the otherwise wan Lattina, Sonia's friend "from a coastal city," with a magisterial grace: "Only Kioka sees how a wooden / Figurehead and a single tree in the forest and Lettina / Can rise together as one, facing straight-on the direction / From which their only motion proceeds." *Legendary Performance* amply demonstrates Rogers's ability to compose narrative verse in sequence, although the result is too gentle in tone to pass for effective satire.

In the poems from *Splitting and Binding*, Rogers returns to her contemplation of the natural universe, without intermediaries such as Felicia. "The Importance of a Whale in a Field of Iris" seizes on the unlikely similarity between the Leviathan and a rippling field of wild flowers: "They would be difficult to tell apart, except / That one of them sails in a single body of flowing / Grey-violet and purple-brown flashes of sun." Not until the poet manages to plumb the depths of the eye does she achieve a fully imaginative and complex metaphor:

> If someone may assume that the iris at midnight sways
> And bends, attempting to focus the North Star
> Exactly at the blue-tinged center of its pale stem,
> Then someone may also imagine how the whale rolls
> And turns, straining to align inside its narrow eye
> At midnight, the bright star-point of Polaris.

A synchronous impulse links iris to whale: Polaris holding steady in the night heavens. In "For the Wren Trapped in a Cathedral," Rogers transforms a soaring religious edifice into a metaphor for the larger cosmos: "during the black moonless nights, / Every flickering star lifts smoke, drips wax." The galleries of votive lights gleam like constellations, as the wren attempts to mimic in song the intricate flourishes worked into the Bishop's throne: "Her song naturally imitates the pattern / Of frills and flutes found in the carvings there, / The hanging fruit, profuse foliage, ripened / Curves." Ultimately, this sculptural splendor or "wooden Paradise" will not do. Rogers implies the wren's need to regain the forest's nave and the stained-glass resplendence of autumn leaves:

> Certainly she dreams often of escape, of reversing
> That process by which she came here, leaving
> An ordinary emissary carrying her own story,
> Sacred news from the reality of artifice,
> Into the brilliant white symmetry
> Of the truthful world.

Rogers's innate capacity for generating wonder at the mere fact of existence continues in *Geocentric* (1993) where her voice is more playful and expansive than ever before. "Life and All the Accordions and Concertinas" is a mock dirge for the cumbersome and unwieldy instruments: "You may wonder yourself what happened to them. / They're at the bottom of the sea." Once jettisoned, the musical cargo with "mother-of-pearl buttons gleaming, / Keys and reeds quivering" emits a plethora of metaphors expanding like bubbles: "concertinas sailed / the salt surface momentarily, bobbing / like a fleet of air-filled jellyfish." Moreover, the poet relishes the suggestion that the sea is the accordion's true element: "They wheeze and blow nightly / with the currents, singing like sirens, / shimmering in their treble." Rhythms collapse and roll as Rogers presses her elaborate conceit to its virtual limit: "soliloquies circle the wide sea, / rippled and meditative / are heard / by nursing blue whales, who answer." On a note only slightly more somber, "By Death" views the sundering of body and spirit as a multiple phenomenon, a metaphorical splitting and binding:

> With the next turning she became
> a hundred and twenty-eight of herself, groomed
> the horse of Orion, dwelled in the light-remnant
> of Vela. She was wind through the scaffold
> of pity, a nesting owl among the eaves of praise.
> Then two hundred fifty-six—she was stone as well
> And zephyr, then legion, then too various
> to be reckoned, too pervasive to be noticed,
> too specific to be named.

In this splendid scenario, microcosm becomes macrocosm, and vice versa. On the other hand, "The Mad Linguist" refuses to accept dissolution, quoting "from an ancient language that pauses / and plunges forward in leaps and lurches / like a prehistoric grizzly that pounces once / in the rushing snowmelt." Rogers translates language into a rollicking brute, a blundering appetite that rends and slakes, fetching its quarry in one quick swipe: "lifting to the shore

/ the sweet flesh of the struggling silver fish / we know so well." Thus, through metaphor, words become palpable. They embody and nourish. They shine.

Rogers gathers twenty-seven previously uncollected poems into a final section titled "Old Spiral of Conception." These poems could easily form a separate volume containing meditations on life, death, rebirth, time, and mutability. Metamorphosis—continual transfiguration—remains Rogers's dominant subject. The speaker of "In my Time" ponders the manifold blessings of a planetary heritage not yet evolved: "How can I extol the nurturing / fragrances from the spires, the spicules / of a landscape not yet formed or seeded?" Rogers imagines "some new creature, / descended maybe from our golden peepers / and white-chinned chuggers" and the song that will be "synonymous, for someone else, / with spring." In "Berry Renaissance," she bestows lavish praise on a brace of sweet intoxicants by delaying the tenor of a many-faceted vehicle:

> Of clustered spears and heart-shaped
> leaves, of terra-cotta-tinted, lavender
> blossoms, of aromatic ovaries, bristled
> anthers and stamens, of probings and fiddlings
> deep within, of open-eyed sun staring,
> of vigil, of transfiguration, of such
> is the palate of raspberry liqueur,
> blackberry cordial.

Cleverly inverted syntax conceals arcane usage in this stanza, the preposition "of" rather than "like" serving as the cue for simile. A metonym for "taste," "palate" savors of deeper wit than the more common locution and makes for a lingering pungency. Indeed, one recalls the curious dedication at the beginning of Rogers's book: *For the celebration, and all the celebrants, every one of them, everywhere.* *Firekeeper* provides us with the occasion to charge our glasses. It is a drinking of healths all around.

Rogers's seventh volume of poetry, *Eating Bread and Honey*, is a paean to both the sensual and sacramental aspects of creation. Deeply versed in geophysics, Rogers affirms yet again that science and religion have a shared aesthetic purpose: to provide a sense of the marvelous. The poet's protean wit, her gift for shifting figurations, embraces everything from the pulsations of a "smelting quasar" to "the plural flickers / of the puss moth's powdery antennae." Her empirical vision of the cosmos never precludes intimations of the sacred in the most minute life forms: "The steady flex and draw of the digger / wasp's blue-bulbed abdomen—I know / there's a fact beyond presence / in all that fidgeting" ("The Fallacy of Thinking Flesh is Flesh").

In "'God Is in the Details,' Says Mathematician Freeman J. Dyson," Rogers lends subversive credence to Dyson's pronouncement, comparing the fabric of creation to a richly embroidered tapestry: "This is why grandmother takes such tiny / stitches, one stitch for each dust mote / of the moon on the Serengeti at night." Even the moon's particle luminescence acquires substance as it settles over the African plain. Rogers extends and embellishes her visual metaphor, switching filaments and expanding the needle's eye to a nimbus-lit sentience: "And this is why she changes the brief threads / in her glass needle so often— metallic bronze / for the halo around the thrasher's eye." The *t* in "metallic" opposes teeth and tongue like flint and steel before rounding the long *o* in "halo," as Rogers's incantation gathers momentum in the rhythmic play of assonance and consonance. Taking up "two slight breaths" of incandescence, her aged protagonist "crochets them around each microscopic / void, invents, thereby, an ice tapestry / of winter on the window." Grandmother breathes into the design of days, her tapestry flowering like frost on a winter pane. Rogers moves from evanescence to a teeming landscape in her closing lines:

> God's most minute exuberance is founded
> in the way she sews with needles
> as assertive as the sun-sharp loblolly
> that she sees with her eyes closed;
> in the way she knots stitches
> as interlocked as the cries of veery
> peewee, black-caped chickadee and jay
> that she hears with her ears stopped;
> in the way she whispers to her work,
> recites to her work, spooling the least
> designation of spicule shade, hay
> spider and air trifid, every hue
> and rising act of her own hands. *Try*
> *to escape now*, it reads, *Just try*.

The insistent cadences with which the grandmother "whispers to her work, / recites to her work" hymns the vast tapestry into being. The intricate marvels or "details" that manifest God's presence arise from an act of supreme artifice. Nature and nurture intertwine with every stitch; indeed, who would want to escape this wondrous bit of handiwork? If Rogers alludes to Greek myth, the fabulous crone who presides over her poem seems more benign than the three Fates who spin, measure, and crop the brittle thread of life in Aegean lore.

Drawing on religion, myth, and folklore, "Service With Benediction" praises the earth's bounty, specifically the varieties of honey from buckwheat to sage: "like glass lanterns / there's enough concentrated summer sun caught / in these jars of comb honey to give us / ample light to travel by on a winter night." More- over, the traditional ritual invoked in Roger's title compels us to delve into Ju- deo-Christian myth. Following his resurrection, Jesus partook of a honeycomb, a source of energy and light, food for the long journey. If the poet shies away from orthodoxy, she delights in the plenitude of the communion table: "heather honey wild- / wood honey gathered by wild bees, hallows / of honey, orisons of bulging loaves." The long vowel in "orisons" swells each loaf with fervor, but also puns on the vocative mode: "O raisins." Such humor betrays the artificer behind these rapt inflections, before yielding to hedonistic revel:

> So I eat sun and earth by the slice
> and spoonful, suck yeast breads soaked
> in alfalfa honey, dip crusts dripping
> from the dish to my mouth, lick gold
> sugar from my fingers. I swallow
> pure flower syrup brought from the sky,
> chew the kneaded spike and germ of fields
> and gardens. Surely I become then
> all the arabesques of bee dances.

Rogers's exuberance confirms the archaic belief that honey imparts eloquence. She usurps the beekeeper's aesthetic role, intervening in the process whereby nectar is transmuted to languorous gold; indeed, she imbibes "syrup brought from the sky." The baker, too, is banished, as the poet returns bread to "the kneaded spike and germ of fields." She even appropriates the bee's arabesques in the intricate pattern of her syntax and diction. But the specter of death intrudes in a manner both dark and enigmatic, quelling the ecstatic tone: "*Two gifts*, I heard the temple bakers say, / when, for immortality, the priests immersed / his dead body naked before burial / in a cistern of amber honey." Before these lines, honey possesses a regenerative or transforming power, but the temple bakers cannot knead the corpse back to life; moreover, the cistern gluts and holds fast, replenishing nothing. Embalming honey fails to preserve the least semblance of vitality, reducing the body to a waxen effigy. Small wonder that Rogers closes with the invocation of a blessing:

> Allow me now in the fullness of this morning
> to consume enough clover honey and white
> wheat fire to see my way clearly
> through the cold night coming.

Rogers's lyric virtuosity fuels every line of "Service with Benediction."

Cognitive power is a key component of Rogers's aesthetic, as she makes clear in her recent essay, "Surprised by the Sacred": "the world provides every physical image and sensation we will ever need to experience the sacred, to declare the holy. If we could only learn to recognize it." However, as Rogers implies, some phenomena go unobserved in our midst. Here is the first stanza of "Creation by the Presence of Absence: City Coyote in the Rain":

> She's sleek blue neon through
> the blue of the evening. She's black
> sheen off the blue of wet streets,
> blue daunt of suspension in each
> pendant of rain filling the poplars
> on the esplanade.

Spectral interloper in a metropolitan nightscape, the coyote blends with the slick spillage of neon tubes, shades off into the bituminous blue-black of wet asphalt. Images of poverty and homelessness attend her passing: "Like the leaping blue of flames / burning in an alley barrel, her presence / isn't perceived before she's gone." Indeed, she becomes a metaphor for the insulted and disenfranchised of the city:

> She cries with fat blue yelps, calls
> with the scaling calls of the ragmen
> screeches a siren of howls along the docks
> below the bridges, wails with the punctuated
> griefs of drunks and orphans.

Not until she slips into a culvert behind an ashbin to give succor and nourishment to her young does the coyote take on an actual presence. She "shakes off the storm in an explosion of radiance, licks / the cold muzzles and genitals of her frenzied / pups, gives them her blue teats, closes / her yellow eyes." Rogers manipulates color motifs with unusual dexterity. The coyote's amber-lit gaze turns inward as her whelps tug at swollen nipples; thus she merges once again with the bleak hues of the city, feeding an alien hunger in its midst. Perceiving her presence is contingent upon accepting the possibility of a phenomenon that moves beyond our ability to explain or rationalize it in everyday terms. Moreover, to see her requires a disquieting glimpse within:

> No one ever sees her face to face
> or those who do never know they do,
> denying her first, pre-empting her lest
> the place of pattern and time she creates,
> like the blue of a star long since
> disintegrated, enter their hearts
> with all of its implications.

Rogers's "blues" are not monochromatic, but rather display an extraordinary range of emotional tonalities. Evocative and poignant, her poem ultimately locates compassion in the desolate reaches of the human heart.

Mastery of figurative language in Rogers's aesthetic evolves from an intuitive awareness of the myriad analogues between life forms great and small. In "Fractal: Repetition of Forms over a Variety of Scales," the ubiquitous blue of the previous poem is strikingly compressed:

> This moment is a single blue jay,
> a scramble of flint, sapphire iron,
> spiking blue among the empty brambles
> and veins wound like skeins back
> upon themselves through the dun forest
> of thistle spurs and thorns.
>
> And this moment is as well the brambled
> skeleton of the jay, anthracite spine,
> thorny blades and femurs, tangle
> of knuckled twigs flittering
> through an equal flitter of jointed
> sticks, vines and husks of wind.

In stanza one, a solitary jay emblazons the thicket, feathers fledged by a "scramble of flint," their luster deepened by a succession of arresting images such as "sapphire iron" and "spiking blue." In the succeeding stanza, the delicate "anthracite spine" seems both fossil fuel and fossil print. Indeed, we would lose the jay altogether in the tangled matrix of "thorny blades," "femurs," and "knuckled twigs" if Rogers did not fuse thicket and skeleton in one sublime gesture: "this split second / is the singular blue-black pod of jay heart / thiddering among a bramble of rib bones." The neologism "thiddering" deftly animates the diminutive heart. Here as elsewhere, Rogers celebrates resemblances, nature's ability to replicate itself on expanding and diminishing scales: "God is a process, a raveled nexus / forever tangling into and around the repeating cry / of loss and delivery." Indeed, metamorphosis proves a volatile force behind all her poetry; in "Opus for Space," she extols "the violent crack / and seed propelling shot of the witch-hazel pod, / the philosophy implicit in the inside out / seed thrust of the sacred sorrel." As always, Rogers combines cognitive power with imaginative and linguistic virtuosity to achieve a poetics at once vigorous and engaging.

In her most recent volume, *Quickening Fields* (2017), Rogers's poetry encompasses several of Harold Bloom's criteria for aesthetic excellence, in particular "exuberance of diction," but she also brings to poems such as "Winter Camping" an altogether new element of erotic love. It begins when her husband shrugs off the encumbrance of frozen slumber in one magisterial gesture and becomes an ardent paramour: "He rises suddenly, naked / and white out of the mountain / drifts." For the enthralled poet, this arctic tryst is paralyzing in its inception:

"Upon me—one long moaning sigh / from his lips under my gown, / and I'm stopped with ice from throat / to knees." Her partner proceeds with a measured and agonizing expertise: "His mouth, moving slowly, / down the back of my neck, sizzles / with subzero burns." The icy sibilants in "sizzles" and "subzero burns" swarm like frost splinters on virgin snow. Ensuing lines awaken in the speaker an exquisite torment: "His fondling / blue fingers tingle six-sided crystals along my breasts." Here we hearken to fricative *f* sounds whispering a gradual thaw and delight in how the voiced velar stop *g* lends a titillating ring to the noun-verb combination "fingers tingle." Once more Rogers plies between microcosm and macrocosm with an unerring facility as she extols her husband's virtues.

> He's the guttural growl of a white
> arctic fox, a froth of white ptarmigan
> smothering against my face, pervasive
> as the inside out on a black polar night
> a white raven circling, making black
> beakings on my belly. A snow hare,
> he crouches at my knees, his white mustache
> maddening as he nips frost-bites
> around my thighs.

Rogers's concatenations subsume and supplant one another when she describes her life-long mate in terms of a feral delicacy, the guttural growl evoking an arctic fox that then gives way to a spume or froth recalling a "white ptarmigan" and so on. Indeed, the lingual cunning of "he nips frost-bites / around my thighs" would be difficult to surpass. Yet, all these are mere prelude to a converging harmony, a devotional air that savors of fleshly communion: "Sucking his earlobe / is like taking a burning pod of frozen / white wine into my mouth." "Winter Camping" is no aubade; instead, it celebrates coupling in darkness on the cold, wind-wrung heights: "his frozen / body— the gaping spires and frigid / temple winds, the icy amnesias—pressed hard / against me tonight."

"The God of Sunday Evening, June 7, 1987," like "Winter Camping," opts for an erotic tone that surprises the reader with a bit of delayed decoding. The opening stanza crackles with kinetic energy: "He roars in red. So I pluck him, pinch / him right at the flat green star / of his fiercest electricity." The speaker quivers with an anticipation so pure it borders on greed. Then she pauses to bestow sedulous care on the object of her desire: "I sponge him all over, gently, / with my thumb, under a spigot / of running water." She works sweet unguents into his flesh, sprinkles him like any other sugary confection: "He lets me soothe him with cream, tap and roll / him once in sweet powders." In the ensuing lines, she becomes the fellatrice in earnest: "he lets me put my lips / around his pudgy tip, bite and pull, suck, / break." Her ardor seems boundless, as the speaker reaches the upper register with the vocative:

> O the sugar and sap in my mouth then,
> the searing blossom-juices spilling, (a napkin
> is required at the corners) the constant ping
> of tiny firecrackers in my mouth.

These pyrotechnics culminate in the classic dying away—"I shiver, swallowing / all of his sizzle"—and both poet and inamorata bask in the afterglow: "He becomes my momentary flush and swell / the same faint draw, the very blush / of my ear napes and nipples." Not surprisingly, she remains as devoted as any acolyte: "All evening long we engage / in our religion. I am his servant. I behold / and dissolve him. I coo in his company." Only in the final three syllables of the poem does Rogers deliver the punchline of this frolicsome satire:

> I hum and he vibrates. He allows me,
> lavishes me, generously bestows upon me
> that which he alone, as God may bestow:
> the power to proclaim
> with a faith so perfect it disappears:
> *strawberry.*

In terms of structure, Rogers's poem is akin to riddle twenty-five from the Old English *Exeter Book;* many of the poems were ribald and sometimes dealt with fruits and vegetables. Thus, the poet goes to the root of the Anglo-Saxon literary tradition with a conceit uniquely her own. Pattiann Rogers is one of the finest poets of her generation.

Blear-Eyed Wisdom out of Midnight Oil

In the final section of William Butler Yeats's "Among Schoolchildren," the Irish Nobel laureate resorts to the line "Nor blear-eyed wisdom out of midnight oil" to refute the notion that late hours and years of studious labor make for perfection of either the life or the art. But therein lies the paradox and essential beauty of his aesthetic. According to biographers, the visionary poet and self-styled intellectual would first set down in prose his artistic ideals and principles; locating these in metaphors derived from worlds both mystical and phenomenal, he would then pace back and forth in one of the rooms in Lady Augusta Gregory's Coole Park estate, chanting them up into song. Interestingly enough, Yeats's closure to "Among School Children" evokes in incantatory rhythms the *topos* of the dancer:

> O chestnut tree, great rooted blossomer,
> Are you the leaf, the blossom, or the bole?
> O body swayed to music, O brightening glance
> How can we know the dancer from the dance?

The Dionysian figure, so ecstatic and ostensibly free from the strictures of any discipline or schooling—the poet's painstakingly evolved concept of the "dance" as opposed to its spontaneous enactment—nevertheless remains like the chestnut tree, the "great-rooted blossomer," forever grounded in an innate wisdom that ripens only with the passage of time.

During his career, Yeats moved from the Pre-Raphaelite dreaminess of his earliest verse to the politically charged diction of "Easter, 1916," eventually arriving at the full-flavored richness of the poetry collected in *The Tower* (1928), a volume that includes "Sailing to Byzantium," "Meditations in a Time of Civil War," "Leda and the Swan," "On a Picture of a Black Centaur by Edmund Dulac," and "Among School Children."

The poetry of *The Tower* and subsequent volumes evolved from a rich and varied life, and for all its esoteric symbols—the Great Wheel, the interlocking gyres or cones, the phases of the moon—*A Vision* (1925) was basically a systemized prose reworking of motifs already present in Yeats's poetry. His participation in the Rosicrucian Order of the Golden Dawn and the Rhymer's Club, the founding of the Irish nationalist Abbey Theatre, and his eventual role as a senator in the Irish Free State—all were the culmination of decades spent squaring the life *with* the art, and could not have been accomplished by a callow youth.

Margaret Gibson's latest book is a model for any young poet who would continue to write beyond the age of thirty: "How stark it is to be alive— / and, although absence is the form you take / in what we call the world, how durable." Of the four poets considered in this essay, only Michael Waters, who falls just a year shy of the mark, has not seen seventy summers wither in their pride. Despite his comparative youth, he tempers in his latest collection a delight in wit and wordplay with a rigorous prosodic training honed and refined throughout a long and distinguished career. Philip Schultz's new tome continues his existential examination of life via his father, who literally worked himself to death by age sixty, from the vantage point of one who has not only survived past that mark but prospered. Stanley Plumly carries on his dialogic relationship with the great English poets from the Era of the Romantic Triumph in his new volume, but also includes remembrances of other accomplished acquaintances such as Jack Gilbert, William Matthews, and Galway Kinnell, all of whom have gone, as Charles Wright would have it, "through the star-filter of memory." Possessing a veritable wealth of talent, all four poets discussed here have not simply aged their way to prominence but, like Yeats in the later stages of his career, continue to display a tireless devotion to their craft.

Not Hearing the Wood Thrush (2018) is Margaret Gibson's twelfth book-length collection in an oeuvre that includes several other splendid volumes, most notably *Long Walks in the Afternoon* (1982), *Out in the Open* (1989), and *The Vigil* (1993). Her engaging memoir, *The Prodigal Daughter: Reclaiming an Unfinished Childhood* (2018), recounts her Presbyterian upbringing in the Southeast and eventual flight from a familial and regional background she considered indifferent to the pressing issues of the day, especially the Civil Rights Movement and the Vietnam War. Gibson has long since transcended the youth-oriented zeitgeist of the mid-sixties and early seventies, particularly the urge to embrace rebellion for its own sake, and, having mistaken one's private ills for public evils, to withdraw from society altogether. Indeed, this new volume finds her reconnecting with her nuclear family and returning to take up the role of caregiver in a household fallen prey the vicissitudes of alcoholism, disability, and old age.

Lest her return be read as a defeat, she refuses to forsake the cultural and spiritual values she developed independently, including sensibilities doubtlessly refined by her education at Hollins College and the University of Virginia. "Playing Mozart at the Town Dump" underscores this while also serving as an ars poetica and a brilliant parody of the narrative exercise termed "composition of place." Gibson treats readers to a proliferation of sensory experience—aural, olfactory, tactile, visual, and gustatory:

> The concerto in D streams out the moon roof.
> Inside the car the air is ripe with Mozart,
> watermelon rind, cat litter, stale beer bottles,
> napkins infused with fish oil, pickle juice,
> loneliness, and a mouse nest I shook free
> from a flannel sheet folded away and meant
> to be saved as a drop cloth. It's andante time
> at the dump. High noon.

James Joyce asserted that a poem is but a simple freeing of a rhythm. Gibson accomplishes this in her first line, but in a manner that is initially self-contained and almost telegraphic. The letter "D" resonates with the long *e* in "streams," and the flowing *u* sounds in "moon roof" seem to buoy up an errant lunar beam. Gibson follows by reeling off a catalog of every day detritus—a polyphony of melon rinds and beer empties, odors of "fish oil" and "pickle juice," the musty smell of a mouse nest "shook free" from a "drop cloth" then slows this cascade of synesthetic images with a pun, the musical directive "andante time," that in this context also denotes the hour: "High Noon."

In the first eight lines of "Playing Mozart at the Town Dump," Gibson subordinates her thematic concerns to a methodology or technique that initially defies logical sequence, a nonlinear naming of parts and blending of high and low brow that accrues only when we pause for mental inventory. But this rest proves brief, as she introduces a note of humor in the guise of a refuse heap habitué: "On the lookout for Ralph, / who likes to ask about my absent husband / with his hand reaching for the small of my back." Thus, the poet conjures then banishes the sly, insinuating Ralph with a single dismissive gesture.

Next, Gibson segues into an overheard conversation reminiscent of the stichomythic exchange between two pub-crawling cockney women in the second part of T. S. Eliot's *The Wasteland* (1922). But this is an instance of allusive imitation with a difference: the interlocutors are male, middle-aged, and paunchy, wearing sweat-stained casual sportswear and their conversation is somber rather that convivial:

> Their talk is
> more contemplative than you'd think.
> One man tells about a friend's recent bypass
> and *renewed* heart—the word's his. He says
> the surgeon split him up the middle like a hog.
> "It makes you think," the older one says.

Perhaps the poet betrays more than a hint of condescension, assuming we would be surprised at the introspective nature of a dialogue characterized by genuine fellow-feeling, but does the graphic depiction of another's diseased but palpitating heart laid bare ("the surgeon split him up the middle like a hog")—preclude empathy? We hardly have time to reflect as the older man heads toward a recycling bin with a "nicked" and "torn" Renoir print:

> It's Renoir's luncheon party on the river.
> Brightly colored parasols and tables,
> the wine uncorked, the women and men florid.
> Renoir—it must be noon in all his paints,

the impression of light so this worldly
it's another world entirely, and ours. Or is it?

Gibson is referring to the *Luncheon of the Boating Party* (1881), an oil painting by French Impressionist Pierre-August Renoir; the scene consists of an intimate yet festive gathering on a balcony at the Maison Fournaise café overlooking the River Seine on the Il de Chatou. A *compotier* of fruit and several half-empty wine bottles that delicately hold the refulgent noonday light sit on the table in the background. Gibson deftly combines two different mediums, blending the painter's alcohol blues with the poet's rich sonority of *o* and *r* sounds in the participle "uncorked" and the adjectival "florid," thus capturing the high color in the faces of the dreamy-eyed revelers, but the Salzburg-born composer remains the *genius loci* of "Playing Mozart at the Town Dump," as shown when Gibson returns to the interchange between the two men:

> I hear the man on his way recycle to Renoir
> say "I feel for the guy." And because
> he's turned his back and cleared his throat
> to hide his feelings, I believe him.
> "It could happen to any one of us,"
> he mumbles beneath the soaring cadenzas
> and inversions, now spritely, now sonorous.

Gibson implies that not even those who are preternaturally gifted in the arts can offer us consolation or elude the literal pitfall of the grave, which the sobering closure echoes: "Mozart, whose body was wrapped in a torn shroud / and dumped into a pauper's grave before sun-up." The proximity of *u* sounds in "dumped" and "sun-up," both abrupt and seemingly final, portends none of the conventional descent with an apotheosis so typical of elegiac poetry. And yet Mozart's transcendent genius continues to inform such Modernist genres as cinema. One recalls the burial scene in Milos Foreman's *Amadeus*, lime dust rising from the depths of cold subterranean clay in Vienna's St. Marx Cemetery as Mozart's body is unceremoniously tossed in. Gibson's "Playing Mozart at the Town Dump" is itself marked by a fullness of *copia*, a lavish application of rhythm, syntax, and diction that is downright Mozartian. It is a scintillating performance, probably the finest poem in *Not Hearing the Wood Thrush*.

If "Playing Mozart at the Town Dump" engages in pure linguistic revel, many of the poems in Gibson's latest collection provide a stark but felicitous contrast. "Snowing," for example, consists of eighteen spare lines, each one the product of subtle, almost exquisite deliberation. It begins with a simple journal entry: "*Mornings are best,* you wrote, *before words, before appetite.*" The morning repast is laid out in the breakfast nook, but it must wait for a numinous encounter with nature and the larger cosmos. Although the moon is down, all the stars still twinkle in the firmament and the landscape lies deep in the season's first snow:

> Your words put on a coat and scarf and stand with me outside
> in the hushed world.

> Snow is silence made visible.

> Where hemlocks edge the dark pond, a fox…intent
> its wind-ruffled russets flecked with silence.

Gibson evokes a silence almost unbearable in the deceptively plain adjective-noun combination "hushed world," and she renews its delicate sibilance in the next line: "Snow is silence made visible." The ensuing couplet (note the slant rhymes "intent" and "silence") proves carefully orchestrated both visually and phonetically, the first line offering a sequence of discrete images—"hemlocks," "pond," and "fox" —meted out and suspended in assonantal *o* sounds. The fox embodies a momentary equipoise and seems intent on some prey other than mouse or vole. Conversely, the phrase "wind-ruffled russets flecked" crackles with kinetic energy, the diminutive canine's pelt coming alive in aspirates and fricatives that in the next instant return to "silence." Gibson's closure is as meditative and lovely as Robert Frost's "Stopping by Woods on a Snowy Evening," but it culminates in a Zen quiescence opposed to the New England poet's western philosophy:

> Slowly the field takes on the color of now your hair, as does
> the fox. The fox

> does not move, yet it grows lighter and appears to float
> nearly to the height of the hemlocks,

> where it hovers. It snows harder. And harder still.

The speaker lives in the breathless interim between the fox's appearance and the slow encroachment of a new cloud cover that effaces the stars. From the brooding stratosphere, the first flakes break into crystal high above the "hemlocks," and the initial aspirates—"hovers," "harder," "harder still"—hush up the whole valley in a pristine whiteness. If Gibson's style seems minimalist here, it invites reader participation in the most emphatic way.

Like two of the other poets considered in this essay, Margaret Gibson has already lived out the promised biblical three-score and ten. She draws, therefore, on an abundance and variety of life experience that reaches beyond that of canonical authors such as John Keats, Hart Crane, Georg Trakl, and Sylvia Plath, all of whom died before or at about age thirty, which perhaps makes their accomplishments all the more remarkable. In addition to her already considerable poetic gifts, Gibson's accumulated experience lends the poems in her latest collection an undeniable *gravitas*. Most recently, she sat vigil at the bedside of her husband of more than four decades, scholar and poet John McKain, whose eleven-year battle with Alzheimer's ended on December 27, 2017. Poems such as "Snowing" clearly derive from the sense of a felt presence, and in their sculptural intricacy resemble a frail yet poignant hermetic scrimshaw. In contrast, "Not to Remain Altogether Silent" is more celebratory, and its profusion of images, at once rustic and extravagantly beautiful, moves toward an unbidden joy:

> All the time I kept you out of my poems,
> you found a way into my body instead.
> Instead of your becoming another word
> for dove or wrist bone, owl or stone,
> you've become the impulse that has me
> raise cairns to mark my way. You're
> what all verbs traverse, a fuse for the urge
> to look for what I can't see within what I can;
> also the stillness inside me as wind-riven
> leaves are driven over the roof shingles
> into the night. Kindled by earth and sky,
> you're the touch of a tongue on my skin,
> contingent and mortal; and the shy,
> reluctant love of faithfulness to what I feel.

The word *metaphor* derives from Greek *metapherein*, "to transfer." Gibson understands intuitively that the vital transfer in metaphor resides in the verb, stating this directly in the alveolar phrase "verbs traverse," which leads in turn to a haunting dispersal of autumn leaves: "the stillness inside me as wind-riven / leaves are driven over the roof shingles / into the night." For Margaret Gibson, poetry is a sacred encoding, and her latest volume attests to a lifetime devoted not only to the craft, but also to close observation, to meditation, and to reconciling inner and outer worlds. *Not Hearing the Wood Thrush* is her best volume to date.

In March of this year, the University of Pittsburgh Press launched Michael Waters's eleventh book, *The Dean of Discipline*, his latest in a series of distinguished titles that include *The Burden Lifters* (1989), *Green Ash, Red Maple, Black Gum* (1997), *Parthenopi: New and Selected Poems* (2001), and *Gospel Night* (2011). Born in Brooklyn, one of the sepia-toned boroughs of New York City, in 1949, Waters as a youth received a rigorous Roman Catholic education and ultimately graduated from the MFA program at the University of Iowa, the first and reputedly foremost of what Yeats reputedly called "singing schools" in his late-phase ars poetica "Sailing to Byzantium." Waters and Gibson share a number of affinities, in particular the desire for transcendence attainable only through contact with the physical world, and an abiding need to confront the inevitabilities of the human condition: life, death, time, and mutability. But there the similarities end. The best way to demonstrate this is by looking closely at "Plein Air and Resurrectionist (1880)," a poem bearing an epigraph ascribed to Renoir: "White does not exist in nature." Here is the first strophe:

> The newly crossed-over retain semblance
> Longer when weather gingers the beech leaves.
> Lips thumbed with beeswax glisten below soil.
> Nostrils puffed with pig fat beckon beetles
> Once the coffin caves.
>   The pine box opens
> And the earth stayed from their eyes tumbles in.
> Moonlight inhabits the skin grown gold.

Waters begins with the exhumation of a young woman's body in Cedar Grove Cemetery in Augusta, Georgia, in 1880, and his approach seems to be that of a voyeuristic necrophile. The dead are referred to as the "newly crossed over," and literally embody the transfer inherent in metamorphosis, just as the season of frost "gingers" the leaves of a nearby beech grove. The third line is perfectly cadenced iambic pentameter: notice how the plosive *p* and *b* in "Lips thumbed" imbue the corpse's mouth with a pouting, full-blooded nubility. The long *e* sound in the noun-verb combination "beeswax glisten" lends a further touch of luster. Phonetically adroit and visually precise, the poet's overall effect would be sumptuous, a Baudelairean feast for the eyes, were it not for the strange and estranging phenomenon of death. Indeed, the fourth line, "Nostrils puffed with pig fat beckon beetles," is fulsome in the extreme; the plosive *p* softened by fricative double *f* in the modifier "puffed" refers to nostrils not flared with breath but rather occluded with "pig fat," food for carrion beetles. But herein lies another paradox, and clear-cut evidence of Waters's love for the polytropic potential of language. In ancient Egyptian culture, the scarab or dung beetle was a symbol of resurrection. Thus, when moonlight finds the corpse, she is nimbus-lit, her "skin grown gold."

Interestingly enough, Waters provides narrative background for this poem only in the book's appended notes. His protagonist is Grandison Harris, a slave purchased in 1852 by the faculty at the Medical College in Augusta, Georgia, to rob graves so that their students would have fresh cadavers to dissect. Here is the poem's second movement:

> Grandison Harris shovels up a corpse
> And wheels her in the cart along the rut
> To the medical school's barn
> Where she'll sway on hooks roped to a crossbeam
> As if ascending, though
> The promised judgment's been postponed again.

Grandison sets about his surreptitious and solitary task in a perfunctory manner; unlike the first gravedigger clown in Act V Scene I of Shakespeare's *Hamlet*, he has no companion with whom he might share a "stoop" of liquor or engage in witty repartee. But the intertextual resonances struck here uncover at least one intriguing similarity: he has been thus employed almost three decades, and the Bard's comic delver has been "sexton here / man and boy, thirty years." Grandison Harris trundles his pathetic load to a churchlike "barn" where she'll "sway," reanimated in a ludicrous *danse macabre* "on hooks roped to a crossbeam." The allusion to Christ's crucifixion and resurrection, not to mention his eventual ascent into heaven is unmistakable, albeit mock-heroic, and irreverent in the extreme. Implicit in the world-weary observation that the "promised judgement's" been deferred again is a certain self-reflexive irony.

Perhaps the most exceptional feature of "Plein and Resurrectionist (1880)" is the facility with which Waters modulates point of view, shifting subtly from third-person into Harrison's point of view, as he "shovels" and "wheels" his burden in what appears to be a somnambulist's trance. The poet's conclusion puts all into perspective:

> The mare grows twitchy and stamps in her stall,
> Hoof-tremor collapsing a spindly box easel
> Upon which a raucous cloudburst of oils
> Shivers a view of the churchyard downhill.
> Grandison studies the weather-bleached stones
> Toothed in rows, shaking his head—
> True if you're standing a few feet away,
> But up close they're blurry and cobalt blue.

Waters displays remarkable skill throughout this final strophe, wherein he plies a virtually flawless decasyllabic measure to telling effect. Of course, this does not imply that he is slavishly devoted to form or otherwise sacrifices to it the necessities of the imagination. The dray horse (read bedraggled Pegasus) that hauls the corpse to the barn grows restive, "twitchy," and "stamps"—an emphatic allusion to Yeats's black Dionysian centaur—in her "stall" a word intimating both structure and stasis. Waters then comes down hard on the metrical register, falling back on the Old English kenning, "Hoof-tremor," and the reverberations collapse "a spindly box easel," upsetting an Impressionist painting described as "a raucous cloudburst of oils." Here the poet leads the prosodist into a deliciously wicked blunder: the plosive spondee, "cloudburst," dissipates into the onomatopoeic "oil," a parody perhaps of the overly fastidious Pointillist technique.

Once more the reader becomes mindful of Renoir's assertion, "There is no white in nature," as perspective shifts to Grandison Harris, who even after Emancipation cracks cribs for anatomists and artists alike. He "studies" the white ledger-stones, each ranged like a tooth at the grave's maw. Illiterate he may be, but Grandison is not inured to his grisly task; indeed, he is, as Robert Frost says, "one acquainted with the night." He has no inkling of Impressionist theory regarding color and light, but he knows from a lifetime of bitter experience—the necessity of earning bread in the sweat of one's brow, regardless of moral implications—the meaning of Water's closing lines: "True if you're standing a few feet away, / But close up they're blurry, and cobalt blue."

In Gibson's "Playing Mozart at the Town Dump," she introduces into her structurally polyphonic poem Renoir's iconic luncheon party on the Seine, "an impression of light so this-worldly / it's another world entirely, and ours." But does she appropriate anything but an interior vignette, a fleeting tableau that illuminates another aspect of Mozart's elusive genius? No, she underscores that portion of the German composer's phenomenal gift that is stylistically akin to her own, "now spritely, now sonorous," as in *Eine Kline Nachtmusik*. By contrast, in "Plein Air and Resurrectionist (1880)" Waters alludes to Renoir only in his epigraph, but his subtle use of verbal shading, his meticulous attention to certain optical effects inherent in language, and his desire to transgress strict linearity ("close up they're blurry, and cobalt blue"), all within the framework of a regular metrical pattern, replicate moralistically knotty themes, and make for extremely pleasurable reading.

"Cautionary Tale," perhaps the most diverting poem in *The Dean of Discipline*, is a four-part reminiscence about a friend's abortive attempt to end his own life and draws its epigraph from French novelist and existential philosopher Albert Camus: "There is but one truly serious philosophical problem, and that is suicide." In section one, titled "The Gesture," Waters itemizes a potpourri of prescription and over-the-counter pharmaceuticals ingested by his "sad-sack buddy": "Ambien, Vicodin, palm-pyramids / Of low-dose aspirin, any capsule / Lodged behind the blurred face in the mirror." This litany of modern cure-alls prescribed by the high priests of healing is rife with apt substitutions and inversions that lead to the desired consummation: "the process of unbecoming, / Its woozy spiral down narrow ice-chutes / Into the final bleb of nothingness." From the moment of conception, we hasten toward our inevitable end, but the poem's dubious protagonist accelerates a process that culminates in an icy "bleb," an artic lens through which he glimpses not the imago, but a grim caricature:

> Then he recalls the science article,
> How the body in death by overdose
> Keeps not the fresh flesh of Sleeping Beauty
> In rosy, plump-lipped, dew-moist suspension,
> But a grotesque, cartoonish parody.

A voluptuary of style, Waters offers us a "rosy, plump-lipped, dew-moist" portrait of his friend's utter self-conceit—recall that Narcissus literally "fell" in love, not with his own reflection, but what he took to be the countenance of his newly deceased twin sister—an allusion exciting more mirth than pity. In this case, the motive is psychological revenge against an estranged sweetheart: "Soon, but too late, she'll find his composed corpse." Here Waters demonstrates that he is not only a genius in the language, but possesses a Dantesque knack for locating the genius *in* the language. "Composed" could denote a self-possession diametrically opposed to the soul-numbing despair that precipitated the act Waters archly terms "The Gesture." Moreover, "composed corpse" suggests a corpus or body of written works attributable to which author we can only speculate. Suicide is the ultimate social protest and implicates us all. Confronted with the reality of his situation and the "grotesque" aftermath, "the face's features / Ravaged as a quake's fissured afterscape, / Bruised as though beaten—moldy pumpkin," the friend reacts before he can lapse into an eternal neural buzz:

> And he bolts upright.
> This is not what he wanted, not *this* death,
> This gesture to declare himself undone.
>
> As shrinking pills release their bridal pull,
> He fumbles his cell to thumb 9-1-1.

Beyond any doubt, the penultimate line quoted above invites the most speculation. As the pills "dissolve" and release or activate what the poet calls their "bridal pull," the despondent friend feels the inexorable allure of the love-death nexus, and desperate to escape its ineffable finality, he ham-handedly, but most emphatically "fumbles his cell to thumb 9-1-1." Maybe it is too picayune to venture that Waters intends "bridal" to be a pun on "bridle," thus lending the line a totally different interpretation, but given his love of wordplay, it bears consideration.

Of the four sections comprising "Cautionary Tale" the second occasions the most levity. Appropriately titled "The Joke," the five tercets are deftly enjambed, and the poet's frequent use of alliteration and repetition of vowel sounds conveys the impression of a formal symmetry that belies content:

> A Times Square hustler's cheap Nikon knockoff
> Strapped like an amulet around her neck,
> My wife dawdled in ciphers of sea foam,
>
> So I draped my arm across Steve's shoulder
> And unbeknownst to my sad-sack buddy
> With a deft left hand lowered my Speedo

> Below the albino cheeks of my butt,
> Knowing my wife would raise the camera,
> Release the shutter to freeze-frame the joke.

Waters sets the tone in the first line, dismissing his wife's camera as a "Nikon knockoff," incisive *n* playing off glottal stops combined in *o* and *k* to catch the flavor of "Times Square" gutturals. Yet he remembers how she "dawdled," luxuriating like Aphrodite in "ciphers of sea foam," at this ocean-side retreat. Here the poet indulges in no elegant circumlocutions but presents in graphic, matter-of-fact detail how he, with gleefully cadenced "deft left hand," mooned the camera, not for all posterity, but for the edification and hopeful delight of his "sad-sack buddy." His wife takes the cue and manages to "freeze-frame" this instance of mad hilarity. His friend nails the print to the wall in "one dark nook of his sparse apartment," punctuating part two of "Cautionary Tale," which significantly leaves off without a period.

Part three is at first less engaging than the other two; it consists of seven unrhymed couplets and an orphaned last line. The police answer the distress call of the hapless friend and attempt to impose order on a chaos of figurations that include "White caps of vials" likened to "poker chips." One cop barks out an imperative *"Stay with us here,"* another's voice is a "soothing syrup." EMTs "whoosh into the room" and the new patient rides the cool slipstream into the custody of "doctors, nurses, psychotherapists, / And the social worker who'll visit him, // Solicitous muse, at least for a while." The epithet "solicitous muse" is an oxymoron awakening dim memories of Petrarch's Cruel Fair.

Waters concludes "Cautionary Tale" with an amusing "Envoi," an earnest imploration to those contemplating the folly of suicide:

> Imagine, friends, if your final vision
> In this gloriously improbable,
> Hourglass'd never-to-be-repeated life
>
> Is not the Lord beckoning you to light,
> Nor the streaked face of this year's beloved,
> But a black and white snapshot of my ass.
>
> *Absurdity trumps misery with time.*
> Weep only once for our living-and-dead
> Selves, and celebrate each failed suicide.

The poet's hortatory tone, "Imagine, friends," both disarms and enjoins the reader to be attentive not to death's self-appointed plenipotentiary, but to a simple messenger who wishes to impart some basic truths. Indeed, Waters earns our attention with a lyric acumen measured out in three tercets that have about them more of gnomic wit than a fearful symmetry. We are creatures of time and chance; life is short, he contends, beautifully glossing this truth with the adjectival "hourglass'd." The orbicular *o* and *r* sounds in "gloriously'" and "Lord" run smack into the "black and white snapshot of my ass." The italicized seventh line says it all; thus, we "celebrate each failed suicide." Perhaps this critic should state unequivocally what he has hinted at before: Michael Waters is the ablest poet of an able generation.

In a compelling instance of serendipity, the four-part, forty-two-page title poem that closes Philip Schultz's *Luxury* bears the same epigraph from Camus as Waters's "Cautionary Tale" but with a significant addition: "All the rest . . . comes afterwards." In that ellipsis lies the narrative gap that separates the two poets. In line after line of "Cautionary Tale," Waters displays a lyrical élan that shuns aureate dictions in favor of a precise but vivid imagery, arresting tropes, and verbal wit. His essential gift is compression, and he writes very few poems that are more than two or three pages in length. On the other hand, Schultz prefers an expansive approach that allows time to pause and reflect; he shares with the novelist the need for introspection in the course of relating a specific chronology enlivened by characters from both his past and present. Perhaps the most striking difference between "Cautionary Tale" and the title poem, "Luxury," resides in the latter's immediacy: "The first / and only life I ever managed to save / was my own." Schultz broaches the subject of suicide from firsthand experience, and his straightforward recitation of events is oddly detached albeit poignant: "when the girl I loved wrote / saying she'd found someone else, / everything seemed unworthy. / I swallowed half a bottle of tranquilizers, / and slit my left wrist, / then watched with cruel fascination / as my future / slowly abandoned me." The repetition of rolling *l* and *o* in proximity to double *u* in the clause "swallowed half a bottle" suggests a more potent opiate than Keats bibbed in "Ode to a Nightingale"; we catch the razor's snick in "slit my wrist" and share the speaker's "cruel fascination" as his heart's blood spends all over the white bedclothes. Schultz sums up his self-negating circumstances in clipped accents: "Twenty and indigent, / living in an attic / and caring for an invalid child," he is sustained only by Nietzschean precepts such as "'virtue, art, music, the dance, reason / and the mind. . .'/ mad, delicate or divine things / that transfigure pain." Unlike the friend in "Cautionary Tale," Schultz's call for aid is a *crise de conscience*: "But fearing / the child's parents thinking me negligent, / and what the god I professed / not to believe in / would think of me, / I called for help."

Schultz's organizing principle in "Luxury" is initially difficult to pin down. In prose fiction—we must remember Wallace Steven's dictum declaring that "poetry is the supreme fiction"—all drama arises (or should arise) from characterization. Schultz introduces a formidable array of characters in "Luxury" giving his long poem a novelistic feel. He is especially concerned with his entrepreneurial father, who virtually worked himself to death by age sixty. Schultz compares the patriarch—with "his black shtetl don't-mess-with-me eyes"—to Sisyphus, the legendary king of Corinth condemned to roll a heavy boulder up a hill in Hades only to have it roll down again as it nears the top. Like many other not-so-humbly-aspiring proponents of upward social mobility, Schultz's father yearns for the emblems of success, its latest manifestation a new 1955 Pontiac station wagon, "its double hooded headlights, / big swerved tailfins, / [and] shiny Ottawa War Chief hood ornament" described early in part one. Schultz's mellifluous enumeration of the automobile's sleek attributes, as the family looks on, is irresistible:

> astonished by the automatic transmission,
> cloth that shines brighter than leather,
> eight powerful cylinders,
> whitewalls reflecting a splendor
> usually seen
> in suburban driveways,
> not deep inside Rochester, NY
> in the inner inner city,
> where snow buries spring
> and memories of war still sour the air.

The poet's rapt inflections mirror his inward vision of the Pontiac's "big swerved tailfins" as it glides like an outsized pike stunned by its own grandeur through the streets of the "inner inner city."

If Schultz's organizing principle at first seems murky, it quickly becomes clear that his poem's narrative is anything but pedestrian; it enables him to manipulate a continuous parallel between time past and time present as he pauses to indulge in gorgeous lyric runs:

> Here
> in East Hampton, NY,
> in the early winter ocean light,
> where stuttering waves play variations
> in the buoyant drift of the moon
> and solitary fishermen cast wistful inquiries
> into an upside-down shadowy kingdom,
> reluctant,
> while the sun is still offering its prospectus
> for the new day,
> to abandon their rituals of satisfaction
> and return to the misgivings
> of mailmen and roofers.

Here in this artist's colony located in the comparative affluence of East Hampton, before the cold but passionate dawn lapses into the prosaic light of day and the poet must "return to the misgivings" of working-class people—"mailmen and roofers"—he looks back on a life that at one time promised a legacy of loss greater than he can now imagine. Rhythmically each line in this passage marks a return from an orbit already traced; the poem builds incrementally, as Schultz lovingly names the properties of light: "early," "winter," and "ocean." The numinous moment lurks between "the buoyant drift of the moon" and the "upside-down shadowy kingdom" so earnestly interrogated by the fishermen's hooks.

After Schultz's father paid the ultimate price for living too long with a single dream, his mother "went back to the same filing job / she worked as a girl, / while I got work on a roofing gang, / dumping truckloads of debris at a landfill." But even in the midst of this grinding toil, Schultz encounters a latter-day rhapsode in the person of Willy, "a one-eyed black man" who sings, "Even a cracked sink is a glory! / A castaway bed a sweetness!" But it is the spectral presence of R, "the son of a white mom / and the black man she cheated on / her white husband with," a prodigy Schulz encounters during his years in Iowa City, that haunts the "the inner voice up-tempo dot-time scale" riffs that occur and recur throughout "Luxury." Through one of R's ostinatos, Schultz introduces Paul Celan, the Romanian-born German poet and translator whose parents died in a concentration camp during the Second World War:

> R, haloed in praise,
> having harvested
> the stuttering strangled breath of the dead
> in his translation of Paul Celans's "Deathfuge,"
> singing: "Black milk of daybreak we drink it at evening . . .
>   we shovel a grave in the air where you won't lie too
>   cramped . . ."

By proxy of R, Schultz captures the gutturals of the German original, particularly in the *u* sound and hissed sibilants in "stuttering strangled breath of the dead." The construction "we shovel a grave in the air" embodies a play on "air," meaning in this context, the song itself. On the subject of Celan, R and Schultz discover common ground: "R, noticing me reading him, / said: 'Yes, Celan, / Babel and Mandelstam / because Jews know death.'" Three years after R and Schultz discuss the peculiar angst of his poetry and translations, Celan drowns himself in the River Seine. Perhaps the arduous and scriptorium-slow process of carrying over into English—"each word a dark psalm / a thorn of mercy / the naked center of nothing / that dwells in the almond"—the gists and piths of Paul Celan's German takes its toll on R. Schultz wistfully remembers his friend's last moments: "Could R / in his last moments, / parked on a cliff overlooking the Pacific, / appreciate the strength of the will / that had taken him that far?"

"Luxury" deepens its distinctly contrapuntal structure when Schultz brings into his long poem Ernest Hemingway, Nobel Prize winning novelist and former journalist, proponent of anti-fascist factions during the Spanish Civil War, aficionado of the arena sands that drank the blood of far-famed toreador Ignacio Sanchez Mejiás, and author of *A Farewell to Arms* (1929), *Death in the Afternoon* (1932), *The Old Man and the Sea* (1953), and *A Moveable Feast* (1964). Schultz relinquishes all the cynicism surrounding Hemingway, depicting him as the master of "luminous sentences" whose prose-style infects his own poetry:

> This Christmas,
> a seventieth birthday present,
> my wife and two sons took me
> to Finca La Vigía,
> Hemingway's house in San Francisco de Paula, Cuba.
> Where, I, among tourists from Canada,
> China and Sweden, was utterly happy,
> peering through fragile windows
> at roped-off furniture, belligerent trophy heads,
> decaying books and photos
> of matadors and movie actors,
> a ghostly Royal portable typewriter.

Perhaps "utterly happy" is the most poignant utterance by this septuagenarian poet obliged in his youth to subsist along with his mother on two hundred dollars a month. By "peering" through the delicately glassed windows, he aspires to participate vicariously in Hemingway's privileged posthumous existence, unaware that he has already replicated a portion of the latter's genius with his juxtaposition of richly sonorous locutions such as "matadors" and "portable." Although he refers to "Papa" as "death's foremost connoisseur" he credits the memoirist and fiction writer with instilling in him "codes of honor and courage / and gracious appetites," coming full circle with a terse but heartfelt tribute: "Hemingway, / who like my father and R, / chose death / would show me how to live."

The counterpoint to Schultz's veneration of Hemingway and his fascination with R's intimate knowledge of the jazz subculture's hip parlance lies in his own love of the surfaces and textures of language: "The light / at Louse Point / this cloudless February morning / is crystalline / a harvest / of frozen silence / the bleaching velvet rinse the painters came for." Brilliantly synesthetic, these lines inculcate the wonder that accrues in the mere act of looking, and a joy in the nominal properties of the natural world: "clouds coalesce into vibrant silhouettes / and birds—gulls, ducks, piping plovers, and the tentative Least / Terns—/ crisscross the sheer white sky." Both wonderfully chromatic and delightfully polyphonous, these sights and sounds serve as prelude to a converging harmony: "clouds perform dream symphonies / to the raucous applause of the waves."

Like William Butler Yeats, Schultz has come to mythologize the people and seminal events in his own life, especially his father's endless round of labors that began anew each day: "Camus asks us to imagine Sisyphus happy, / in fact / he says we must, / all is despair otherwise." He no longer sees his parent's unrelenting pursuit of prosperity as a form of slow suicide, but rather an inbred desire for something better about to be, an act transformative in and of itself. Nor is Schultz reluctant to usher in humor in the person of Osiris, a conflation of the Greek psychopomp Hermes and the Egyptian god of the underworld: "the ice cream parlor / Osiris, our guide, dreams of / will only serve one flavor, / his favorite, strawberry, / which tastes of the future, / sweet and quickly passing." In the mythologies of the ancient world, red fruits such as strawberries were exclusively the food of the dead. One delves into and savors a concupiscent dollop of the poet's wit: "In Bulgaria, they add buttermilk, he explains / in St. Petersburg, vodka, to give a kick / in Venezuela, coffee bean extract." Osiris appeals to our best instincts with a self-deprecating humor: "'Forgive me,' he laughs, / 'everyone here dreams of only one thing.'"

By any reckoning, "Luxury" is a dark and disquieting poem; even in his use of color motifs Schultz often insists on the bleaker hues: "One Sunday morning / a used blue Ford station wagon / was parked under the big oak / instead of the gold Pontiac." The father's financial fortunes have taken yet another downward turn, leaving the son to engage in musings both abstruse and recondite: "Blue, / after all, / wasn't conceived billions of years ago out of asteroids, / isn't a symbol of balance and divine principles." Perhaps the elder Schultz feels the pressure of expectations, sometimes a difficult load for a man to bear: "Blue / was the color of Mother's eyes / as she tried to smile / and then looked away / and sighed." The headlong momentum of his father's varied career comes to rest in chiseled-out initials on a marble slab: "The woman / from whom I ordered Dad's stone / insisted *Rest in Peace* / was more fitting than *In Last Relief*." A biting irony is implicit in the blue-veined monument's legend. In this context, *relief* connotes a final respite from an onerous burden, but another possibility is a payment made by a feudal tenant to his overlord on succeeding to an inherited estate. Will Schultz's father, having literally "paid his dues," take his rightful place in the nether regions? Perhaps the last word on the matter of suicide, whether by a desperate act or slow attrition of body and spirit, belongs to Camus. The only courageous or morally valid response to the Absurd is to go on living: "Suicide is not an option."

At the age of seventy-three, Philip Schultz is not about, as Yeats would put it in "Easter, 1916," to resign his place in the "casual comedy." Founder and director of the Writers Studio, he is master of his own "singing school" and lives with his wife, the sculptor Monica Banks, and two sons in East Hampton, New York. His sixth volume of poetry, the disingenuously titled *Failure* (2007), won the Pulitzer Prize for the same year. As for acquired wisdom over the decades, he probably puts it best in these lines from "Greed," one of the shorter poems in *Luxury*: "Happiness, I used to think, / was a necessary illusion. / Now I think it's just / precious moments of relief."

The title of Stanley Plumly's most recent volume, *Against Sunset*, suggests that he is no more inclined than Philip Schultz to yield readily to the vicissitudes that time and chance foist upon us in the course of a life by turns spiritually impoverished or steeped in self-actualized good luck. Like Schultz, Plumly mythologizes a larger-than-life father—though his died of alcoholism in addition to overwork—and skillfully avoids the Confessional tendency toward what James Dickey dismissed as "scab-picking." This is especially true in poems such as "For My Father Dead at Fifty-Six, on My Fifty-Sixth Birthday" and "Drunks," both of which appeared in his new and selected poems, significantly titled *Now That My Father Lies Down Beside Me* (2000). Unlike Waters and Schultz, in *Against Sunset* Plumly's initial approach to the notion of suicide is ostensibly theoretical, even abstract. Here is "Suicide" entire:

> Something to think about, an abstraction,
> like being, therefore I am, I am whatever.
> Like the spirit bird in reaction to nothing
> it can see except flying over and over
> into the icy window. Perhaps the sunlight
> in the room reflected in the glass that brings
> to life what otherwise looks cold is fire enough.
> Break the bright window and everything changes.
> Those things days we think we want to die and know,
> this, too, passes are like those images of flight
> the imagination loves, as there we are, watching
> the winter cardinal so suddenly out of breath,
> taking a moment, taking it in, its sunlit wings
> unfolding on the branch, ready to try again.

Structurally speaking, "Suicide" taps the Continental lyric tradition; since it runs fourteen lines, it is architectonically in the form initially adopted into English from the Italian of Francesco Petrarch by Henry Howard, Earl of Surrey, and Sir Thomas Wyatt. Notwithstanding the fact that Plumly often extends their decasyllabic line by as much as a metrical foot and introduces a looser, more colloquial tone, "Suicide" remains in essence a sonnet. Although prosodically less rigorous than Waters in "Cautionary Tale," Plumly is richly allusive and often no less clever. The second line of "Suicide" merits closer scrutiny: "Like being, therefore I am, I am whatever." Plumly offers a variation on the Cartesian

Cogito ergo sum, only to dismiss it with an almost flippant "whatever." But the poet also awakens more ethereal echoes. When Moses in the Book of Exodus asks of the burning bush whom he shall say has sent him, God's answer is "I am that I am." Perhaps for this reason Plumly invests the bird continually buffeting itself against the frosted window pane with the qualifier "spirit." Lines five through seven are subtly inflected; the hard *i* in "icy," the "sun" in the anapest "sunlight," and the brilliantly oxymoronic unit "cold is fire" kindle and culminate in the traditional turn in line eight, which is a discrete sentence: "Break the bright window and everything changes." To shatter the simulacrum of self is to break through to oblivion; therefore, best discretion lies in renewal, the intrepid (perhaps Sisyphaen) daily willingness to try again: "Those days we think we want to die and know / this, too, passes are like those images of flight / the imagination loves." Ebullience is the quality that enables the red-crested avian spirit to batter repeatedly its double locked in the frozen glass: the winter cardinal so suddenly out of breath, / taking a moment, taking it in, its sunlit wings / unfolding on the branch, ready to try again."

But for Plumly, the subject of suicide is more than an abstraction, a mere postulate that provides a point of departure for meditation on an act at once futile and irretrievable. "With Deborah in Amherst" limns in twelve heartbreakingly lovely quatrains the epiphanous moments that seem to foreshadow the demise of his former wife, the poet Deborah Digges, who reportedly leapt to her death years after their divorce and her subsequent remarriage:

> Out of the blue, out of the marble blue
> of her eyes, the sudden tears—we'd be talking
> about dinner, where to go, already driving,
> the forsythia burning sunlight into evening,
>
> passing—of all possible places—
> Emily Dickinson's house and what was once
> The Evergreens, where Austin and Sue Dickinson
> wore a daily path back and forth.

Charles Simic once remarked that it is the dream of every cliché to make its way into a great poem, and the prepositional phrase "out of the blue" leading into the marmoreal splendor of Deborah's eyes brimming tears—salt quotidian tears that nevertheless wed pang to fire—prompts one to venture that the Yugoslavian-born poet's words have at last borne the shape of prophecy. Most arresting is Plumly's fourth line—"forsythia burning sunlight into evening"—in which the delicate blossoms flare up with a temporal light that smolders into the blue hour. Also of signal interest is Plumly's juxtaposition via geographical and psychic terrain of his own troubled domesticity and the outwardly sedate lives of the Dickinsons, who suffered their own peccadillos. If Plumly's languorously cadenced blank verse implies that he is at leisure from his emotions, the lapidary cut of his imagery insists otherwise:

> If fear is a cover word, pain is a better word,
> a blood word, that cuts like paper or a clean razor.
> It wasn't tears exactly, or only, but her body
> breaking open the whole hurt length of it.

The precision of velar *k* sounds in "cuts" and "clean" make the preceding adjective-noun combination "blood word" seem a sanguine afterthought. The first line of the next stanza is a wordless *cri de coeur*. "as if, in that moment, she'd halved her heart." Moreover, in "With Deborah in Amherst,"—in fact, throughout *Against Sunset*—Plumly enters into a dialogic exchange with the great granite dead, interspersing his own words with those of Emily Dickinson: "The Things that can never come back are several." The poet mourns his inability to snatch his former wife from a literal and metaphorical abyss in the classic language of the English elegy:

> a time-line as a lifetime, as if our lives were linear,
> ours or anyone's. I remember, most of all, the trees,
>
> their classic stature, their first-growth size, and how,
> in late September, they seemed to die with color.

In the first line quoted above, Plumly's artifice remans speculative as he muses on the meaning of coinages such as "time-line," jargon belonging to the world of business or politics, and bloodless substitutes for appraising the inherent worth of a "lifetime." Indeed, he has finished with the notion that our lives are "linear," that time, whether personal or historical, forms a seamless continuum to be traced in someone's palm or the lineaments of a text. Instead, he looks to the cycle of the seasons, the prospect of seed-time, floribundance, and the inevitable hastening toward ends not our own. As the ninth month draws toward a close, the trees "die" with color, a locution bearing a number of connotations. Perhaps the most obvious is the play on "dye," which does not lend itself to Plumly's purposes at this point in the poem. More intriguing is the Renaissance meaning of "die," the moment when coitus reaches its highest intensity followed by a dying fall. Plumly concludes, "With Deborah at Amherst" with an almost plangent memory of another time and place:

> that outsized oak that took up all the lawn
> in front of where we lived on Blue Hills Road,
>
> beautiful, like weather or wild nature, and again,

always to be blamed. The trees, everywhere around,
loom like other century presences. Who knew, in such
an old, deep place, how quickly trees humiliate our loses.

As befits the larger contours of the elegiac tradition, Plumly finds himself caught up in identities such as "weather," "wild nature," and "other century presences." Here, Deborah's memory is subsumed and transformed by a landscape that radiates the stained-glass resplendence of autumn leaves. How better to assuage pain and irrevocable loss?

Almost the whole of *Against Sunset,* like the poems in Yeats's *The Tower,* betrays a valedictory tone that yearns to reclaim the past by way of vital interaction with those alive only in the far recesses of time. In "Jack Gilbert," Plumly retrieves through associations both sensory and cerebral, the one occasion he met his pugnacious fellow artificer at the residence of *Antaeus* editor and Drue Heinze beneficiary, Daniel Halpern:

> Dan would roast
> a pig and we'd drink to the open sky
> or the cumulonimbus clouds drifting
> full-blown on parade—Gilbert came right
> at me, white wine tight in one hand, almost
> nose to nose, "I'll bet it's Stevens,
> not Williams," a bet he would have won.

Plumly anticipates a repast of succulent pork and heady libations under the drift of typically anvil-shaped cumulonimbus formations—one thinks of the forge and fire-blast of the imagination—when he finds himself virtually "nose to nose" with Gilbert whose smug intellect tempered with "white wine tight" trumps his own: "He wasn't tall, though he / had a face sharpened with an edge of mind / that seemed to cut the air, like the quartz / cut to flint inside his poems." Plumly regales us with his uncanny knack for recall, notwithstanding the fact that once he could not sort between William Carlos Williams's late-phase triadic line and a passage from Wallace Steven's *Auroras of Autumn.* Self-effacing on the surface, he too can "cut the air" with a critical insight no less penetrating than Gilbert's searing lyric acumen. Plumly ruminates about the company the elder poet kept in his youth, his own mind's eye honed precise as any camera lens:

> I remembered his picture on the cover
> of Gerald Stern's *Red Coal,* the two of them,
> as young men, walking toward the camera,
> talking with their hands, completely
> unaware they'd live a whole day longer,
> with Paris at their backs.

No doubt, the title blazoned above the jacket photo of Stern's *Red Coal* awakens in Plumly's imagination the slow tick of carbon toward the diamond lusters of the creative intelligence. After all, he grew up in the mining community of Barnesville, Ohio—a far cry from the tree-lined lamplit boulevards of a Paris. For now, he feels he has had a privileged glimpse into the lives of an older generation of artists who themselves live in the shadows of a Modernist pantheon: "old / age would mean they'd both survived, / like Jeffers, Pittsburgh, as Stevens, at the end, survived Hartford, Williams, / East Rutherford."

Plumly demonstrates rare insight into the concept of canonicity, proffering Gilbert an unusual compliment as well: "If poetry is one silence / speaking to another silence or otherwise / Gilbert's is somewhere in between." If Gilbert has a plot on the slopes of Parnassus, he still seems to be oddly sequestered: "He lived on islands / of his own making. White islands / in waters crystalline." Plumly's inversion of the adjective-noun combination lends emphasis to the clarity and refinement of Gilbert's vision. On the other hand, he cannot resist a deft albeit affectionate last jab: "His obit quotes / a friend that Gilbert was our 'greatest / living poet,' a large and loving claim, / which we all are, ditto, until we're dead." All poets must at last negotiate the terrible *agon* with Homer, Dante, and Shakespeare, and no less a master than Yeats found a middle way in "To a Young Beauty": "There is not a fool can call me friend / And I may dine at journey's end / With Landor and with Donne." As Plumly attests in a similar poem about ingesting brie, crackling Italian red, and fine literature with William Matthews one evening: "At one point, / maybe this one, we'd reached the hour of wisdom."

Beyond all question, "Brownfields" is the finest poem in *Against Sunset,* a sixty-six line meditation and retrospective about the years Plumly spent in Hampstead, Rome, and Barnesville, Ohio. Organized into eleven six-line stanzas, each structure owns a chiseled perfection that lies in its rich profusion of detail, tiny eloquent reminders that we are but poor passing facts in the larger sweep of human endeavor. Plumly remembers how he and a companion went picking among misplaced artifacts in

> what has been a landfill
> for eighteenth-and-nineteenth century
> cracked or flawed Wedgwood—serving bowls and cups
> tureens and dinner plates with scenes
> of rural life, bric-a-brac perhaps
> and lavish urn-like shapes

> meant for death or human waste,
> festooned with flowers and bunch-of-grapes
> and the full and tender leaves of Arcadia,

> now broken down to broken bones
>   and carried in house buckets to a bath
>   in order to be picked among again.

Plumly chances upon a trove of cast-off and forgotten "bric-a-brac," discarded curios no longer of any save sentimental value even to those who lie beneath the cold sod of Hampstead. In effect, these are fragmented grave-goods waiting to be reconfigured in the poet's word-hoard, an Anglo-Saxon kenning for poetry itself. Particularly compelling is the nuanced catalog introduced by the double -adjective and noun combination "cracked and flawed Wedgwood." "Cracked" is a Proto-Germanic voiceless fricative now rare in modern English but still extant in Chaucerian locutions such as "licht" or "light." "Wedgwood" functions as a historical and cultural synecdoche for the jasper or bone Chinaware fired in the kilns of Tom and Josiah Wedgwood (whose annuity of 150 pounds underwrote Samuel Taylor Coleridge's "Frost at Midnight," "Rime of the Ancient Mariner," and part one of "Christabel"). Plumly's aptly florid repetition of long vowel sounds in "tureens," "scenes," "festooned," "bunch-of-grapes" and "Arcadia"—a region of ancient Greece noted for pastoral poetry—evoke a new industrial epoch already nostalgic for the sylvan loveliness of previous centuries. His mention of "lavish urn-like shapes // meant for death or human waste" proves most disquieting. These highly decorative wares served as both crematory urns and chamber pots; whether the end be inhumation or bodily waste even to these decorative receptacles we must return.

The concluding stanzas of "Brownfields" find Plumly back in Ohio, sleuthing down foundry garden rows after his father, intent on the effluvia of his American heritage:

> I'd see things no one else could see,
>   which may be why my father made me
> follow him down foundry garden rows
>   of digging, pulling, picking,
> waste not, want not, though what I'd found
>   among potato vines
>
>
>   and corn was coins
>   and Shawnee arrowheads and ingots into stones
> and flints and rusted cartridges—
>   and coral-colored shells scattered
> into seeds, as if a sea, upon a time,
>   had planted them.

Plumly has made the circuit from England to Italy to North America and rediscovered the wonder and delight of childhood, and of poetry itself, in the freshly turned furrows of his native soil. But remembering these things has been the outcome of a life spent arduously devoted to the craft. As Yeats observed in "My House," the second part of the title poem to *The Tower,* "Benighted travelers / From markets and from fairs / Have seen his midnight candle glimmering."

Plumly's overall career as scholar, critic, and poet has been quite extraordinary; in addition to original verse, it includes *Posthumous Keats* (2008), a critical biography destined to supplant the canonical work by the late W. Jackson Bate, and most recently *The Immortal Evening: A Legendary Dinner with Keats, Wordsworth, and Lamb* (2014), about the failed enterprise of Benjamin Robert Haydon, England's leading history painter of the Regency Period, an artist now forgotten apart from his intimate connection with the literary luminaries of the day. Insofar as practical criticism and general observations about the making of poetry are concerned, Plumly's *Argument & Song: Sources & Silences in Poetry* (2003) rivals Donald Hall's *Goatfoot Twinbird Milktongue* (1978). *Boy on the Step* (1989) was the finest collection published by an American poet during the eighties, and *Old Heart,* a National Book Award finalist for 2007, should have won. Perhaps *Against Sunset* will garner Stanley Plumly the accolades for which he is long overdue.

Vexed Heritage: Two Southern Poets
R.T. Smith and Natasha Trethewey

Southern poets necessarily live in the aftermath of slavery, an economy that relied on the enforced servitude of virtually a third of its population. Therefore, all Southern poets must develop a historical awareness akin to the one T. S. Eliot set forth in his essay "Tradition and the Individual Talent": "The historical sense involves a perception, not only of the pastness of the past, but of its presence." Of course, Eliot's treatise urged the need for the poet to cultivate a current sense of identity with the literary tradition of Europe dating back to Homer, but it is at once amusing and sobering to relate that the St. Louis-born Eliot considered himself a Southerner, and was known to sing "I'm a Good Old Rebel" when drunk.

Both R.T. Smith and Natasha Trethewey share the dilemma of the Southern poet who must negotiate a vexed heritage that endures well into the present century. In *Summoning Shades* (2019), Smith, a white male born in Washington, D.C. and raised in Georgia and North Carolina, delves into the lives of both prominent and little-known historical figures, among them Mary Todd Lincoln, Thomas Jefferson, and Joseph Mason. In the book's second part, he draws on childhood epiphanies and the natural world peculiar to his native region and also evokes the music, folklore, and popular culture of his youth. Trethewey—the daughter of a mixed-race marriage between Canadian-born poet Eric Trethewey and black social worker Gwendolyn Ann Turnbough—bears witness to the domestic and workaday lives of marginalized people, especially in Mississippi and Louisiana. She also brings a robust historical sensibility to Storyville, the fabled red-light district of New Orleans, and the Native Guards, a regiment made up of black soldiers from Louisiana who fought on the Union side during the Civil War.

R.T. Smith's Mary Todd Lincoln is finely drawn, blending her intelligent, sophisticated, and determined character with her spendthrift ways and bizarre forays into spiritualism, contradictions often presented in her own haunting voice, as she shoulders the grief of a nation along with her own. Mary Todd Lincoln was the wife of the nation's martyred sixteenth president. Born in 1818 in Lexington, Kentucky, she was a staunch Unionist and supported the abolition of slavery, although her wealthy family supported the Confederacy throughout the conflict. In the poem that opens *Summoning Shades*, "Mary Todd Lincoln Suite: Gloves," Smith—innately aware of the textures of language—adopts the "Hellcat" voice of the divided nation's first lady, who has been told that expensive, custom-made gloves are the best means for arousing envy among Southern "senator's / ladies" in a time of private mourning and national crisis:

> ribboned gloves, those open at the wrist with pearl buttons,
> dove-colored, Chantilly, seamed, hush-blue, those suited

for the opera or riding, mittens for frost, every cut and cloth,
gloves … and fans—the Italian, the Japanese laced,
with figures like fantastic shadows and spreading
wing-like with one flick of my wrist.

The phrase "mittens for frost" takes on a scintillant edge in the locution "cut." The assonantal short *a* and incisive *n* in "fans," "Japanese," and "fantastic" culminate in "flick of my wrist," capturing with synoptic clarity Mary Lincoln's almost flippant profligacy in matters of attire during a period when soldiers in the night fields lacked blankets.

Smith's passion for reveling in the phonetic richness of English never overshadows his considerable gift for the dramatic monologue, a narrative tradition traceable to masterpieces such as Robert Browning's "My Last Duchess" and Eliot's "Journey of the Magi." Neither is he altogether unsympathetic with the plight of Mary Todd Lincoln, who—having previously lost her sons Edward, William, and Thomas to childhood illness and typhoid—is prompted by the president's tragic death to seek refuge in spiritualism. She visits a medium "under the *nom de guerre* of Mrs. Tydall," and when he captures her photograph, he perceives

nothing unusual
through the lens, but when he lifted the silver print
from its chemical fixer, he was amazed as I
to see Mr. Lincoln clearly visible behind me, hands resting
on my shoulders in his former fashion, face placid
in death.

Smith conjures here Mary Todd Lincoln's fascination with the otherworldly, a trait that many Southerners still share.

Perhaps even more poignant is "A Serpent's Tooth," in which Smith's gift for ventriloquism allows him to recount how Mary Todd Lincoln was consigned for several months to an asylum at the behest of her eldest son, Robert, whose ruthless intent to collect what he considered his rightful patrimony evoked the laws of primogeniture dating back to the feudal system of medieval Europe. Mary, afflicted with a veritable catalog of maladies that include "tortuous headaches, joints aflame, palpitations, / the fitting grief of one who has lost so many," decries the "masculine quackery" of physicians who connive with Robert to place her in an institution where she must submit to a soul-numbing regimen of "opium, morphia, cannabis, indica, belladonna, / ergot, conium and Bellevue's celebrated whisky-laced eggnog, / all dispensed to suspend the patients in harmonious lassitude." No one realizes that she has already devised a getaway plan: "a pistol, / my one white trunk stored at the station and ready / for escape—a hooded cloak, emeralds, gowns, the Todd silver." But this stratagem proves moot when she signs over the Lincoln inheritance to her grasping offspring with a blessing that is also a curse: "the will, witnessed and signed lovingly, /

'Your dearest Mother.' Let him finally comprehend and suffer / the sting: I will leave him all."

In "At Shadwell," Smith eschews persona to address slavery directly, the deadly canker in the heart of the Republic from its earliest days. Shadwell was the birthplace of Jefferson, who drafted the Declaration of Independence, served as the nation's third president, and (through the Louisiana Purchase) doubled the stolen territory that is the United States. The poet once more resorts to a first-person perspective as he describes life on the Jefferson plantation with an arson detective's seeming detachment:

> Shards and hearthstones, letters scratched
> by a brant quill dipped in mulberry ink—
> all the remnant evidence suggests
> the Jefferson children learned minuet
> and equestrian manners from "servants"
> dressed in livery or crinolines—
> when to serve Madeira or hang harateen
> to hunt and dress and elocute like gentry
> where empire and frontier met. Clay
> pipes and bone combs, a rickle of cat ribs,
> a buckle, smudged buttons—all somehow ditched.

The glottal *c* and *k* in "rickle" and "buckle" awaken the Germanic gutturals that linked America to northern Europe, although the disaffected colonies still clung to the slavery alluded to in the euphemism "servants." The first lines of the ensuing stanza state that outright "near that threshold dwelled some seventy-six / in bondage"—and if the Tidewater inhabitants of Shadwell were benevolent masters, some of their hirelings were not: "those who will never / whisper it have heard of Bates, the new / overseer who on the Snowden property / whipped poor Hannah to death."

In the second part of *Summoning Shades*, Smith reminisces about his upbringing in rural Georgia during the late 1940s and 1950s, a post-World War II milieu now living only in the minds of a dwindling number of Southerners. "Tube Rose" recalls how the poet's great-aunt dipped snuff, a habit few women now indulge in even along the remote back roads of arcadia. He sets the tone for this country idyll when he describes her makeshift spittoon and the ubiquitous upright radio of the period:

> In spats and monocle Mr. Goober danced
> across the blue tin of a Planter's peanut can.
> Aunt Emma's rocker kept a cradle's cadence
> while the radio evangelist ranted.

Here Smith employs a loose decasyllabic line to telling effect. Of particular interest is the locution "spats," which not only denotes the leather gaiters covering the instep and ankle of "Mr. Goober" (a Southern colloquialism for "peanut"), but also suggests Aunt Emma's practice of expectorating into a repurposed can. The lulling "cradle's cadence" provides a neat counterpoint to the "radio evangelist" with his hell-fire and brimstone sermon, as in defiance of the fiery orator Aunt Rose would intone her secular hymns: "Silver pins and golden / needles will not mend this heart of mine." Moreover, she relished her one vice: "She'd spit a golden ambeer into the cess / of her silver-rimmed can and never missed." Smith's choice of a little-known Southern and Midland term for tobacco juice, "ambeer" with its long *e*, catches the viscous sheen of the elderly woman's spittle. But she also remembers balmy evenings when she was young girl being courted beneath the elms: "She spat and laughed and spoke again / like a devotee of fireflies and summer / love with her lonesome voice." Like James Dickey's "Buckdancer's Choice," "Tube Rose" amounts to a poignant remembrance of a time when preachers declaimed with a meetinghouse fervor, and old people took their ease on screened porches at twilight. Smith's intimate knowledge of Southern idioms, coupled with an unerring mastery of traditional prosodic skills, makes for an unbeatable combination throughout this volume. "Owling," for example, consisting of fourteen tercets and an orphaned last line, speaks to an encounter with the numinous familiar to anyone raised in Georgia or the Carolinas. According to the region's folklore, the winged nocturnal predators may be harbingers of phenomena as welcome as rain or as foreboding as death. The poet listens for their crepuscular cries—"All month I'd been hearing them call / from the woods of a neighbor"—as he anticipates a break in the weather that would be "a blessing / in the record heat." He proceeds to recount how

> I'd sit at twilight by my high window
> and wish they'd approach, until at last
> one dusk a soundless wing passed beyond
>
> the trees. At first I knew it was a bird
> but never guessed which species, since
> screech owls are secretive, built for stealth
>
> and lethal surprise.

Downy-feathered but equipped with talons keen to facilitate the kill, the gray-tufted raptor whose passage from tree to tree Smith intuits at dusk is doubtless intent on little more than picking the bones of careless mice; it is the myth and lore of the poet's Southern forebears that invest the avian spirit with a meaning beyond its place in the endless cycle of life and death. Indeed, the poet has come to regard its intermittent calling as a longed-for benediction, "because on the sill / of darkness we will all stand equal, // in need of the world's heartening trill." Even more so than previous books such as *Outlaw Style* (2008) and *The Red Wolf* (2013), *Summoning Shades* is a landmark volume in R.T. Smith's distinguished career.

In *Monument: Poems Selected and New*, Natasha Trethewey draws on her five previous collections—*Domestic Work* (2000), *Bellocq's Ophelia* (2002), the Pulitzer Prize-winning *Native Guard* (2006), *Thrall* (2012), and *Congregation* (2014)—and also offers a carefully winnowed selection of recent work. Trethewey's facility for employing received forms is commensurate with Smith's, and she writes variations on the sonnet, villanelle, and ballad with a metrical dexterity difficult to surpass. Her "Enlightenment" provides an interesting contrast to Smith's "At Shadwell," as both poems touch upon Thomas Jefferson's uneasy relationship with the South's "peculiar institution." Touring the Monticello estate with her white father, Trethewey remarks on the statesman's portrait: "Against a backdrop, blue // and ethereal, a wash of paint that seems / to hold him in relief, Jefferson gazes out / across the centuries." If that "gaze" seems imperturbable, both the poet and her father, as well as the other tourists, are aware of the former president's liaison with his mixed race chattel:

> talk of Sally Hemings, someone asking,
>
> *How white was she?*—parsing the fractions
> as if to name what made her worthy
> of Jefferson's attentions: a near-white,
>
> quadroon mistress, not a plain black slave.

Significantly, Trethewey accords the slave girl the dignity of a last name, which many people living in bondage did not have. Nevertheless, we can detect the hushed irony and even outrage underlying the italicized question and the locution "fractions," which implies the fragmentation and division along racial lines still existing in America today. Moreover, this poet delights in the bass resonance of "quadroon," proclaiming in its proximity to "mistress" the one-quarter of blood that marked Sally Hemings as a woman of color. Notwithstanding Jefferson's purported abhorrence of slavery, he never legally acknowledged the six children she bore him. Thus, the title "Enlightenment" itself is also fraught with irony:

> *Imagine stepping back into the past,*
> our guide tells us then—and I can't resist
>
> whispering to my father: *This is where*
> *we split up. I'll head around to the back.*
> When he laughs, I know he's grateful
>
> I've made a joke of it, this history
> that links us—white father, black daughter—
> even as it renders us other to each other.

The tour guide's evocation of the past incites Trethewey to only half-jokingly relegate herself to the back entrance that was still in use until a comparatively short time ago. Her father's gratitude that she sees some element of humor in their precarious connection is undercut when the poet adds that each remains the "other" in spite of their blood ties.

R.T. Smith approaches the Civil War that divided our troubled nation via the persona of Mary Todd Lincoln, a Kentuckian born to a life of privilege, but Natasha Trethewey appropriates the voice of a fugitive black who served in the Louisiana Native Guards during the conflict. Regardless of his official status as a Union soldier, he finds himself relegated to hard labor that recalls his years of servitude:

> Still, we're called supply units—
> not infantry—and so we dig trenches,
> haul burdens for the army no less heavy
> than before. I heard the colonel call it
> *nigger work*. Half rations make our work
> familiar still.

In this sonnet-length entry titled "December 1862," Trethewey opts for the epistolary mode. If the designation "supply units" is dehumanizing, the ensuing racial slur proves downright demeaning. The Native Guards' C.O. apparently bears little resemblance to Colonel Robert Gould Shaw, commander of the Massachusetts 54th, extolled by Robert Lowell in his poem "For the Union Dead," and the "[h]alf rations" are even more familiar than the labor of plying retrenchment tools and shouldering ammunition crates that Tretheway references. The black soldiers must resort to looting to obtain the essentials: "We take those things we need / from the Confederates' abandoned homes: / salt, sugar, even this journal." The poem becomes multilayered and complex when Trethewey's speaker reveals that his first-person account is a palimpsest, a diary entry "near full // with someone else's words, overlapped now, / crosshatched beneath mine." Ironically, the previous record belonged to a secessionist, and even now, the Negro infantryman's recitation of events cannot efface it: "On every page, / his story intersecting with my own." Thus the poem becomes symbolic of slavery, the shared predicament of all Southerners that began when the holds of ships filled by slavers embarked for the New World with their living cargo.

Even more compelling are the poems from *Bellocq's Ophelia*—with Ophelia being the made-up name of a young prostitute who posed circa 1912 for photographer E. J. Bellocq's portfolio, later published under the appellation *Storyville Portraits*. A light-skinned black woman, Ophelia lives in a "colored" bordello in New Orleans, possibly Lula White's Mahogany Hall. (According to the Blue Book, a guide to the red-light district, Lula's "house" was also known as the Octoroon Club.) Trethewey displays her extraordinary lyric acumen in a sequence of eight sonnets titled the "Storyville Diary." In "Naming," her Ophelia rehearses her origins through the medium of writing.

The daughter of an affluent and dissolute white man, she gets the benefit of an education unavailable to most children of color in that time and place. She dwells painstakingly and lovingly over each syllable of her name as it flows through her pen nib, transforming via the magic of metaphor those first "tentative strokes," which become "a banner / slanting across my tablet at school."

In the nominative properties of language lie the aspirations of a people marginalized by the circumstances of their birth: "like the naming of a child—*Queen, Lovely,* / *Hope*—marking even the humblest beginnings / in the shanties." In the declension from *Queen* to *Hope*, a certain pathos inheres, mediated by *Lovely,*the one attribute that enhances an impoverished woman's potential to transcend her roots:

> My own name was a chant
> over the washboard, a song to guide me
> into sleep. Once, my mother pushed me toward
> a white man in our front room. *Your father,*
> she whispered. *He's the one that named you, girl.*

Not only does the locution "chant" chime with "shanties," it also connotes the liberating power of the lyric itself, whether intoned at a "washboard" or over the tuned ivories of a grand piano in a brothel. This grace is undermined when Ophelia's mother urges her to embrace her biological father and hence a future wherein she becomes the degraded object of men's desires. The closing lines of the next sonnet in the cycle cast her situation a more somber light: "I search now for his face among the men / I pass in the streets, fear the day a man / enters my room both customer and father."

Ophelia is only one of the book's many inhabitants listed under various pseudonyms. In "Blue Book," Trethewey introduces yet another voice into this stunning sequence: "I wear my best gown for the picture— / white silk with seed pearls and ostrich feathers— / my hair in a loose chignon." Sibilants lend the second line a lurid sizzle, and the "loose chignon" seems intended to bewitch as surely as the "erring lace" in Robert Herrick's "Delight in Disorder" centuries before. Of course, men are not the only peddlers of flesh in Storyville: "Countess writes my description for the book." The old madam knows precisely how to pique the prurient interests of the white Southern male, and her neat appraisal of Violet's attributes reflects this:

> *"Violet" a fair-skinned beauty, recites*
> *poetry and soliloquies; nightly*
> *she performs her tableau vivant, becomes*
> *a living statue, an object of art—*

Trethewey's cadenced pentameter evokes Violet's evening recitatives that elevate her above the condition of mere *objet d' art*. Yet every time Papa Bellocq draws her into lens of his camera, she must "pose as I think he would like—shy / at first, then bolder." Nor is the youthful octoroon deceived about her eventual fate: "I'm not so foolish / that I don't know this photograph *we* make / will bear the stamp of his name, not mine."

The ekphrastic poems in *Bellocq's Ophelia* may beguile with their conflation of pathos and tawdry eroticism; selections from *Domestic Work* vividly depict the lives of working-class people in the Deep South. Trethewey's subject in "His Hands" could be a dock laborer of any race, a man obliged to earn in the sweat of his brow a bare subsistence for his family: "he tries to prove himself in work, / his callused hands heaving crates / all day on the docks, his pay twice spent." In the initial aspirates—"hands heaving"—we catch the weariness of a stevedore struggling to unburden both his loved ones and himself of bills perpetually a week in arrears. The man endeavors to supplement his meager income by any expedient: "He brings home what he can, buckets of crabs / from his morning traps," and every evening he comes home late to a house already battened down for the night: "His supper waits in the warming oven, / the kitchen dark, the screens hooked." Lacking even the dignity of a latchkey, "he raps lightly on the back door"—but the wordless greeting he receives makes it all worthwhile:

> Putting her hands to his, she pulls him in,
> sets him by the stove. Slowly, she rubs oil
> into his cracked palms, drawing out the soreness
> from the swells, removing splinters, taking
> whatever his hands will give.

Trethewey also chronicles the lives of women from working-class backgrounds, including her grandmother "pumping the stiff pedal / of the bought-on-time Singer." In "Expectant," the poet imagines her mother pregnant in the "Delta heat," longing "for the Quarter—lights, riverboats churning, / the tinkle of ice in a slim bar glass." Big with child and dreading the responsibilities of parenthood, the young mother-to-be yearns late at night for the lounges of the French Quarter, the "tinkle" and click of gin rickeys full of ice, but she must bid farewell to rain-slick evenings on Bourbon Street, with its bars drifting like luxury liners in the spillage of their colored lights: "Each night a refrain, its plain blue notes // carrying her, slightly swaying, home." Trethewey then recalls her grandmother, a seamstress who spent each morning "pacing the cutting table" of her cottage industry: "And now, grandchildren— / it's come to this—a frenzy of shouts, / the constant *slap* of an old screen door." However, there are small consolations: "At least the radio still swings jazz / just above the noise, and / *ah yes*, the window unit—leaky at best." In the heat and humidity of the Mississippi Delta, a working-class woman must derive relief from any source at hand:

"Sometimes she just stands still, lets / ice water drip onto upturned wrists."

Unlike R.T. Smith's, Trethewey's life has been marred by a violent personal tragedy—the execution-style murder of her mother at the hands of her stepfather, a brutal man Gwendolyn Ann Turnbough married after divorcing the poet's biological father when Trethewey was six. In "Reach," the grownup child tipples rum and coke "late nights on the front porch" with her surviving parent: "We are at it again, father / and daughter, deep in our cups, rehearsing / the long years between us." Eric Trethewey, with a guitar pick in his right hand as he works the ache of taut strings into the callused fingers of his left, becomes an Orpheus figure attempting to lead his daughter's mother back from the nether regions:

> My father
> saying, *If only I'd been a better husband*
> *She'd still be alive today,* saying, *Gwen and I*
>
> *would get back together if she were alive.*
> It's the same old song. He is Orpheus
> trying to bring her back with the music
> of his words, lines of a poem drifting now
> into my dream.

"Reach" evolves into a blend, at once artful and heartbreakingly guileless, of the voices of both father and daughter lamenting the death of a beloved one. Most affecting of all, the father—who died in 2014—must now embark on a solitary quest:

> I know where he is going. I cannot call
> him back. Through the valley the blacktop
> winds like a river, and he is stepping into it,
> walking now toward the other side where
> she waits, my mother, just out of reach.

Both R.T. Smith and Natasha Trethewey eloquently negotiate the difficult, often unique heritage of Southern poets by confronting head-on the racial and class divisions that continue to be part of the culture. Smith witnessed firsthand segregation's myriad inequities, but he is never at leisure from his emotions, even when exploring these particular problems from a perspective more historical than personal. Because of Trethewey's mixed-race background, she knows more intimately than most of her contemporaries the ineffable despair of a disenfranchised people and the indomitable spirit that can enable many of them to confront on a daily basis what seem to be insurmountable ordeals. Extraordinarily gifted, she is undoubtedly one of the finest poets of her generation.

When one takes into account the prodigious skills that R.T. Smith brings to the craft of poetic making, in particular his uncanny knack for ventriloquism that makes for dramatic monologues in the Southern vernacular surpassing those of any poet in his generation, it would seem appropriate to comment here on both *Outlaw Style* (2007) and *The Red Wolf : A Dream of Flannery O'Connor* (2013). *Outlaw Style* is his twelfth volume in a career that meets all three of T. S. Eliot's criteria for poetic excellence: abundance, variety, and complete competence. Smith is a quintessentially Southern poet who employs a conflation of lyric and narrative techniques to bring his native region under a relentless and thoroughgoing scrutiny. From the argot of cockfighting and snake-handling to the hip parlance of the jazz and blues subculture, much of his figurative language inheres in his subject matter, and it requires a constant effort on the poet's part to be inventive beyond the colorful metaphors already in place. Needless to say, Smith proves up to the mark; moreover, he shows himself to be a genuine adept at the dramatic monologue, no easy form to master.

In "Shepherd Ollie Strawbridge on the Chicken Business," Smith's first-person narrator—despite the poem's benign title—reveals from the outset that the topic of his spellbinding oratory is not common poultry: "Brothers, I have seen two Pruvells whirl a brown cyclone / in midair and slash their gaffs into each other for no cause / except God invented them for combat and no quarter." Here the poet exhibits an extraordinary command of Southern fundamentalist vernacular. Lean-thewed, muscular in thigh and groin, these are not pullets for the Sunday pot, but banty roosters fitted with gaffs honed to a lethal niceness. Smith's headlong rhythm, syntax, and diction gather momentum in the following stanza: "and I have seen one blue-stripe flat-out assail a stupid man / who stepped between that bird and its close-bred cousin, / and they will flail at the mesh of cages for blood contact." Despite the internal rhyme of "flail' and "assail, ultimately, the phrase "for blood contact" catches the true flavor of Strawbridge's rhetoric. For he goes on to avow that the birds have "pea-wit chicken / brains," despite his vivid trope extolling the beauty of "those red-headed birds with the question mark tails, / and the gold feet," a sublime bit of ventriloquism on Smith's part. We then learn that the sermon is not only an apologia for cockfighting, but also a plea for the congregation to get up bail for a shiftless breeder named Cortez Darlington:

> so now let's stand and reach
> deep into our pockets, yes, and open the hymnals
> and lift our voices for the Word and our brave new
> world, praise Jesus, say amen. Now page one-oh-one
> for a full-emersion anthem of our perilous survival.

The speaker of Smith's chawbacon dramatic monologue could well be modelled on Chaucer's Pardoner. Taking the pulpit to espouse a way of life based on an inhumane blood sport, Ollie Strawbridge emerges as a charlatan of the first order.

Smith demonstrates a definite virtuosity with language in "Gypsy Fiddle," a poem that unfolds in twenty-two unrhymed and cunningly wrought tercets. The fiddle casts a "spell" over anyone that touches it: "hewn in evergreen and ebony, / Alpine maple, an hourglass sawed, whittled, / and assembled in some lamp-lit forest camp." One senses the seasoned grain of carved "Alpine maple" quicken in locutions such as "whittled" and "lamp-lit." But without the amber rosin-block and horsehair bow, something ineffable yet slumbers in the finished instrument: "nicks and scars in the varnish / almost tell the secret history / of Cain's progeny, the lost tribe vagrant // on a moonlit mountain road." Only when the poet's wife begins to play does the pearl-inlaid fiddle come fully to life:

> It can freshet, shirr, and flurry,
> pattern like a spider and conjure a silk shawl,
> black with red tassels, or a knife
>
> under the jerkin, and I'm actually happy,
> or nearly, that my wife has little time
> to work its magic, to grip its edge.

Just as his spouse coaxes the spirit of the Romany from handworked wood and strung catgut, so Smith's every locution sets forth intricate and lucid patterns.

The second section of *Outlaw Style*, titled "The Booth Prism," comprises the book's centerpiece, a sequence of eleven poems. A number of these are dramatic monologues, either spoken or in the epistolary mode. The subject is Lincoln assassin John Wilkes Booth; even one hundred and fifty years after his death, he remains one of the darkest, most enigmatic figures in American history. Of course, any poet who writes about historical persons or events must beware of the pitfalls inherent in a transcriptive retelling, a mere recapitulation of the "facts." Smith manages this admirably, resorting to language heightened from life, but subtly modulated to convey the impression of verisimilitude.

"Booth: A Quick History" dispels the prevailing portrait of the assassin as a lonely and disaffected madman: "History miscasts him as a misfit, / but he rode a crest of success until Gettysburg, / a prosperous celebrity, though his love of the Confederacy / led him to anger and brandy." The pitch and timbre of these lines, their synoptic clarity and elusive rhythms, elevates Smith's writing from the realm of prose. Indeed, he communicates Booth's prowess as an actor with stunning brevity: "when he stepped out limping as Richard or blackfaced / for the Moor, his anthracite eyes in the lamplight flashed / like Mesmer's and ladies in the front row swooned." Syntactical inversion in the penultimate line accentuates the hard glitter of Booth's gaze. Indeed, the poet enables the reader to detect the first glimmer of a feverish obsession with The Lost Cause beneath the handsome thespian's grease paint. This effect, coupled with both aural and visual nuances, throws the staged scenario into sharp relief.

Smith's dubious protagonist is a *bon vivant* attached to fine liqueurs and the blandishments of silk; a reputed rakehell and whoremaster, he insists that his "valet clip the names / off any letter from 'a true lady'" ("Exhuming Booth"). Naturally, other gentlemen admire "his manners, his equitation, fencing, and diction." Popular history views Booth as a sort of malign Richard Cory who goes out and puts a bullet through another man's head. However, Smith's depiction of the Southern sympathizer is far more complex. In "Asia," a letter written from Pangloss Cottage near London by Booth's beloved sister fifteen years after his tragic end, we learn the true depth of his devotion to the Confederacy:

> I never guessed at the plot nor heard him utter
> anything of murder. Of his sense of mission,
> however, I was not wholly in the dark. So many
> nights he slept on our sofa in those high boots
> with sewn-in holsters and counseled strangers
> in the parlor all godly hours. They called
> him "Doctor," and when I inquired, he confessed
> to carrying quinine in horse collars to his Rebels,
> chamomile, morphia, all manner of contraband.

Smith's speaker is a lady of learning and refinement, and throughout this passage, her ordering intelligence is brought to bear on language. Nevertheless, one wonders whether Asia is a reliable narrator. The poet portrays her as guileless, though not unbiased, betraying her emotions in the seemingly innocuous but eloquent details of memory: "I miss him still, the boy who embraced / the sadness in a jew's harp as Joe twanged out / a tuneless noise in the kitchen." Notice that the letter *j* in the adjective-noun combination "jew's harp" is lower case, perhaps indicating that Booth's sister regards a musical instrument traditionally associated with the black subculture to this day with a certain brow-raised hauteur. On the other hand, the alternate designation, "juice harp," would mark the speaker as one who indulges in vulgar colloquialisms, which Asia Booth would never do. Nevertheless, her abiding affection for her disaffected brother who was shot by a Union soldier in Richard Garrett's theater-like tobacco barn on the morning of April 26, 1865, indicates she cared for her sibling despite the heinous nature of his crime. More than most Southern poets, Smith understands that his native region still participates in the ways of a fallen culture well into the twenty-first century.

In *The Red Wolf: A Dream of Flannery O'Connor* (2013), R.T. Smith adopts the voice of acclaimed fiction writer Flannery O'Connor, who was afflicted with lupus and lived with her mother on a farm called Andalusia near Milledgeville, Georgia, until her untimely death at age thirty-nine. The poems are not a rehearsal of actual events in O'Connor's short life but are instead a series of monologues and letters describing plausible incidents that ultimately take shape in Smith's own words. A Southerner himself, the poet deftly captures O'Connor's sardonic wit and essential scrappiness, as well as her personal and imaginative courage, in an idiom that he playfully terms "cracker mouth music."

The book opens with "Accordion Days," a humorous poem in which twelve-year-old "Mary Flannery" submits to music lessons in "Miss Neva's parlor." The elderly spinster, "her wattle / wagging," emerges as an exacting and querulous teacher: "'Your / accordion,' she says, "works like / a piano with lungs. To make it breathe / you've got to practice.'" Smith's diction is so compelling that it conjures the reedy wheezing of an old accordion, pearlescent buttons shining like beaded rain: "Hold that chord. / *Susurrante*, / Miss Lazy." Despite her later knack for storytelling as an adult, the young O'Connor is no musical prodigy; she yearns for the moment when she receives ginger cookies, curtsies, and bids her frustrated mentor farewell.

In "Corn, the MFA," a poem that reads like a superb bit of ventriloquism, Smith appropriates O'Connor's voice to describe her experience as a writing student at the University of Iowa. Men in the program, many of them veterans of World War II, tend to be scornful of a woman in their midst: "*Hick, wallflower, muskrat / nun* (after my fury coat), *Sister Mary Revisa*— / they aimed to keep me cowed." But the pugnacious O'Connor persists under the tutelage of Andrew Lytle: "Mr. Lytle was a guide / I could follow, to a point, though I thought / he might quail about the buzzards at Heaven's / Gate." Smith's striking image alludes to the commingling of the sacred and profane that would soon become so prominent in O'Connor's work, especially in her novel *Wise Blood* (1952). Indeed, throughout Smith's volume the poet refers *sotto voce* to O'Connor's deep knowledge of Catholic doctrine and exegesis. In closing the poem, Smith suggests a learning experience altogether different from the one in Miss Neva's parlor:

> I kept self and church in balance whenever
> obstacles arose and recited for my sanity.
>
> *Ors et labora and eat no fish come Friday*
> *I am forever Flannery Flannery Flannery.*

Smith's gift for writing in the Southern vernacular comes to the fore in the remainder of *The Red Wolf*, as he assumes O'Connor's mindset and speech patterns in a series of cunningly wrought monologues. In "Ash Wednesday at Andalusia," she goes about feeding the ubiquitous peafowl on the farm: "The king flashes his straight flush / of gems, as if accusing—all this in my yard / under the smut-struck peach tree and the sun." The repetition of short *u* sounds enlivens these lines; moreover, the "straight flush" of the peacock's spread plumage not only provides an arresting image, but also reminds us that in Christian mythology this bird with its feathers that resemble starry beaten metals, is a symbol of immortality.

Such meaning is not lost on O'Connor, who goes about her tasks on the farm even though illness gains ground on her: "Humming my little hymn, I try not to be just / another cracker smitten with the family stain / my sawbones calls *lupus*." Flannery's dilemma is twofold: "The wolf in my bones means me harm, / and readers reckon me an enigma at best." She intuits that her time is short and that hard work is the only remedy in the interim: "The life you save / must be your own, but you have / to behave / and get busy quick, lickety-split if you can."

"Tryst" puts to rest once and for all the notion that O'Connor was what has elsewhere been termed an "isolated Dixie Dickinson." The poem comprises equal portions of the "hick ridiculous" and tender poignancy as the poet describes an encounter between his protagonist and a gentleman caller, deploying dialect that summons up an evening full of dewy hydrangeas and serenading jar flies: "All gentleman, manly but sweet, Eric read / *Wise Blood* at last, and it plainly made him antsy, but he asked again, whispery, and 'Yes,' / I said with just my fluttery eyes." However, the kiss the speaker and her beau share is not one of salty eroticism and celestial sweetness:

> famous
> for being chaste, medicined bald as a possum
> and already starting to limp with a stick,
> nothing sent from Venus, my head swole up
> like a muskmelon in July, but we tried, and yes
> that kiss was chilly with just a smidgen
> of desire.

The richness of Smith's diction and his feel for the rhythms and argot peculiar to O'Connor's region make for captivating reading. Subsequent lines hint at an intertextual resonance between "Tryst" and O'Connor's well-known short story "Good Country People": "I did not swoon, but asked how a textbook drummer could know to utter such palaver." Indeed, Smith's closing dispels any doubt regarding such reference: "that Hulga story came easy, I confess / both his presence and the absence brought me Joy // who showed me then how less is more." R.T. Smith's *The Red Wolf: A Dream of Flannery O'Connor* is one of his most accomplished books, a painstakingly researched and lovingly written paean to one of the most renowned American authors of the twentieth century. Smith's facility with language, coupled with his selfless devotion to O'Connor's life and work, should earn *The Red Wolf* the accolades it unquestionably deserves.

Auspicuious Beginnings, Sure Arrivals:
Beth Ann Fennelly and Eavan Boland

William Wordsworth closes stanza seven of "Resolution and Independence" with a resolving couplet that ominously portends his winter of aesthetic and philosophical discontent—a period spanning four decades—perhaps the longest withering of major poetic genius in history: "We poets in our youth begin in gladness / But thereof come in the end despondency and madness." Perhaps he had no thought for the two-faced nature of Janus, god of auspicious beginnings and sure arrivals, whose month is January when the sap recedes, and snow reconfigures every bough with an edge like glittering cutlery. A few months after Lord Byron's death, William Hazlitt compared the late master of the Satanic School to the aging poet of Lake Windermere: "The author of the *Lyrical Ballads* describes the lichen on the rocks, the withered fen, with some peculiar feeling he has about them: the author of *Child Harold* describes the stately cypress, or the fallen column, with the feeling that every schoolboy has about them." Indeed, Wordsworth's gnomic utterance privileging youthful exuberance over mature vision is too much in Byron's facile manner and rings false as a brass shilling. He forsook the powerful originality and magisterial grace so arduously attained in "Tintern Abbey," eventually yielding to the slow encroachments of time and mutability with a sentimental complacency that would have outraged William Butler Yeats.

If Beth Ann Fennelly's first book-length collection, *Open House*, reaffirms Wordsworth's early enthusiasm for each new-fledged hope, Eavan Boland's tenth volume, *Against Love Poetry*, belies his fear that breadth of imagination and genuine lyric acumen dissipate with the passing years. Despite differences in tone and temperament, Fennelly and Boland explore the full linguistic register with unerring dexterity, mingling syntactical verve with apt diction and vivid imagery. Moreover, each poet sustains an ongoing dialogue with personal and cultural inheritances, often interrogating the patriarchal cast of history and the Western canon.

Beth Ann Fennelly's *Open House*, winner of the 2001 *Kenyon Review* Prize in Poetry, marks an auspicious debut for a poet not yet thirty years of age. Her work appears in a surprising number of anthologies—*Poets of the New Century*, *The Penguin Book of the Sonnet*, *The Best American Poetry 1996*, *The Pushcart Prize XXV, 2001*—so many, in fact, it would seem that her youthful enterprise could hardly fail to prosper. In poems ranging from blank verse variations on the traditional sonnet to sustained meditations in the highly elliptical and hauntingly polyphonous Postmodernist mode, Fennelly tempers cognitive power and sensual wordplay with a subversive wit born of wry self-knowledge. Unlike Wordsworth's *The Prelude*, Fennelly's verse *bildungsroman* begins with the sequence of vignettes titled "The Impossibility of language." In section one, a trinity of wine "connoisseurs" ceremoniously sets about naming the gustatory and olfactory qualities of what sounds suspiciously like a fine Bordeaux, a *premier cru* such as Chateau Lafite: "Blackberries says one, rolling it in the barrel / of the mouth. 'Yes,' says the other, 'oak.' 'Well aged, aroma of truffles,' says the third." Fennelly never overtly mentions gender, but the orotund metaphor "barrel of the mouth" implies that a conclave of male parvenues have broached and pronounced upon a vintage with more bombast than élan. Subsequent lines dispel all doubts: "They nod. Discuss the legs of it running / down the glass." In wine parlance, "legs" is a convenient trope for rivulets that supposedly confirm richness and body. The tipplers resort to a prescribed idiom, thus betraying their tendency to intone ritually rather than to evoke imaginatively. Indeed, each of these "legmen" is a smug poetaster who believes that the *Logos*, the divine wisdom of the creation, even now cloys his palate and tongue: "They roll it and roll it, the way / God must have packed the earth in his palms." They refuse to trace the ruby, amber-lit claret's translucence back to its roots in the Latin *claritas* or the cultivated rows of the vineyard, preferring to filter the sacraments of soil and sunlight through the high artifice of institutional adornment: "They bring the valley into it. And color: 'The light / staining the glass at Saint Chappell.'" The robust aficionados cannot resist garnishing their impressions with esoteric clichés—"Back to taste: / 'Earthy. A finish of clove'"—prompting Fennelly to descant archly on elegant circumlocutions that preclude the genuinely communal: "They leave nodding —/ such faith in the opaque bottles of their words." Does the critic come away with new insight into the foibles inherent in his own sphere of discourse? One certainly hopes so.

In the poem's second section, subtitled "How I Became a Nature Lover," Fennelly's speaker neatly subverts the patriarchal aplomb of the three "experts" mulling over the virtues of an official ferment. In fourteen lines ostensibly charged with a surfeit of sweetness, her persona recalls a moment of wondrous initiation:

> Suppose I said, "Honeysuckle,"
> meaning stickysweet stamen,
> the hidden core you taught me,
> a city girl, to find. How I crave
> the moment I coax it from calyx,
> tongue under the bulbed tip
> of glistening stalk, like an altar boy
> raising the salver under the blessed bread
> the long Sundays of my girlhood,
> suppose my tongue caught that mystery,
>   that single swollen drop
>   O
>   honey-
>   suckle,

Deft enjambment, internal near-rhyme, and dense alliteration offer rare aural delectations richly evocative in their own right, but Fennelly brings us up short with a three-line coda: "The ironies of metaphor: / you are closest to something / when naming what it's not." The aphoristic comment on the slipperiness of metaphor ultimately proves to be a bit of delayed decoding, an invitation to a risqué subtext reminiscent of Henry Reed's "Naming of Parts," especially when one remembers the "stickysweet stamen," a floral organ that produces the male gamete. Previously innocuous locutions—"core," "crave," "coax," "calyx"—become laden with new connotations. One imagines the poised "tongue" teasingly restrained by the labial *p* of "tip." The poet then momentarily subsumes and effaces the double entendre, "glistening stalk," with a simile likening the speaker's tongue to a "salver" waiting to catch the least particle of the sacramental host. It serves as a deferred oral metonym, eventually precipitating the "swollen" ambrosial "drop," a vocative "O" that ends up a numinous ideogram for "honey- / suckle." Perhaps the emphasis on the adjective-noun combination should be shifted from "Nature" to "Lover." Fennelly delights in the polytropic potential of language, the power of words both to embody and transmute meaning.

Despite her adept and relentless pursuit of the myriad figurations intrinsic to lyric poetry, Fennelly opts for a sustained blank verse narrative in "Mary Speaks to the Early Visitor at the Laying Out." In a dramatic monologue patterned on Robert Browning's "My Last Duchess," the speaker welcomes a visitor calling to pay homage to John Milton, last of the English Renaissance humanists, whose major works—*Comus*, "Lycidas," *Areopagitica, Paradise Lost,* and *Samson Agonistes*—raised him to an eminence among British authors shared only by Chaucer and Shakespeare. His second daughter, Mary, greets the early mourner in a deceptively winsome manner:

> You're welcome here, kind sir, take off your cloak.
> It seems you've traveled far to pay respects—
> a friend from Cambridge? No? Well, never mind.
> Anne, Deborah, and I have baked the day
> and you shall be refreshed, though father died
> and left us, orphaned, with the larder bare.

Like Browning's Duke of Ferrara, Mary is an unreliable narrator, whose curious acrimony initially melts into the rhythms of Fennelly's mellifluous blank-verse lines. Weighing her late father's fame as a man of letters against his notoriety as a sectarian and political activist, Mary answers the visitor's unvoiced question with a smart drollery and playful impertinence bordering on coquetry:

> Yes, you're right. He'd taken a third wife—
> three wives and three daughters, he loved
> his trinities. So, no, we're not quite orphans,

his wife is here to share my share of naught.
Have a glass of elderberry wine?

Mary's sportive reply to the effect that Milton "loved / his trinities" is also a piquant barb aimed at the poet's adamantly patriarchal beliefs, both domestic and theological, including his antitrinitarian argument in *De Doctrina Christiana* asserting that even Christ reigns subordinate to God the Father. She knows her father would wince to hear such caustic wit, nor would he fail to glean the ambiguity in the remark that his surviving widow shares his daughter's "share of naught." Of course, "naught" literally means "nothing," but in the seventeenth century could also imply "indecency" in certain contexts. Actually, Milton bequeathed an estate of one thousand pounds (no mean sum in 1674) to his third wife, Elizabeth Minshull, but because his will was oral or nuncupative, his disinherited daughters challenged in court and collected a third of the legacy for themselves. A sweet intoxicant, the proffered elderberry cordial loosens the visitor's inhibitions, thus emboldening his inquiries:

> Well, yes, I'll tell what happened,
> despite my lack of skill at giving speeches—
> I haven't had much practice. Our mother died
> while laboring; she took with her the boy
> inside her. Papa, longing for a son,
> soon met a second wife who stayed two months,
> that's all, then fled home to her mother.

Mary earlier told the young gentlemen that she was twenty-three; in fact, she was twenty-six at the time of her father's demise. But from here, she moves from clever repartee and white lies to a tale fraught with barefaced mendacity. Milton's *first* wife, Mary Powell, left the dour and cloistered Milton in 1642 after only two months of marriage, returning to the conviviality of her parents' Anglo-Catholic and Royalist household. She reconciled with Milton three years later, but not until Charles I capitulated to Parliamentary forces in the field. She subsequently bore the Puritan poet and polemicist four children: Anne, Mary (the poem's speaker), John, and Deborah. Mary Powell died in 1652, three days following Deborah's birth. Deborah survived, but fifteen-month-old John expired with six weeks of his mother. Milton endured four years as a widower, then married his much-beloved Katherine Woodcock in 1656. She died within two years, the result of a tragic childbirth, and was buried with her infant namesake, Katherine. Most scholars consider her the inspiration for Milton's elegiac sonnet, "Methought I Saw My Late Espoused Saint." Does Fennelly's narrator despise Milton for canonizing Katherine Woodcock rather than her own mother? Perhaps so, but Mary seeks to dismantle her father's reputation for more personal reasons. She speaks the unvarnished truth when she relates how the blind and querulous Milton compelled Mary and Deborah to scribe down his verses. Moreover, he reputedly schooled his daughters to read six languages phonetically, but neglected to teach them a single word:

> He rose at four. Which meant we rose at four.
> We'd lead him to his seat before the fire.
> "Girls," he'd say, "I need my morning milking."
> He'd recite new lines, our hands worked fast
> To yank them into pails of parchment paper.
> When he was empty, he would have us read.
> We got to where we could sound out Italian,
> Latin, Hebrew, Spanish, French, and Greek.

When Mary repeats the patriarchal taskmaster's mock-jovial and oddly passive metaphor for dictation—"I need my morning milking"—she exposes an incongruously soft bovine underbelly. Small wonder his classmates at Cambridge dubbed Milton "the lady of Christ's College."

Fennelly's narrator continues to enlarge upon her father's insouciance regarding his daughters' social and intellectual development: "Papa drove us from the parlor / when men came to talk politics / or hear how he met aged Galileo." She also insinuates that her father discouraged potential suitors: "Andrew Marvell once spied me in the kitchen, / but Papa said, 'She's my amanuensis.' / Which put an end to that." Marvell was twenty-seven years Mary's senior. This brief anecdote is almost certainly apocryphal, but nevertheless points to a paternal selfishness almost pathological in its intensity. One listens for the incisive *n* sounds and hissed sibilants in "amanuensis," the vehement possessiveness of an artist bent on sacrificing his progeny's happiness to attain his goals. Fennelly describes with disingenuous verve how relentlessly the blind poet would drive his pubescent copyists: "He kept us up all night to write of Samson, / 'Eyeless in Gaza at the mill with slaves.'" Ultimately she makes no bones about her intention to topple one of the triple pillars of English literature, even as Milton's protagonist brought the columns of Dagon's temple crashing down upon the Philistines in *Samson Agonistes*: "We saw the parallels, but we, not him, / would brace in doorways dreaming of the push / that'd cave the house." Mary then concocts a deliciously wicked tableau in which the dead Milton—strapped to his cooling board—must be tackled down from a second-story window by rope and pulley, simply because the spiral staircase proves too narrow to accommodate his passing:

> I never will see a stranger sight: Papa
> swinging into sunshine, wings of gauze
> aflap his shoulders, bed sheets billowing.
> I wept, which I did not expect to do.

In the above passage, Milton begins as a laughable *deus ex machina*, but through a paradoxically descending apotheosis, he is transfigured from Satan to Lucifer, the light-bearer and morning star. Mary abruptly dismisses her poignant invention: "That's the story, best as I can tell it. / I'd like to sleep late but still wake at four, / my tongue outstretched where Babel has been razed." Through a brilliant architectural metaphor, the speaker compares the foreign languages she once learned by rote to the ancient tower raised in Babylon to challenge the heavens. Now the edifice lies in ruins, so many vowels and consonants irretrievably scattered. Nevertheless, Mary brightens at the prospect of life without Papa: "If you pass this way again, / you'd be welcome, sir. Perhaps some whist? / You could be our fourth, if you desire. / We plan to keep a lively parlor now." One can scarcely imagine whist, a card game wherein the object is to score "tricks," as a pastime befitting a literary salon. Indeed, the coy turn of phrase "if you desire" suggests that this will be a petting parlor. Fennelly's 114-line dramatic monologue is wonderfully iconoclastic, its sprightly and duplicitous narrator delightfully engaging in her ability to "Tell all the truth" and "tell it slant."

Fennelly combines an acute historical awareness with a multilayered conceptual depth to address social and cultural issues, occasionally attributing the recurrence of civic chaos to corrupt power structures. A long poem in the epistolary mode, "Madame L. Describes the Siege of Paris" exploits intertextual resonances and tonal felicities to chronical the slow starvation of the general populace during the 1870 Prussian investment of Paris. Suffering the privations of a siege essentially provoked by Louis Napoleon's dissolution of the Second Republic in favor of a government modeled on his illustrious uncle's Grand Empire, famished Parisians eventually storm the municipal zoo:

> We turned upon the zoo inside
> our zoo. Trumpetings and ape-cries from the ark:
> the hippopotamus, the kangaroo,
> wapiti, bear, and wolf—all mustard-doomed.
> We killed them two by two. We cheered the boys
> who drove the weeping zoo keeper away
> and broke the locks made strong to keep us safe.
> On fire, we roasted camel on a spit,
> danced palm to bloody palm.

In a macabre scenario that conflates the carnival and carnivalesque, Fennelly's Madame L. vividly depicts the mad hilarity of common people run amok within a decadent regime. Indeed, the bloody 1789 Revolution has come full circle: "What's wrong? What's right? To live was right. To know / that you could take the heart and eat it raw." Other splendid poems include "The Insecurities of Great Men," "The Snake Charmer," and "Why I Can't Cook for Your

Self-Centered Architect Cousin." Beth Ann Fennelly's *Open House* betokens a bright future for one of the better young poets in America.

Against Love Poetry is Eavan Boland's tenth book-length collection, a watershed volume in a long and distinguished career. Boland was born in Dublin during World War II. Her father, a senior diplomat, served as Irish ambassador to the court of St. James and later to the United Nations. Educated in England and Ireland, she continues to write against the grain of a dual literary heritage that often consigns women to the role of Muse. A lovely apparition haunting the medieval Irish bardic tradition, the feminine *genius loci* undergoes certain ominous permutations—historical, cultural, political—in both William Butler Yeats's Kathleen ni Houlihan and Seamus Heaney's Bog Queen of Moira. According to *Object Lessons*, Boland's profoundly introspective memoir, "A woman has to grow old in poems in which she has been fixed in youth and passivity: in beauty and ornament." As a corrective, Boland believes that she must inevitably "write her poem free . . .of the object she once was in it."

Part one of *Against Love Poetry*—titled "Marriage"—consists of eleven vignettes spanning twenty pages, almost half the book's length. By turns meditative and anecdotal, several poems in the sequence endeavor to debunk the Petrarchan ideal celebrated in Sir Edmund Spenser's "Epithalamion." A British imperial agent stationed in Ireland during the reign of Elizabeth Tudor, Spenser composed a passionate lyric for his own marriage in 1594. The 365-line wedding song honoring bride and bridegroom remains the exemplar of its kind in English after four hundred years. In section one of "Marriage," subtitled "In Which Hester Bateman, 18th Century English Silversmith, Takes an Irish Commission," Boland fashions an austere counter-sublime to Spenser's highly stylized and richly ornamental paean to connubial bliss. Boland's protagonist, Hester Bateman, was born in 1708, and learned her craft under the tutelage of her husband, John, whose smithing tools she inherited at his death in 1760. In the ensuing years, she evolved into a master artisan in her own right, emphasizing the importance of strong lines and neoclassical precision rather than the absurdly lavish patterns of the popular rococo style. Boland opens her poem with a description of the artist engraving silver fresh from the annealing fire and sintered to near-perfection:

> Hester Bateman made a marriage spoon
> And then subjected it to violence.
> Chased, beat it. Scarred and marked it.
> All in the spirit of our darkest century.

Boland's chaste, spare diction and incisive rhythms—especially the frequent playing of short *i* sounds off glyptic *t* in the repetition of "it"—capture beautifully the percussive strokes of Bateman's characteristic "bright cut" technique. However, Boland disdains the purely aesthetic resonance of these lines when she refers to "the spirit of our darkest century." Indeed, eighteenth-century Irish Catholics suffered Great Britain's introduction of the Penal Laws and absentee landlords, not to mention floggings and tar cappings (the cauling of recalcitrant peasants in pitch-coated leather skullcaps). These abuses culminated in the 1798 Croppie Rebellion and the brutal annihilation of the insurgents on Vinegar Hill. Yet Bateman appears unaware of the civil conflict, as Boland depicts her blithe preoccupation with an earlier part of the creative process:

> Far away from grapeshot and tarcaps
> And the hedge schools and the music of sedition
> She is oblivious to she pours out
> And lets cool the sweet colonial metal.

Bateman watches the molten silver cool in the clay crucible with no thought for the brass and iron cannon cast in the foundries of industrial Birmingham or the Irish agrarian rebels massacred by leaden scattershot on the green slopes of County Wexford. Hester Bateman died in 1794, never imagining that Catholic dissent wedded to Jacobin radicalism could threaten the Protestant Ascendancy in Ireland. Neither could she see how the impending Act of Union would eventually destroy any potential for concord between Ireland and Great Britain. Contemplation of the "sweet colonial metal" seems a palliative for Bateman, as does anticipation of the graceful refinements her artifice will endow on a household object at once symbolic and practical. In the next two stanzas, Boland traces the precious mineral worried from veins of subterranean rock to the intricate contours of a finished product:

> Here in miniature a man and a woman
> Emerge beside each other from the earth,
> From the deep mine, the seams of rock
> Which made inevitable her craft of hurt.
>
> They stand side by side on the handle.
> She writes their names in the smooth
> Mimicry of a lake the ladle is making, in
> A flowing script with the moon drowned in it.

The second stanza quoted above maintains an exquisite tension between lyric and narrative elements. Like twin homunculi conjured from the earth's core, a "man and woman" adorn the handle. Moreover, the liquid sonority struck off the internal half-chime—"handle" / "ladle"—rounds to fullness the limpid vowels in "smooth" and "moon." The deft confluence of participle and noun in "flowing script" overbrims the polished concave surface. Interestingly enough, Bateman could neither read nor write, signing her commissions with "the cross of the illiterate"; nevertheless, her ability to inscribe foliage, festoon, medallion, and finial patterns made sinking the sinuous ripple of the couple's name into the silver "ladle" an act of pure mimesis. Thus, she transcends the plight of Milton's daughters, who were obliged to lend utterance to words they could not possibly apprehend. Boland fuses prosodic rigor and lexical burnish to reflect the durable splendor of Bateman's commemorative spoon: "The silver bends and shines and in its own / Mineral curve an age-old tension / Inches towards the light." The nuptial pair reproduced in miniature becomes the emblem of vicissitudes that few could weather:

> Past and future and the space between
> The semblance of empire, the promise of nation,
> Are vanishing in this meditation
> Between oppression and love's remembrance
>
> Until resistance is their only element. It is
> what they embody, bound now and always.
> History frowns on them: yet in its gaze
> They join their injured hands and make their vows.

Boland and Bateman embody neither Muse nor object: like James Joyce's Stephen Dedalus, each artist is bent on forging the "uncreated conscience" of the race. In one sense, Boland prevails in her *agon* with Spenser, a leading proponent of empire, whose "Epithalamion" reduces his betrothed to an assemblage of Petrarchan figurations such as ivory, marble, and sapphire. Even the lady's hair provides occasion for a gorgeous conceit: "yellow locks like gold wyre / Sprinckled with perle." By proxy of her protagonist, Boland adheres to the neoclassical ethos that insisted on ornament without ostentation. In their respective approaches to the shaping art, both women shun patriarchal mystifications of love and the marriage contract, but only Boland can be completely aware of the larger forces that impinge on Irish identity today.

In "Quarantine," section four of the sequence titled "Marriage," Boland persists in subverting the mythical perfections and false ideals of traditional love poetry. Moreover, she consolidates her theme against the backdrop of Ireland's troubled history. This time her dramatic setting is the Great Famine of 1845-49, a phenomenon accounting for the deaths one million Irish people and the eventual emigration of an additional one and a half million. The fungus *Phytophtora infestus*, shipped from America in a dank hold stocked with infected tubers, destroyed the staple of Irish life in September 1845. More often, the crop went bad before harvesting: "In the worst hour of the worst season / Of the worst year of a whole people / A man set out from the workhouse with his wife." Consigned to a public works shelter for the poor and dispossessed, a couple must depart for a quarantine center because the woman shows signs of cholera or "famine fever." Obliged to carry his wife upon his back, the man journeys through a barren nightscape where the stars seem to twinkle in a void: "He walked like that west and west and north. / Until at nightfall under freezing stars they arrived. / In the morning they were both found dead. / Of cold. Of hunger." Here the poem acquires the dimensions of a tragic folktale: "But her feet were held against his breastbone. / The last heat of his flesh was his last gift to her." Caught in the bone-chilling throes of an absurd *danse macabre*, she treads her last measure to the faltering cadences of his heart. Their death consummates a pact, both spiritual and physical, an affirmation of intimacy beyond the coital embrace. In the truncated rhythms of her closing stanzas, Boland achieves a rectitude and grace wholly alien to the eulogies of thwarted love:

> Let no love poem ever come to this threshold.
>   There is no place for the inexact
> Praise of the easy graces and sensuality of the body.
> There is only time for this merciless inventory:
>
> Their death together in the winter of 1847.
>   Also what they suffered. How they lived.
> And what there is between a man and a woman.
> And in which darkness it can best be proved.

In a later poem, "Once," Boland reprises her story of the outcast mendicants in another context. She decries the fate of lovers in medieval Irish romance, her opening lines possibly referring to "The Pursuit of Diarmaid and Grainne" from the Fenian cycle: "The lovers in an Irish story never had good fortune. / They fled the king's anger. They lay on the forest floor. / They kissed at the edge of death." The poet sees nothing salutary in the destiny of star-crossed lovers: "I do not want us to be immortal or unlucky, / To listen for our own death in the distance." In her closure, she resorts to a mode of direct address:

> I want to show you what is hidden in
> this ordinary, ageing human love is
> there still and will be until
>
> an island coast so densely wooded
> not even the ocean fog could enter it
> appears in front of us and the chilled-
> to-the-bone light clears and shows us
>
> Irish wolves: a silvery man and wife.
> Yellow-eyed. Edged in dateless moonlight.
> They are mated for life. They are legendary. They are safe.

Boland describes a land of virgin forest still extant in the time of Elizabeth I, though wooded areas occupy less than five percent of Ireland today; moreover, she evokes native fauna hunted to extinction in the intervening years. The spectral wolves undergo an extraordinary transmutation, the color motif "silvery" consonant with the symbolic man and wife meticulously chased into the precious metal of Hester Bateman's rare artifact. Their bond is primal, driven by the exigencies of mere survival.

Although Eavan Boland embarked on her career before Beth Ann Fennelly was ever born, both poets confront dubious historical and cultural inheritances, especially the vexed question of gender hierarchies. If she lacks Fennelly's subversive wit, Boland seems less scathingly iconoclastic at times. Her poem "Called" insists on presiding geniuses other than the dual-visaged Janus to signal her arrival as a poet belonging to the generation of Seamus Heaney, Derek Mahon, and Michael Longley. "Called" begins with Boland's search for the overgrown plot of her grandmother "who died before my time." Her quest amid a labyrinth of graveyard slates, "smashed lettering / archangel wings," reveals nothing. She deems her forebear lost to history ("Unloved because unknown. / Unknown because unnamed.) and determines to efface in her imagination the storied landmarks of Ireland's turbulent past: "To the west the estuary of the Boyne— / stripped of its battles and history—/ became only willow trees and distances." Driving homeward, the poet experiences a startling epiphany:

> I drove back in the half-light
> of late summer on
> anonymous roads on my journey home
>
> as the constellations rose overhead
> some of them twisted into women:
>
> pinioned and winged
> and single-mindedly holding high the dome
> and curve and horizon of today and tomorrow.
>
> All the ships looking up to them.
> All the compasses made true by them.
> All the night skies named for their sorrow.

With a synoptic clarity at once visual and aural, Boland depicts the prismatic tints of "winged and pinioned" constellations glittering on the far horizon. Thus, the nameless and disenfranchised dead attain apotheosis; however, their sorrow, albeit ineffable, does not connote the "despondency and madness" of Wordsworth's "Resolution and Independence." They define and magnify "today and tomorrow," eloquent harbingers of promise and fulfillment for those who would listen generously.

Esperanza and Hope: I Am My Own Country

Esperanza and Hope, Esperanza Snyder's first volume of poetry, conveys the varied life of an artist living with borderline poverty and cultural displacement. The book opens with a twelve-page biographical sketch that depicts the author's quest for identity. Born in Bogotá, Colombia, Snyder's parents baptized her Hope, although she was not initially called by that name. Although Snyder's father spoke fluent Spanish and her mother enough English to get by, "they never really learned each other's language." The poet's parents were incompatible almost from the start. "Showing my mother his large, white hands, his long fingers, he would say, 'these hands will work for you!' But they didn't." Perhaps the most compelling passage of the poet's prelude to *Esperanza and Hope* describes her relationship with her maternal grandfather, Papá Régulo: "I grew up with a grandfather who loved poetry." From the old patriarch, she learned "Neruda's 'Poema XX' and Alfonsina Storni's 'Capricho.' He also taught me Lorca, and the meaning of *duende* (the power to attract, to have magnetism, have soul)." He taught her entire stanzas from the Andalusian poet's *"Llanto por Ignacio Sánchez Mejías,"* the elegy for the gifted toreador who was killed in the bullfighting arena.

"My Grandfather, 1910-1982" consists of nine quatrains that privilege narrative immediacy and quiet introspection over lyrical effects: "His picture, on my desk, to me, he never died. / I didn't make it to his funeral, never visited his grave, / yet all the poems I learned from him remain fragmented in me." Here the poet fractures the mold of form as she contemplates, in lines plying between five and seven metrical feet, the likeness of a man whom she still reveres. The ensuing stanza is perhaps the most evocative in the poem:

> Teatro Colón. How small the stage now seems, how empty
> the velvet seats, how far away the front row,
> faded chandelier, dull wood floor where Berta Singerman
> stood that night—diaphanous blouse, red hair, scarf.

Snyder metes out every syllable like Diana Krall, reaching inside each key for the notes. Her composition of place inheres in these laconic accents—"Teatro Colón"—conjuring the theater's plush red velvet seats, the once-prismatic tints of a chandelier that dripped crystal and nickel, but has long since lost its luster. Even the wooden boards of the stage, redeemed in wax before every performance, are now "dull." But the poet captures the numinous moment when *duende* came alive for her in the person of Berta Singerman: "diaphanous blouse, red hair, scarf." These haunting metonyms summon up the charismatic performer who recited the feminist poet Alfonsina Storni's

"Capricho" to a spellbound audience. Snyder then reveals her grandfather's transcendent soul and all-too-human flaws:

> My grandfather loved women but didn't know how to love them.
> Living apart from my grandmother, another woman in his bed,
> he loved Alfonsina and her words, like he loved
> Singerman, the way she repeated Alfonsina's lines.
>
> All those times I recited "Capricho" for my grandfather
> I didn't know this poem he loved, lines he longed to hear
> me say, were written by a woman who jumped into the sea
> forever. *The sea we carry sea inside often floods our eyes.*

Whatever his flaws, Snyder's grandfather apparently relinquished all cynicism when he nurtured young Esperanza's passion for the language arts and drama:

> The year Berta Singerman performed "Capricho" at the Colón,
> poetry was born for me. The actress spoke to an absent lover,
> on an empty stage, laughing, explaining away her sadness.
> *Don't ask me why I cried so much last night.*
>
> All these years, carrying lines of this poem inside me,
> lines I learned from Singerman and Papá.
> I thought it was for fun—to make Papá Régulo laugh—
> that I stood in the middle of the sala in Bogotá, reciting.

The prepubescent Esperanza believed her recitatives of Alfonsina's rapt inflections were solely for the amusement and delight of her Papá Régulo. She was unaware he discerned in her the seeds of the bardic gift at an early age. Under her grandfather's loving tutelage, she learned pitch-perfect diction to complement the innate flair for image and metaphor that defines the true maker. She became part of the human chain in which love is a vital link, shaped in the forge and fire-blast of the imagination. Yet, she also concedes the immense complexity of such love:

> I was too young to understand that love
> can drive you mad. Now, I sense a touch of madness
> in Alfonsina's words, madness in Singerman's laughter
> when she said them, madness in my grandfather.

Notice the half-chime in the locutions "young" and "touch," as well as the repetition of "madness," doubling back syntactically no less than three times. Though Snyder's homage to her grandfather acknowledges his faults, Papá

Régulo's indomitable spirit embodies for us the primacy of art. His abiding presence guides us into and through the compelling world of Snyder's volume.

In her volume's second section, "Europa," Snyder recounts in mellifluous cadences the particulars of her star-crossed courtship and marriage with her second husband, Stefano, during her time in Tuscany. In "Honeymoon in Ischia," Snyder opts for a third-person perspective: "How small the island was, how hilly, / how cold in May." The poet's daughter, born out of wedlock two years before, can scarcely be aware of the occasion's import. The speaker recalls the brief sojourn primarily through sensory impressions that portend an emotionally sequestered existence:

> She doesn't remember making love,
> but she remembers the terrace
> had French doors, kept open
> so she could breathe the sea air.
> So she could breathe. The wedding
> dress was white, short, and tight.
> At Ponte Vecchio, her light raincoat
> couldn't keep her warm.

The bride does not recollect any nuptial embrace, but she remembers the open doors, the scent of brine from the calm sea, a detail that subtly connects her with Alfonsina. Her favorite wedding picture depicts her daughter's "green eyes shaped like white grapes." In another snapshot, the poet is stepping out of a car parked curbside, and describes herself as "a straniera, / more mistress than wife, / more girlfriend than mistress, / wearing sunglasses, red lipstick." "[S]traniera" denotes a foreign woman, and if the designation holds a certain allure for men in Tuscany, her status remains tenuous at best. Her new husband basks in the plaudits of his countrymen: "Stefano has gotten lost in the crowd / that came to see her marry him, / a duke's grandson, a true *signorino*."

In "Il Mio Marito Italiano," Snyder offers deeper insight into failure with Stefano. The speaker confesses that for her the very act of cognition derives from the region's dialect. She begins each day gazing out at "Spring mornings in front of our window: hills, vineyards, / backroads." The previous night seems in retrospect an evening of tawdry eroticism and celestial sweetness: "Behind me, our empty bed, rumpled sheets / smelling of sweat, pillows, blankets." But for now, the poet sees her new husband and old paramour through rose-tinted lenses.

> He painted our bedroom walls white, the trim blue,
> covered the mattress with rose colored sheets,
> chained it to the ceiling under a mosquito net.

Empty bed where we first lay, where I discovered his skin
—soft as a woman's, hard underneath, discovered his beauty,
his Tuscan villa, fragrant grapes, his Santa Christina,
his room, his presents, his love-makings and whisperings,
his Milanese accent, his gold ring.

Tactile pleasure yields to olfactory sensations as we savor the repetition of long *a* sounds in the adjective-noun combination "fragrant grapes." However, Stefano's wedding ring is not gold to airy thinness beat but a massive weight that also encircles Esperanza's finger. Her efforts to exorcise the presence and purported transgressions of his previous wife have been futile:

I stand by the window, study
the darkness of the open night, and for an instant I forget
his lies, his screams, his gun, his stories about photographs
she left behind, about *her* drunk, driving her Skoda
into the rain. I want to ask. Was this also *her* bedroom?
Also *her* bed. How long had *she* been gone when we met?

Stefano's mendacity, verbal abuse, and threats to bang off a clip of .45 caliber rounds at the least provocation have become intolerable by this time; moreover, the speaker fears that she will never supplant her husband's former wife in his heart. She drives this fact home prosodically through the exact rhymes "forget" and "met."

One of the most beautifully wrought and delicately refined poems in this collection, "Portrait of a Youth: Lucrezia Borgia Duchess of Ferrara" is an ekphrastic meditation about the painting by Dosso Dossi at the National Gallery in Victoria, which was authenticated on November 25, 2008:

I can hold what's left of her hair, what Byron didn't take,
read her letters, recite the Spanish poem
she copied out by hand, open the locket she used to wear,
"est animum" carved on it, the way Bembo asked.
I can wear her gold rings, read St. Matthew,
drape her shawl across my shoulders.

Snyder's poem about the Spanish-Italian noblewoman, who was the daughter of Pope Alexander VI, is particularly telling. During her third marriage, Lucrezia had an affair with the Renaissance courtier and poet Pietro Bembo, who presented her with a gold locket inscribed "est animum," invoking both mind and spirit. Lord Byron read their amorous correspondence in the Ambrosian Library of Milan in mid-October 1816, and the expatriate author of *Don Juan* pronounced them "the prettiest love letters in the world." Snyder's identification with the supposed *femme fatale* is implicit in the way she slips the lady's "gold rings" onto her fingers and lets the intricately knit shawl settle like a mantle on her shoulders. Even though Esperanza and Lucrezia are both omnilingual and gifted poets, the speaker cannot yet light upon the affinity she feels for this portrait: "it's not her face, beautiful, and so much like a boy's, / with rosy cheeks, and lips, small, and full, almost / pouting, as if she might start crying at any moment." However, in an abrupt instance of *ut pictura poesis,* the speaker undergoes an epiphany: "What it is, is the infinite sadness in her large, dark, almond eyes, looking at me, trying to tell me something. / What it is, is her sadness speaking to my sad almond eyes." The pictured countenance that Snyder regards so earnestly doubles her own ineffable dolor that can be attributed to love never quite reciprocated by the men in her life. Snyder rounds out her narrative by describing the Italian noblewoman's death at age thirty-nine soon after the birth of her tenth child: "A nurse soaks linen cloths in water, spreads them on her chest." If flights of angels do not sing Lucrezia to her rest, a little songbird's sliding treble will do: "Tomorrow, at dawn, before she flies away, / she'll hear the swallows sing outside her window."

The third section of Snyder's volume, entitled "Estados Unidos," marks her return to America and her first husband. "Fireflies" depicts a summer evening when adults take their ease on lamplit patios while children cavort on new-mown lawns. Among tangled switchboards of honeysuckle vine, the winged insects light up:

> Out of nowhere, fireflies, their conspicuous
> bioluminescence, which is to say, their living light,
> light in living beings. Inside their abdomens,
> these small creatures carry cold lights,
> scientific miracles of enzymes and chemicals
> lighting up as they dance, helping them find
> and love each other in the dark.

The electric stroke of fireflies that the poet invokes, "their living light," their lanterns of emerald or "bioluminescence," makes them rise and fall like rootless stars over the terrace. Embedded in the adjective-noun combination, "scientific miracles" is an oxymoron so clever one misses it at first. In "Fireflies," it would seem the "scientific" and "miraculous" do not belong to mutually exclusive realms of discourse. Each insect's cool radiance becomes an extended conceit for the nexus between genders regardless of species: "helping them find / and love each other in the dark." However, the poet demurs when she considers these phosphorescent entities in light of her own experience: "Capture them, / seal them in glass jars the way children often do, / and they're gone. Like me, they'd rather die / than live in cages." She longs for those idylls of late July that now seem to belong to another time: "That summer evening / centuries ago, we tried to catch them / with our hands, feel their wings against / our palms, peek inside our fists to see / their light." These lines are wonderfully tactile and kinetic, as children peer into cupped palms pulsing with an alien radiance. Note the succession of long *e* sounds in the locutions "evening," "feel," "peek," and "see" that imbues these lines with an astonishing luminescence. In her conclusion, Snyder resorts to direct address in this poem, dedicated to her first husband with whom she has reconciled after almost a decade's separation:

> I didn't know that as a child you
> sat on the same porch with your father,
> watching fireflies light up the night, the sky,
> his words while he smoked, the German
> Shepherd at his side. And you, how
> did you know that in those summers
> there was so much we didn't know.

The rhythmic loveliness of this passage, the dulcet strains and repeated hollow *o* and long *i* sounds enhance the inner serenity that the speaker shares with her auditor. But no amount of phonetic richness quite equals the poet's new insight into the depth of her first husband's mind and character. Every time his father dragged on a cigarette, the fireflies seemed to signal back from the thick grass and dense foliage. The speaker is now aware that knowledge comes and goes but true wisdom not only lingers, it abides.

Esperanza comes full circle in her odyssey from North America, to Spain, to Italy, and back when she arrives in Wisconsin to dispose of her father's belongings following his death: "After the call came, we drove straight to Green Bay, / fourteen hours to his empty place, to clean out / his refrigerator, meet his friends, decide / which coffin would suit his body best." In "Candle," her insight into another's inner loneliness is once more the catalyst for compassion and understanding: "This is the closest I ever came / to loving him, standing in his empty room, / looking through his things, learning." Like a female acolyte before an icon, she strikes a match and grafts the little hell-blossom to a candle wick:

> I light a candle
> in front of them, dressed up and dancing
> in a night club in New Orleans.
> He holds her close. Even in high heels,
> she doesn't reach his shoulder.
> Behind them, on a dinner table,
> champagne, unfinished wedding cake, candles.

"Candles are for the dead," *para los muertos*
my mother says.

End-stopped rhyme in the first two lines quoted above promises yet another incantatory lyric, but the poet dispels this expectation when she constructs a *tableau vivant* wherein her parents slow-dance in a photograph with the white cake that rose on a simple note now a ruin of shattered scroll and fluting in the background. The Spanish phrase *para los muertos* neatly subverts its English equivalent, thus reasserting the Hispanic origins of both mother and daughter. The poet then recalls her deceased father's brief stint in a Brazilian prison, and how he reached out to her from a cell that had not much music in its bars: "He wrote to share the news from a Brazilian jail, / as if he suddenly remembered he had / a daughter, and prison could bring us closer." Her father's wayward journey now at an end, she catalogs his various stops throughout the decades: "The stamps on his passport, Amsterdam, Buenos / Aires, Spain." Here Snyder comes down hard on the metrical register, especially in the locutions "stamps" and "Amsterdam." Her father's mortal remains consigned to the refining fires of the crematorium, she and her spouse disperse his ashes in the likeliest spot: "Late spring, to please my husband, we went / to the river, poured my father, one scoop at a time, / on the towpath, on the bluebells, in the water." "Esperanza's Country," the penultimate poem in *Esperanza and Hope*, sums up this volume:

> Once, in a cab in Paris, I let the driver think
> I was from Madrid. My ride was free.
> All those years trying to be Colombian, a waste.
> I am my own country.

Like Neruda, Esperanza's identity crisis resolves itself once she realizes that self-actualization is an awareness that our origins outline but do not define who we are. In "We Are Many," the Chilean poet declares: "I am going to school myself so well in things / that when I try to explain my problems / I shall speak, not of self, but of geography." Esperanza's odyssey begins in Bogotá, Columbia, and the years she spent under the tutelage of Papá Régelo.

Carolyn Forché: A Poetry of Witness

In the Lateness of the World, Carolyn Forché's first poetry volume to appear in almost two decades, derives its title from line fourteen of Robert Duncan's "Poetry, a Natural Thing." Denise Levertov, some of whose finest poems vigorously protested U. S. intervention in Vietnam, said of Forché's second collection, *The Country Between Us* (1981), "there is no seam between the personal and political, lyrical and engaged." Duncan quarreled with Levertov over what he perceived to be her own privileging of political values over aesthetic ones. However, Forché has built her reputation on "the poetry of witness," which expresses a moral or ethical imperative to address events such as war, genocide, racism, dictatorial tyranny, and other acts of injustice. Why then, the titular nod to Duncan, when Forché's "poetry of witness" seems to come down on Levertov's side of the debate?

Perhaps the answer lies in *The Country Between Us,* the crown jewel of which is "The Colonel," a prose piece describing a sumptuous repast at the home of a hedonistic Salvadorean officer who after dinner spills a grocery sack full of human ears on the table: "They were like dried peach halves. There is no other way to say this. He took one of them in his hands, shook it in our faces, dropped it into a water glass. It came alive there." That the quickening of dried fruit to an organ of sense requires only water to undergo this metamorphosis is as memorable an image as any in contemporary poetry. Having preyed on hapless *campesinos* who gathered ripe produce for cheap export, Forché's cavalier representative of death squads clears the table with a swipe of his arm and theatrically raises his glass of cabernet: "Something for your poetry, no? he said." Her response, which ends the poem, implies that many will discern little of consequence in his dismissive gesture, whereas others will hearken to the palpable evil that lies beneath it all: "Some of the ears on the floor caught the scrap of his voice. Some of the ears on the floor were pressed to the ground."

This poem appears to represent a marked departure from those in her first volume, *Gathering the Tribes* (1976), which focused on familial relationships, sexual awakening, and the haunting remembrances of Old World customs. But even these quasi-confessional efforts dealt with the themes of cultural displacement and hasty immigration. Simply put, Forché's oeuvre has always embodied both personal and political concerns. For humanitarian reasons, "the poetry of witness" holds an irresistible allure for her, as is evident in her third collection, *The Angel of History* (1994), as well as her most recent, *In the Lateness of the World.*

While her detractors dismiss Forché as an ideologue unconcerned with aesthetic matters, this is blatant nonsense. In an interview conducted by this critic on 17 November 1982, at the University of Memphis's Faulkner Lounge, Forché stated, "Journalists attempting to write about El Salvador at the time were viewed as 'the witting and unwitting dupes of international Communist propogandists.'" "Elegy for an Unknown Poet" laments the death of Daniel Simko, a Czech poet and translator who defected to the United States after the Soviet invasion in 1968. She enters into a dialogue with her friend Simko when she adopts the color motifs employed by German Expressionist Georg Trakl, whose verse her friend lovingly rendered into English: "Black is the color of footsteps, frost, stillness, and tears. / It modifies branches and wings. Blue appears as cloud, flower, ice." Typically associated with bereavement, here black actually connotes translation to a higher plane without necessarily being about the end of physical existence. Moreover, Forché is subtly attuned to the repetition of fricative *f* in "footsteps" and "frost" as well as the sibilance of "stillness" that congeals to an icy bleb in the locution "tears." One envisions "branches" glazed with frozen precipitation after a winter storm. "Blue" evokes spirituality and undergoes several permutations from evanescence of "cloud" to the pattern of lacy ferns that "flower" on winter panes, which returns us to the ineluctable image, "ice." Forché mourns the death of a friend obliged to seek political sanctuary, but she deftly sidesteps partisanship through aesthetically nuanced tropes of astonishing beauty. Her closure embodies what Jahan Ramazani termed compensatory mourning: "What is left us then but darkness? Oneself is always dark and near."

"Visitation" is perhaps the most compelling poem in Forché's new volume. It depicts the creatural existence embodied in the Central European upbringing of her paternal grandmother, Anna Sidlosky. This ethnic genealogical piece lends amplitude to the "poetry of witness" espoused in *The Country Between Us*, even as it revisits the folkways initially broached in *Gathering the Tribes*. Forché remembers a Christmas fir that stood in her cramped living room as a young girl: "On the nativity tree, a tiny lute, a French horn and painted egg, / a crèche carved from olive wood, a trumpeting angel." Forché's disarmingly quaint inventory includes a teardrop-shaped instrument of resonate wood, a "painted egg" that recalls the jeweled ornaments designed by Peter Carl Fabergé for the corrupt Romanov dynasty under the reign of Czar Nicholas II, a tableau of Christ's birth carved from olive wood that conjures the rough-hewn beams of the Crucifixion, and the seraph whose trumpet signifies burst cerements and erupting graves on the Last Day. Forché's opening images trace Christ's journey from birth to resurrection, resonating with T. S. Eliot's dramatic monologue "Journey of the Magi." In Eliot's conclusion, his Magus is "no longer at ease here, in the old dispensation, / With an alien people clutching their gods." If the Redeemer comes a dark way, early Christianity had socio-political as well as religious implications. Thus Forché introduces her grandmother's irrepressible and subversive character into her corpus for the first time in several decades: "Anna is there, crocheting smoke, not speaking English anymore, as if / English had put out her memory like a broom on fire." The old Slovak woman fires up her pipe and begins a yarn about the Yuletide rituals of her homeland:

> She tells us that on this night in her village, they would carry home
> a live carp wrapped up in paper that had just been swimming in a barrel.
> The fish would silver the snow and have its life taken by a sharp ax.
> The potatoes that had grown eyes in the cellar would be brought up
> and baked with the fish, and there would be beet soup, bread, and wine
> made from mulberries.

Something mellifluous inheres in Forché's straightforward narrative. The carp shunned as trash fish in this country is netted from a chilled cask and fetched home wrapped in butcher's paper. The colors silver and white connote spiritually even as the axe's abrupt stroke severs the scaly denizen of boreal cold from all being. The tubers that sprouted eyes in the cellar go well with the apportioned fish, beet soup, baked loaves, and wine fermented from dark berries. The meal the poet describes by proxy of her grandmother summons up the Christian commensality seldom encountered in America's largely secular milieu. Forché's numinous remembrance of Anna's presence in her household proves deeply affecting, as the old matriarch leaves behind a token of her ghostly visitation: "a holy card with her own birth and death dates so we would know / she hadn't visited us, that her satin-pillowed coffin lay still in the ground." The poem's ending is one of sublime loveliness: "and in every glass bulb, there we were—children descended from her on a winter night."

If "Visitation" is reminiscent of the turf-fire snugness of the Gaeltacht so prominent in the poetry of Seamus Heaney, Forché's poem "The Refuge of Art" conflates aesthetic and political concerns much as he did in "A Dream of the Solstice," depicting the megalithic passage tombs at Newgrange. It is not surprising that the Irish Catholic Nobel laureate's work would inform hers. Their religious upbringing provided both poets with a grounding in the Judeo-Christian mythos that pervades their writing about injustice. Indeed, Heaney's poetry, both about the primacy of art and about the ongoing extreme violence between Protestants and Catholics suggests that he is a crucial literary predecessor for her. Before Forché's first volume ever appeared, he was writing poetry about the insulted and marginalized in poems such as "Punishment," which portrays the Windeby Girl who was strangled and drowned in a peat bog for merely having committed adultery. Forché's poem opens with a description of an unknown artist who sets the walls of his studio blazing with rich pigment: "In his atelier once a shoe factory, an artist paints walls, / cromlechs, and cairns." Her protagonist brings his subject to life in the manner of a prehistoric shaman animating the Lascaux caves in the Dordogne region of France: "Slate tiles light his vigil over stags in flight, / bison stampeding, wild aurochs with lyre-shaped / horns." Forché's cadenced hard *i* sounds capture the clatter of the stag's cleft hooves and the rumbling gait of even-toed ungulates such as bison. But the real masterstroke comes into play when she invokes the "lyre-shaped'" horns adorning the shaggy-headed aurochs. One immediately calls to mind the untrammeled power of the lyric, its capacity both to celebrate and subvert. Although the paleolithic chambers she alludes to were not burial crypts, the poet proceeds to illustrate those that were: "In the dawn of humanity, children built passage tombs / for the dead: stone hives in the earth for the hum of spirit." The beehive tomb or *tholos* can be traced to Agamemnon's Mycenae; moreover, Forché's trope "hum of spirit" is deceptively facile. If we delve into Heaney's lexicon and read "hum" as Irish slang meaning a bad odor, Forché implies that the realms of the spirit and flesh are one. According to scripture, the dead shall be raised incorruptible, but even Christ lay three days in the tomb. Forché's poem is ultimately a testament to human suffering in times of political upheaval:

> In the hollow pits the dead repose, bones whitening
> in utter dark, where not even bats sing, and until
> seen from the air by pilots during the Great War
> the domes slept, round and risen in the field.

To the casual reader bats would seem to jibber rather than sing, but these chiropterans do emit multisyllabic trills and chirps as complex as any songbird's. Forché is not engaging in mere poetic license, but offering us a poem that is aesthetically pleasing and at the same time vigorously interrogates the plight of humankind when ideologies come into armed conflict.

The poetry of witness embraced by Forché in *The Country Between Us* is revisited in a number of her latest efforts, but the poet provides her readers with a new point of departure when she advocates for animal rights in "Water Crisis." Here she decries the barbarity of a blood sport that exploits the gamecock's natural propensity for combat: "The gamecocks are forced to fight with knives taped to their feet. / This is illegal." These are not plump fryers for the Sunday table, but banty roosters, lean-thewed and muscular, bred for the pit and fitted out with steel spurs to facilitate the kill. Moreover, Forché's unadorned accents are all the more efficacious for their straightforward simplicity: "They transport the cocks in baskets covered by plastic bags— / their entire lives tethered to the ground, / trapped in wicker." But one does catch the speaker's outrage in a run of plosives and glottal stops: "cocks," "baskets," "plastic," "wicker"—that lays bare the pyrotechnics embedded in discrete locutions.

In the Lateness of the World also serves as a verse intertext for *What You've Heard Is True* (2019), Forché's prose memoir about the social and political upheaval in developing nations, which she dedicated to the memory of Leonel Goméz Vides, the man who encouraged her to visit El Salvador during the late seventies. What she terms "the poetry of witness" became an integral part of her own life at that time, and all the more so because Vides insisted that the crisis required the voice of a gifted poet to chronicle events. Forché would soon join her lyric powers to those of Wilfred Owen following the 1916 Somme Offensive, Osip Mandlestam during the Stalinist purges, and Pablo Neruda before the 1973 coup in Chile that ushered in the military dictatorship of General Augusto Pinochet. "The Ghost of Heaven" recapitulates the beauty and atrocity that Forché encountered during her sojourn in Central America. Although Vides is never specifically named, he is the *genius loci* or presiding spirit of this poem. The fifth section is remarkable for its clipped diction and brevity of phrasing: "Walking through a firelit river / to a burning house: dead Singer / sewing machine and a piece of dress." We listen for the cicada clack of the antique Singer's treadle and the sibylline whisper of thread stitching both the dress and the poet's narrative together. Lightning bugs hover in the twilight: "Outside paper fireflies rose to the stars." In section six, Vides itemizes a survival kit:

> Bring penicillin if you can, you said, surgical tape,
> a whetstone, mosquito repellant but not the aerosol kind.
> Especially bring a syringe for sucking phlegm
> a knife, wooden sticks, a clamp, and plastic bags.

Medical aid is apparently self-administered in these environs; especially ominous is the syringe for siphoning the body's corruption, the necessity for clamps that secure severed arteries in surgical emergencies, and the "mosquito repellant" for fending off pestilential insects. Other parasites are abundant, and measures for coping with them extreme: "When a leech opens your flesh, it leaves a small volcano. / Always pour turpentine over your hair before going to sleep." Moreover, Vides's final admonition is all the more eloquent for its directness: "If they capture you, talk. / Talk. Please, yes. / You heard me the first time." Forché's closure echoes the penultimate stanza of Eliot's "The Hollow Men": "All who come / All who come into the world / All who come into the world are sent." However, her *Weltanschauung* is more auspicious, inasmuch as it holds out the hope of redemption for those determined to make a difference in such turbulent times. *In the Lateness of the World* bears witness to the courage and dignity of Carolyn Forché's vision as well as her preternatural gift for the language arts.

Michael Waters: Wit and Wordplay

Because the essay included in this text titled "Blear-Eyed Wisdom Out of Midnight Oil" omits some key biographical information on Michael Waters, it would be beneficial to augment the gap. The poet graduated from SUNY-Brockport with both a baccalaureate degree and an M. A. in English. He subsequently earned an M. F. A. from the Iowa Writers Workshop and eventually took a PhD. at Ohio University. Along with the late A. Poulin Jr., Waters is co-editor of *The Contemporary American Poetry Anthology*, which is now in its eighth edition since it first appeared in 1971. His honors include grants from both the Fulbright and Guggenheim Foundations and an National Endowment for the Arts fellowships. Like William Matthews before him, Waters is a poet of wit, candor, and grace, and his prosodic skills are second to none in his generation. His volumes include *The Burden Lifters* (1989), *Bountiful* (1992), *Green Ash, Black Maple, Red Gum* (1997), *Gospel Night* (2011), and *The Dean of Discipline* (2018), perhaps his finest to date. Some poets and editors have taken me to task for declaring him "the ablest poet of an able generation," but few could deny that he ranks in the top five.

Although he had previously written noteworthy collections, Waters came into his own with the publication of *The Burden Lifters* (1989). In this volume, his subjects include the life-transforming experiences of childhood, the wonder and despair of other lives, and a longing both sexual and spiritual. He desires to recover the numinous quality of experience through language, often relying on the brand of empirical knowledge derived from a Roethkean "long looking." "Horse," the first poem in *The Burden Lifters*, speaks to a child's attempt to square reality with his earliest conception about the relationship between words and images encountered in picture books. The poet recalls his first encounter with the word made flesh in the form of a junk dealer's nag, and there is no disappointment in the meeting: "I had seen horses in books before, but / this horse shimmered in the Brooklyn noon." Despite the fact the horse's eyes are "caked and rheumy," the boy is awed by the terrible span of its nostrils, as he breathes in the animal's "inexorable, dung-tinged fume." But the vital infusion occurs only when the child actually touches the beast as it waits patiently at the curb:

> I worked behind his triangular head
> to touch his foreleg above the knee
> the muscle jerking the mat of hair.
> *Horse*, I remember thinking,
>
> four years old and standing there,
> struck momentarily dumb,
> while the power gathered in his thigh
> surged like language into my thumb.

Even though the word is not spoken aloud, here the very essence of the horse answers to its name. It is interesting, too, that of all the fingers on the boy's hand, the opposable thumb serves as the comprehending one; for Waters, language is a way of grasping, in both literal and figurative terms. However, this child's questing imagination is certainly benign; there is no danger of his developing the aberrant mentality of Peter Shaffer's dubious protagonist in *Equus*.

Elsewhere, Waters longs for what seems ephemeral but is somehow palpable, for the quality of poetry that, in the words of W. H. Auden, "survives, / A way of happening, a mouth." "Lipstick" is a sensual reminiscence that is Confessional in tone, Oedipal and autoerotic in its implications. In this poem, the persona is once again a child, this time enchanted by the scent, color, and variety of his young mother's lipsticks. He wants to "hold her hand across cinnabar avenues, / whisper in libraries of peach frost and ruby." He even engages in an act of childish fetishism, so strong is the impulse to transform the almost molten tastes and aromas into a tactile experience:

> She'd sit in her bra and half-slip,
> elbows propped on the vanity top,
>
> brushing the flames across her lips,
> first one flavor, then another—
>
> forbidden strawberry, crushed orange, café au lait—
> then close her lips on a tissue.
>
> I'd steal the paper from the wicker
> basket to taste the exotic
>
> spices, the delicious
> mocha, crème caramel, glazed papaya,
>
> and when I was older, ten or twelve,
> I'd wrap tissue after tissue
>
> around my small, preening member,
> smudging the lipstick on my flesh.

The cool spices painted on the young woman's lips, then pressed into tissue thin as membrane, transform her simple gesture of artifice into something numinous for the boy. This time he is the one to deliver a surge by way of his "small, preening member." The exotic hieroglyph is flesh made word, again unspoken, but capable of awakening in the boy an unrelenting wonder.

Perhaps the strongest poem in *The Burden Lifters* is a two-part ode titled "Keats's Lips." We recognize from tributes by previous authors Keats's rapid decline, the ill-starred fate of a man who died in the froth of his own lungs without ever leaving his bed. Unlike other poems on this subject, Waters's verse centers not upon the dramatic, real-life situation but upon a tangible object, the "death mask by Gherardi." It is the dead poet's swollen lips that draw Waters's attention; they are "what's left / of Keats's tumultuous spirit." In the poem's second part, the meditation shifts to a quarrel between the speaker and his wife. Afterward, the pair make up in bed, and in a commingling of Eros and Thanatos, the speaker again becomes a medium for the corporeal and the divine:

> Let me tell you this—
> when her face flushed with orgasm
> as we briefly lost all control,
>   I was praying for Keats, his lips,
>
>   the language touched with fever
> that bears us away from our bodies
> and soothes the bruised soul,
>   if only for a few moments.

Bountiful (1992), Waters's third collection with the Carnegie Mellon series, is an apt successor to the *Burden Lifters*, seizing upon the sacramental vision that began to emerge within his work during the mid-eighties and developing it further into an idiom of resounding richness and abundance. Quarried from memory, the cornerstones of Brooklyn tenements exude an eerie light in the full blaze of noon; hummingbirds converge like daubs of watercolor on a bed of lilies, and a gray fox, its pelt "tarnished silver" in moonlit sawgrass, renews for dinner guests "the romantic / childhood urgencies long ago given over / to the conservative wishes of adults."

"Hummingbirds" maintains the tenuous flux between spirit and flesh everywhere apparent in Water's recent poetry: "When I read the translation from the Russian, / *razdirat' dushu*, literally, to 'tear out' one's soul, / I understood the genesis of hummingbirds." Here Waters revives the ancient connection between breath and the soul, extending the concept from something as basic as the element that sustains life to a metaphor for high artifice:

> How the elements conspire to create them:
> the blue-green pearl of molten sand
> —that miniature globe, swirl of smoke—
> hovering at the tip of the glassblower's rod
> seems forever on the verge of cooling
> into final form, the almost-shape of the hummingbird.

The vivid color motif, "blue-green," provides not only animation but also offers a wisp of heat and luster. The repetition of *o* sounds in "molten," "globe," and "smoke" infuses the stanza with a breathing viscosity. However carefully modulated the glassblower's exhalations, as an ocular phenomenon the hummingbird hovers perpetually on the brink: "Who has ever seen a hummingbird arrive?" Nevertheless, this blurred atomy proves real when Waters proceeds skillfully to dissect each particle of its infinitesimal being:

> Who has seen a hummingbird at ease, though
> its metaphysical dollop of flesh
> must grow heavy, weighted with gravity, even
> the saffron seed of its eye, the cork skeleton,
> the heart like a ball bearing in its feathered case.

In English, the poet intimates, the word hummingbird connotes a harmonious order, a subtle blend of dross and ether.

The desire for communion, those numinous moments in the midst whereof we encounter our own strangeness, endows "The Fox," with a clarity at once radiant and haunting. Indeed, the poem's psychic field emanates from a shared hunger, as the speaker and his wife linger at the tableboard of their beloved but isolated host. Having tasted the succulent heart of an artichoke, the company broaches the *genius loci* of midnight:

> uncorking another light-proof
> bottle of homemade plum wine, we began
> telling our dreams, those that surprise us
> or bring back the romantic
> childhood urgencies long ago given over
> to the conservative wishes of adults—
> the wish to be simple, to hurt no one—
> when, low to the earth, scavenging the frost-
> lit bristles of sawgrass for torpid mice,
> the fox appeared beyond the glass door,
> tarnished silver, mottled with mange,
> a rough rag torn from the hillside,
> a storybook fox cut out with blunt scissors.

Like a loping phantom answerable to a secret invocation, the gray fox suddenly materializes. Perhaps once the ablest hunter of an able clan, the diminutive listener in the frost is now "mottled with mange," prowling with ears cocked for dollops of brown fur, "torpid mice" overtaken by the autumn freeze. The sly orchestration of rhythm beginning in the eighth line of this passage abruptly shifts to the mincing syntax of the ensuing line, "frost- / lit bristles of sawgrass," thus mimicking the stalking canine's deft padding. At first, hardly a smudge of moonlight on the glass door, in a play of sibilants clipped by *t* sounds, the "tarnished silver" apparition suddenly shears off into the image of a "storybook fox." The resulting mystification is nothing if not agreeable: "leaving us / astounded, more than pleased, aware / of a mild blessing bestowed upon friends."

At this juncture, the piece is accomplished but somehow incomplete. However, the speaker moves beyond anecdote to allegory when he relates the depth and intensity of his friend's longing: "Later that night, I glimpsed our host's face / pressed to the guest-room window / while my wife and I undressed." The speaker's startled outcry precipitates the voyeur's hasty retreat. Yet the awkward explanation forthcoming at breakfast is not so specious as it appears on the surface: "he'd gone out in search of the fox, / but found nothing but scat, / the autumn earth too hard for tracks." Only the fecal droppings confirm for their host the previous night's visitation. But his desire to relive the mute wonder of that late hour magnifies his loneliness and makes him the presiding spirit of the speaker's dreams:

> Sometimes I dream of the fox in his lair,
> that secret, interior life
> growing thinner, losing hair, starving,
> the alert intelligence sharpened by need
> helpless not to transform itself into grief,
> humiliation, the sense of silence among friends
> in return for a moment of mournful
> revelation, the chimera of a child,
> however naked and heart-rending, however
> impotent and wild.

Thus, the speaker looks in turn upon his friend's nakedness and discovers an almost sacred yearning prey to the compulsions of both flesh and spirit.

The dual themes of loss and redemption dominate Waters's next collection titled *Green Ash, Red Maple, Black Gum* (1997). In a series of memorable vignettes, the poet chronicles the dissolution of a long marriage, the subsequent estrangement from his daughter, and the impending death of his father. At least one critic has described Water's recent poetry as belonging to "the tradition of masculine Romanticism," but such easy categorizing fails to account for the emotional complexity and cognitive singularity of vision apparent throughout this volume. In the title poem, words become a compensatory element in the speaker's life, even as his sense of alienation grows: "How often the names of trees consoled me, / how I would repeat to myself *green ash* / while the marriage smoldered in the not-talking." For Waters, silence is the nullification of love; only the talismanic resonance of *"green ash"* and the recollection of pensive afternoons in a forest can forestall the inevitable breakup:

> Those days I tramped the morass of the preserve,
> ancient ash smudging shadows on stagnant pools,
> the few wintery souls skulking abandoned wharves.
> In my notebook I copied plaques
> screwed to bark, sketching the trunks' scission,
> a minor Audubon bearing loneliness like a rucksack.

The speaker recalls the names of trees indelibly tooled in brass, each placard's screws sunk deep as grubs in the bark. The bitter allusion to Andrew Marvell's "The Garden" is unmistakable: "How far these beauties hers exceed! / Fair trees wheresoe'er your barks I wound, / No name shall but your own be found." Like Marvell, Waters refuses to sunder the thing signified from its signifier. Sketching bole and bark into his notebook, he appropriates both a sacred object and a numinous lexicon: "And did the trees assume a deeper silence? / Did their gravity and burl and centuries-old patience / dignify this country, our sorrow?" The poet transforms the name of each tree into an earnest conjuration, an incantation that sustains him in his grief:

> So as I lay there, the roof bursting with invisible
> branches, the darkness doubling in their shade,
> the accusations turning truths in the not-loving,
> *green ash, red maple, black gum,* I prayed,
> in the never-been-faithful, in the don't-touch-me,
> in the can't-bear-it-any-longer,
> *black gum, black gum, black gum.*

Waters offers the frail dignity of his mantra—"*black gum, black gum, black gum*"— in place of the buffetings so prevalent in domestic quarrels.

On the other hand, Waters shuns any tendency to mistake his private ills for public evils in the comically libidinous "Snow Cone," a tableau reminiscent of Odysseus encountering the princes Nausikaa on the beaches of Phaeacia:

> Her tongue mimicked the color of her bikini
>   after she'd licked the cherry
>   snow cone, & the tip of the paper cup
>   dripped fluorescent beads of syrup,
> cool pinpricks, onto her oiled belly,
>   the electric swirl pooling her pierced
>   navel where the gold ring flashed.

The speaker vividly depicts the naïve ardor with which the nymphet addresses her frozen confection. Adopting an aural and visual delectation uniquely his own, Waters seems to be puckishly reviving Robert Frost's quaint axiom: "Like a piece of ice on a hot stove the poem must ride on its own melting." As the poem goes on, the speaker—bemused by the younger generation's penchant for body piercing and hoping to pursue the sticky rivulet beyond her twinkling navel—regales the pretty girl with a harrowing anecdote:

> I told her its glittering would attract
> sharks, how a novice scuba diver
> skimming the reef off the Caribbean
> coast of Costa Rica—I smiled at her—
> had been taken headfirst into the maw
> of a six-foot mako & blamed the attack
> on the cluster of studs rimming one ear.

His wit more barbed than the "cluster of studs" adorning the unfortunate diver's ear, Waters describes the grim aftermath of the shark attack: "The scars raking his skull seemed tribal, / hewn in some Land-That-Time-Forgot coming-of-age / ritual, but the raw stubs of his lobes / oozed a milky gel that caked his cheeks." Here the poet tries his rhythms on the pulse of another and registers more than a shudder of revulsion: "the icy / flavor overflowed her belly button, / ruby rill snaking toward her tan-line, / then under the rim of triangular cloth." The sinuous trickle fails to vex the nubile sunbather, who remains enthralled with the tale of brutal scarification inflicted by the cruising mako:

> She gazed at me now, propped on both
> elbows, the snow cone like a splintery bulb
> generated by body heat, its slow leak
> shape-shifting her pubis into a relief
> map of a savvy Third World country
> that exports slashed fins for soup
> but saves, for the occasional tourist
> blundering through the market square
> in search of a cheap souvenir
> the sun-bleached, primeval hoops of teeth.

If the speaker indulges certain fantasies, he also alerts the young woman to the dangers of fetishism, and leaves her with an inkling of her own vulnerability: the "primeval hoops of teeth" gleam like a necklace on display.

Waters parodies the literary theorist's notion regarding the "pleasures of the text" in "Snow Cone," but the self-reflexive qualities of his poetry imply that language itself often provides redemption from the inevitable sense of loss and disillusionment that attends middle age. In "God at Forty," however, he portrays the poet as a divine creator undone by too much introspection and the relentless pursuit of excellence: "a brooding being whose creative pulse / drove Him inward, whose silence— / that dour guest—too often graced their bountiful table." Loneliness and ritual austerity are the wages of perfection: "Now God keeps His meals simple, / noodle soup simmered on the single coil, peppered brie / slabbed on chunks of broken bread." Once more, Waters's wry sense of humor redeems the moment: after God "opens / his black binder to erase some easy metaphor," he dozes, becoming a portrait of the artist as a scabrous lout: "He scrapes His pocked, / bristly cheek along the splinter-shot table, eyes shut, / allowing His vast yearning / to wash over the planet. A more somber mood governs "Wasps," a brief elegy for the poet's father:

> Dead C battery, souvenir lighter, spool of thread,
>   lipstick tube lacking a smudge of red:
>   we'd rummage junk drawers to fill the squares.
>   But the lost chessmen?—
>   they click against glass, black
>   bishops bidding me open the window,
>   wheedling a wary God to release them
>   to crusade for their king gone ahead to Jerusalem.

Intrigued by the mellifluous catalog of household flotsam that apparently substituted for elegantly carved pieces of ivory and ebony, we initially miss the fact that Waters employs spatial form to contrive a pattern poem in the tradition of George Herbert's "The Altar" or "Easter Wings." Moreover, the stanzaic shape could as easily resemble a chiseled monument on a cemetery lawn as any chess piece. Chess, like music, is basically an art of development, combination, and continuation; thus, the poet imagines that his father longs beyond the grave for his lost chessmen. Apparitions pinched between abdomen and thorax, the "black / bishops" click tactilely at the windowpane, heraldic figures "wheedling" for one more opportunity to assail the crenelated towers of Jerusalem. The gift for improvisation acquired from his father early in life now lends the poet a haunting image, a lingering assurance that he is not alone. Indeed, Waters's resourcefulness and facility with language afford redemption from the losses that attend even the most serene existence.

In *Gospel Night* (2011), Waters is closely attuned to nature, bringing a painstakingly developed and singular idiom to bear on a fallen bird nest in "Young John Clare": "Not often do I find a nest fallen / Among seed pods in autumn, three blue-white / Eggs broken." The poet gains a tentative footing on the piece through repeated trochees such as "often," "fallen," "autumn," and "broken." His protagonist's capacity for wonder comes to the fore when he discovers a survivor amid the delicately woven debris: "One egg sealed, the fluids of birdmaking / A milky galaxy bundled inside." The egg contains a "galaxy" in little, a marvelous evocation of the microcosm / macrocosm trope so prevalent in metaphysical poetry. Obviously, the youthful John Clare reads his books with diligence and a genuine ardor. The fragile, bluish oval in his palm awakens an impulse borne of an ineffable yearning:

> So smooth and dry I want to swivel it
> Wholly into my mouth despite dirt-flecks,
> Lave the vowel-sheen off the oval shell,
> Tumble that globule of starling within
> Until its unspooled trill begins to boil,
> Slips its bony case and kindles my voice.

The adroit pun on "globule" (from the Latin *globulus*, diminutive of *globus* or sphere) is delightful, as is the *cri de coeur* that rounds out this short poem: "O then would I sing! I would have no choice."

Waters explores the fine boundary between the carnal and carnivalesque in "Cannibal," a darkly humorous work. His speaker recounts the secret hungers of some who survived the ill-fated Donner Party, ruminating on forbidden desires once masquerading as necessity: "Who developed a secret taste for flesh / Flaked between the fluted bones of the wrist? / Who for organs: charcoaled tongue or poached heart?" A dense musicality marks these lines, specifically alliteration—"flesh," "flaked," "fluted,"—as well as the subtle internal rhyme of "charcoaled" and "poached." Aspirates and fricatives seethe throughout, whispering of unspeakable urges. But Waters quits this veritable Feast of Fools, moving forward a century to the ghoulish spectacle of Jeffrey Dahmer ladling a decapitated head into a pot: "The water simmering, lightly salted, / New potatoes, leeks, and scrawny carrot / Floating past eyes uplifted toward Heaven." Despite the humor inherent in the image of the young victim gazing heavenward like a choirboy rapt with song, the poet speaks to a physical craving almost spiritual in its intensity, as he describes having coitus with his wife: "Who can fathom the such inexplicable / Hunger? How my mouth covets your body, / Teeth grazing buttocks, shoulders, each nipple?" For his speaker, making love amounts to fleshly communion, a partaking of mysteries beyond any language save the sacred encoding of poetry: "What can I do but write these poems for you?"

Aquatic motifs form an integral part of *Gospel Night*, especially in "Rio Savegre," a poem set where the river in Costa Rica meets the Pacific Ocean. The speaker has been swimming the stream's limpid waters when he perceives an ominous change in the current: "Where the Pacific seized the river, tugged / Limbs then torso toward murkier waters / I turned back." The sudden undertow thwarts the swimmer's intended goal: "I'd wanted to cross to the cloistered beach / Where turtles oared ashore to bury eggs." Here Waters manifests via the metonym "oared," one of the many small touches distinctive to an achieved style. A less accomplished author would have chosen a more obvious verb. Meanwhile, his persona senses an inchoate evil lurking in the dark confluence of waters. "That night I learned what the voices counseled: / Where salt and fresh waters tumble and stir, / Shark and crocodile sunder together." By heeding indigenous lore, Waters avoids the crocodile's gaping jaws and the toothed gullet of the shark:

> I was lucky to leave that turbid bath.
> Now I awaken when church bells worry
> To recall my shade taken by current,
> Riven on the waters' skin, wrenched apart
> Black rag by black rag, as the soul is torn,
> The heart bitten, as I stumble away,
> Too dumb to know which creatures seethe below
> And how whitely the body must beckon.

The apt manipulation of long and short vowel sounds enriches this passage, words accruing a palpable surface and texture. Such easy familiarity with the concept *ut pictura poesis* in this instance calls forth a Yeatsian "terrible beauty." If only in Waters's imagination, not since the Maenads ripped Orpheus to shreds has the poet suffered such a fearful rending of body and soul. In a similar poem, titled "Diogenes," Waters opts for a tone altogether more benign. He snorkles in fire-blue waters "so clear / You could swim far out past the coral reef." He spends his spare time in bars imbibing "colorless liqueurs" in a half-hearted search for an ever elusive "truth":

> In the morning, when clumps of flies
> Blackened honeyed scrolls tacked to rafters,
> When truth prodded me again
> With its trumpet blare of heat and light,
> I snorkled toward families of green squid,
> Alert, throbbing, horizontal, lit-from-within
> Coke bottles teasing me forth.

For one of the few times in *Gospel Night*, the poet abandons his characteristic decasyllabics to telling effect. Select imagery enlivens these lines, from the fulsome but cloying sweetness of the improvised flypaper to the palpitating formations of squid. For the speaker, the quest for truth resides in the various wonders of the natural world: "I might join those inky creatures / To spend my days reaching always for the nothing / That remains just beyond my grasp."

Waters seldom writes poems more than thirty lines in duration, but this does not imply that his ingenuity is readily exhausted. Instead, he makes a virtue of compression, lending every locution its due weight and proportion. In "White Stork," for example, he takes the birds' full measure with each syllable expended in describing their buffeting ascent: "the white storks' / Plosive and gorgeous leave-takings suggest / Oracular utterance where the blurred / Danube disperses its silts." Indeed, he invests the waterfowl with a near-mystical aura:

> Then the red-
> Billed, red-legged creatures begin to spiral,
> To float among the thermals like souls, wrote
> Pythagoras, praising the expansive
> Grandeur of black-tipped wings, of dead poets.

Waters comes down both hard and lightly on the metrical register, first favoring the startling color motifs and then the storks' gentle capacity to glide the high thermals. His speaker then relates how generations of the white birds return for centuries to the same nests.

> built on rooftops, haystacks, telegraph
> Poles, on wooden wagon wheels placed on cold
> Chimneys by peasants who hoped to draw down
> Upon plague-struck villages such winged luck.

Mentioned in proximity to chimneys from the medieval period, a telegraph pole seems a stark but delightful anachronism. In his closure, Waters notes that no stork has hatched in Britain since the visionary Julian of Norwich died in 1416: "that final / Stork assuring, even while vanishing, / 'Sin is behovely, but all shall be well.'" The internal quote originally derives from Julian's *Revelations of Divine Love*; her incantatory saying echoes throughout T. S. Eliot's "Little Gidding," and its appropriation by Waters endows "White Stork" with an intertextual resonance dating back a half-millennium.

Elizabeth Spires: *Annociade* and *Worldling*

In my thirty years of writing critical prose for quarterlies such as *The Georgia Review, The Gettysburg Review,* and *The Kenyon Review,* I have encountered few poets as gifted and versatile as Elizabeth Spires. Born in Lancaster, Ohio, in 1952, she graduated from elite institutions—Vassar and Johns Hopkins—and holds a distinguished professorship at Goucher College in Baltimore, Maryland. She cites John Donne, Robert Frost, Elizabeth Bishop, and Robert Lowell as seminal influences, but has assimilated these exemplars so effectively that she arrived at a voice distinctly her own by her third volume titled *Annociade* (1989). Here Spires's passion to incorporate history and transform it into myth is rivalled only by her longing to create—or recapture—what Donald Hall so aptly called "the dark mouth of the vowel by which the image tells its secret rune." Spires demonstrates a keen interest in the artist as subject, particularly the manner in which the life of Peter Carl Fabergé, whom many consider one of the finest goldsmiths and jewelers of all time, was transformed by the upheavals of 1914-1918. Spires's poem, "Fabergé's Egg," is epistolary in nature, taking the shape of a letter written from Lausanne, Switzerland, by the Russian expatriate in the year of his death, 1920:

> Before the Great War,
> I made a diamond-studded coach three inches high
> with rock crystal windows and platinum wheels
> to ceremoniously convey a speechless egg to court.
> All for a bored Czarina! My version of history
> fantastic and revolutionary as I reduced the scale
> to the hand-held dimensions of a fairy tale,
> hiding tiny Imperial portraits and cameos
> in eggs of pearl and bone. Little bonbons, caskets!

This diminutive coronation coach was presented by Nicholas II to Alexandra Feodorovna in 1897. With the outbreak of the Great War, the Fabergé workhouses were given over to the manufacture of small arms and medical supplies. When the Bolsheviks took control of private business, they considered the world of enchantment envisioned by Fabergé too brittle and reductive: "My version of history / fantastic and revolutionary as I reduced the scale / to the hand-held dimensions of a fairy tale." Here Spires points to a subtle irony. According to A. Kenneth Snowman in *The Art of Carl* Fabergé (1952), Fabergé's ideas were, indeed, revolutionary: "In the matter of objects of *virtu* and jewels generally, the emphasis placed squarely on sheer value shifted, without compromise onto workmanship. In other words, the sincerity of a gift was to be measured by the imagination shown rather than by a noisy demonstration of wealth." Moreover, Spires's speaker is at heart a realist, though his buoyant wit owns that tinge of the macabre often found in the Brothers Grimm. He knows he has locked away the Romanovs by proxy of "tiny Imperial portraits and cameos / in eggs of pearl and bone." His pun on the confectioner's art, "Little bonbons," becomes an undertaker's joke: "caskets!" But Spires's Fabergé is a man less cynical than wise. He relinquishes all bitterness in light of his egg's symbolic significance, exchanging in closure three kisses that follow the traditional Russian greeting on Easter morning, "Christ is risen!:"

> Here, among the clocks
> and watches of a country precisely ordered
> and dying, I am not sorry, I do not apologize.
> Three times I kiss you in memory
> of that first Easter, that first white rising,
> and send this message as if it could save you.
> Even the present is dead. We must live now
> in the future. Yours, Fabergé.

Much of *Annonciade* is set in Europe, particularly England, which Spires does not always view through a lens so delicately ground as Fabergé's. In "Mutoscope," Spires journeys to an East Sussex borough on the English Channel: "I have come to Brighton, / come as the fathers of our fathers came, / to see the past's Peep Show." She strolls as did "veterans and stay-at-homes of the Great War" down the "West Pier's promenade" to the old Penny Palace. There she sees in the crackling light of the mutoscope

> "What the Butler Saw": a woman artlessly
> taking off her clothes in a jerky striptease
> I can slow down or speed up
> By turning the handle.

The speaker views the anonymous stripper as a specter who is not the coinage of her own brain, but nevertheless answerable to the stiff current of commerce ("pennies burning hotly in their hands") after almost a century: "you are your own enigma, victim / or heroine of an act of repetition that, once chosen, / will choose you for a lifetime." We see a dubious protagonist caught up in, yet projected beyond, a culture that has fallen into ruins:

> Dilapidation upon dilapidation, Brighton
> is crumbling, fallen to sepia tones,
> as your unfunny burlesque continues past
> your life, perhaps beyond mine,
> the past preserved yet persevering,
> the sentimental past.

The title poem of *Annoniade* is Spires's most ambitious and arguably the collection's finest. It derives a sense of history and myth from its setting, Le Maison de Repos, a mountain sanitarium near a centuries-old monastery in Menton, France. Here time is suspended between the bell-tones of the canonical hours, where Spires's persona performs "the small tasks a child could do," the daily repetition of "buttoning buttons," ritual gestures that make the future as irretrievable as the past. Here the "ill and the ill-disposed" seem to belong (as in Wallace Steven's "Sunday Morning") to a procession of the dead. Living seems an act of pure will: "I steady myself / at the window, still wanting to be alive," and complacency will not do.

Spires attempts to locate in the third and fourth stanzas of "Annonciade" where the will-to-survive and faith intersect. The speaker watches an old woman climb the monastery, "the 500 worn stone steps / of the Chemin de Rosarie," fingering the beads of her rosary as the speaker does, each day, her buttons. Those who enter "the cool cavern / of the church," perfunctorily lighting "a votive candle for five francs," also find themselves suspended in time:

> Time's silence surrounds them, held
> in the steady flame of the Sacred Heart,
> the armored effigy of a nameless crusader
> who lies in a low altar in the crypt,
> hands clasped in an attitude of prayer,
> as if at any minute the warrior
> soul will wake, leap up, and lead
> the sleeping body to Apocalypse.

But the soul of the nameless crusader cannot reanimate its flesh simply because an effigy assumes an attitude of prayer. For Spires, the spirit is not separable from the body's dross, of which the will-to-survive is a part. Still, the visitors to the monastery avert their eyes and

> move quickly past the apocryphal
> remains of martyrs, splintered fragments
> of bone and strands of human hair
> in shining jewel-encrusted caskets,
> the stoppered crystal vials of blood
> and tears, relics handed down for centuries.

Relics of the past, "splintered fragments / of bone," are necessarily parts of the past and future. Moreover, the speaker believes the residents of the Maison de Repos " live closest to annunciation"; they submit daily "to the omniscient x-ray eye that searches / for the small dark spot on the lung, / the glowing bone that will not mend." The way back to health means returning to the things of this world, enjoying the fullness of the seasons, tasting wine and meat, sharing the fellowship of others. Body and soul are finally inseparable: "Surely the spirit chooses its affliction / and makes it manifest" in bone, hair, and blood cells. In its refusal to choose resignation in the presence of illness, "Annonciade" becomes a poem of redemption.

The act of seeing serves a dominant motif in *Annonciade*, though Spires's method of color and shading is primarily aural. She expresses determination to avoid purely visual techniques in "Victoriana: Gold Mourning Pendant with an Eye Painted on Ivory: " I will turn from the art // of eye-painting, so distant / from hands, lips, heart." Despite an overall tone of affirmation, many lines in this book border on the elegiac, hollow *o* sounds almost swallowing the consonants. In "Bells" Spires asks, "What moments are these / tongued wholly with inexpressibles?" The answer is not long in coming: "The signs are there if we would listen, see."

In her fourth book-length collection titled *Worlding*, Spires locates the paradigms of the human condition within her own personal experience. The volume's first section focuses on conception, pregnancy, birth, and early childhood from the perspectives of both mother and daughter. Several of the poems emanate the fantastic aura of German *Marchën*, fairy tales, and Spires's intrinsic feel for the surfaces and textures of language typically culminates in striking tropes and images: "Shall I forget this night, this dream? / Forget the wink and tear of the doll / crying at the shard of moonlight in her eye?" Of course, a particle of risk inheres in such domestic themes, and Spires waxes downright effusive in "The Robed Heart":

> They come in white livery bringing the sun,
> the Robed Heart astride her white mount,
> crowds lining the royal road in anticipation.
> Ahead, the castle flying the new colors,
> a queen's great labors come to an end.
> A shout and the cord is cut,
> The crown placed on my head.
> And I am, Mother, I am!

"The Robed Heart" is set in a realm too remote from Spires's everyday, phenomenal world. How is a woman caught up in birth pangs, her heels braced in delivery-room stirrups, to gain a foothold in this abstract domain? Do newborns announce their arrival in complete, albeit simple, sentences? Sylvia Plath's speaker in "Morning Song" engaged this subject in a manner much more compelling and believable. Fortunately, the blissful hyperbole that somewhat mars "The Robed Heart" occurs but rarely in *Worldling*.

Spires writes most convincingly about the singularity of birth when she shuns ecstatic conceits and allows actual experience to shape her idiom. In "The Summer of Celia," mother and unborn child move in perfectly synchronous rhythms:

Is this a dream? The August sun,
the trees in the moment before their decline,

the high bodiless clouds skimming the horizon,
the water a second skin my strokes

slough off, and Celia swimming
her small strokes inside me as I swim?

These couplets embody beautifully the mutual yet discrete worlds of both beings. Through deftly enjambed lines Spires expresses a fervent desire for perpetuity, as her speaker proceeds in luxurious strokes toward an inevitable sundering. As surely as she "slough[s] off" the membranous "second skin" of the pool, the fetus will soon slip from warm amniotic waters and shed its birth caul:

Speak to me, Celia. Speak. Speak.
Before birth erases memory and suddenly

you are taken from me, then given back
wrapped in the white gown of forgetting,

changed, utterly changed. As I will be.
This is our summer, the summer of the dream

We will, too soon, awaken from
shocked and surprised, in our separate bodies.

In this instance syntactical precision complements the pristine loveliness of the imagery. The trope "white gown of forgetting" would be darkly elegiac in another context, and even here life and death are woven into one seamless fabric. Indeed, the prospect of childbirth awakens the mother to her own mortality. Spires achieves a similar fine excess in "Celia Dreaming": "I watched a bee tunnel into a Rose of Sharon, / summer's late-blooming flower, watched its head, / then furred legs, disappear completely." The bee vanishes like a swollen note into the bell-shaped flower: "back beyond / the body's origin, as if it could be unborn." This startling reversal causes her to ponder the spiritual origin of the infant asleep on her shoulder: "before you were with me, where were you?" The child answers with a gesture ephemeral as the flower's balmy fragrance: "Waking, you reached to touch the white face / of the flower, then another, and another, faces / quickly flowing past us, or held and stared into."

When Spires confronts the flawed grandeur of life beyond the nursery in section two of *Worldling,* her poetry becomes much more engrossing. In "Maison Beach," she converts an ordinary stroll along the shore into a vision of mythopoeic beauty. Her speaker spots some jellyfish stranded on the beach, globules of protoplasm almost seraphic their translucence:

> Englobed, transparent, they litter the beach,
> creatureless creatures deprived of speech
> who spawn more like themselves before they die.
>
> I peer into each and see a faceless
> red center, red spokes like a star.
> They are and are not, like what we are.

Though capable of reproducing, the jellyfish seem neither flesh nor spirit. Before the sun absorbs them, leaving only filmy rings, the medusae pulsate like heavenly bodies. But the true epiphany occurs when the speaker happens on "a dripping castle, all towers and crenellation," and sees how children have left the gelatinous creatures to guard the moat: "death and potentiality entwined forever." Staring at the crumbing battlements, she remembers an unfinished cathedral in Barcelona, the *Sagrada Familia* undertaken in 1883 by the Catalan architect Antonio Gaudi:

> Travelling once, I stood under the open sky
> inside a great unfinished cathedral.
> Stonemasons, there for generations, clung
>
> like ants to thin scaffolding, carving
> griffins and saints, the rising spires and portals
> dripping like hot wax, and birds flew
>
> freely in and out of lacy walls, like angels
> thrown down from heaven. Gaudy and grand,
> it was a vision of eternal mind. Its maker
>
> dead for a long time, left no finished plan,
> design, but work went on, days turning
> into years, the century coming to a close.

Spires's thick massing of images, set in motion by present participles in the second tercet, captures the molten plasticity of Gaudi's carvings; moreover, successive short *i* sounds—"thin," "griffins," "dripping,"—intimate the subtle patterns worked into the stone façade of the eastern portal. The pun on the architect's name, "Gaudy," shows that Spires senses the potential for humor in even the grandest language. "Lacy walls" alludes to the bonelike character of Gaudi's structure, especially the supporting columns and ribbed arches. But this does not imply a massive ossuary. For Spires, the *Sagrada Familia* is the *ban-hus,* of the Old English tradition, the living bone-house, the abode of the spirit. The sand castle no longer drips, nor do the jellyfish evaporate beneath the poet's sometimes caustic gaze. In a moment of redemption, she recalls the sculptures adorning the cathedral: "I touched each twisting vine / and leaf, / marveling at what had been done, / and what was yet to be, and wished, // as I do now, O never let it be complete!" Spires recognizes that the soul expends and renews itself in the very act of creation, thus her plea that the edifice never be finished in the terminal sense of that word.

In "Roman Lachrymatory Bottles," the poet wonders at the antique custom of preserving tears in elegant miniature vessels: "Of glass, of alabaster, these phials / that held the tears of this one, that one." Keats urges us to "glut" our sorrow on objects of natural beauty in his "Ode on Melancholy," and Spires goes a step further: "O let us make a gift to each other: / our stoppered tears, liquid and alive." The distillate of grief, tears become a rare quintessence free from any taint:

> There is a liveliness in weeping,
> and tears admit no stain, no pediment.
> A face shatters, a countenance dissolves,
> and wave after wave breaks against the shore.
> Our tears rise out of the spray, hang
> for a second of grand illumination,
> a cherished face, a picture held
> in every one of them, and are gone.

The slow dissolve from a countenance wracked by sadness to the myriad images suspended in sunlit spray is powerfully kinetic. The extended metaphor links teardrop to fire, each "cherished face" briefly illuminated in the mist. Spires strives for a similar clarity in "Two Watchers":

> Dusk. The light on the water contracts to a tear
>   where only a minute before
> it lay like a long spill, and out of the shadows
>   the great blue heron appears
> to stand on the periphery of what is and what is not.
>
> Heron, I met you once before on a summer morning
>   in the North. You were wading
> the shallows of Round Pond when you heard my footsteps.
>   Your neck tensed to an "S,"
> and then you flew, great wings flapping, toward heaven.

It is worth noting how the "tear" in stanza one appears to focus the speaker's vision, enabling the "great blue heron" to emerge from the deeper shades of evening. Phonic inversion, as in "Heron" and "North," enriches the word music of stanza two. Like a recurved bow, the taut "S" prefigures the lithe fisher bird's release and flight. Momentarily bereft of the feathered apparition's presence, the speaker harks back to a forgotten dream: "After that, you came to me...standing over me as an angel would, wings furled." Now winter makes a second parting imminent; the blue heron, poised on the brink of autumn, disappears in the encroaching darkness: "night closes in, and cold cuts to the marrow, / and, distantly, the lights / begin to come on in the great houses of Baltimore." At once stark and voluptuous, the nightscape implies anything but warmth. Soon a bone-slashing cold will turn the pond's surface to Arctic plate, and the heron migrate further south. Although the visionary impulse, the willingness to credit marvels, proves difficult to sustain, Spires insists upon it in the second part of *Worlding*. Her most successful poems surpass anything from her previous volume, *Annonciade*.

David Baker: Midwestern Counter-Sublime

David Baker is a distinguished author of both poetry and critical prose, the former including *Sweet Home Saturday Night* (1991), *Changeable Thunder* (2001), *Never-Ending Birds* (2009), and *Swift: New and Selected Poems* (2019). His *Heresy and the Ideal: On Contemporary Poetry* (2000) is the most well-written and insightful collection of essay-reviews to appear since Helen Vendler's *Part of Nature, Part of Us* (1980), and contains an excellent appraisal of the often neglected Miller Williams. Marilyn Hacker calls Baker "the most expansive and moving poet to come out of the American Midwest since James Wright," and that astute estimation is not far off the mark. Whereas Wright, the Ohio native, often dealt with the lives of the insulted and marginalized, Baker, who lives in Granville—he was born in Maine and grew up in Missouri—writes in his earliest work about the ennui of daily existence in the region—"All you can eat for a buck at the diner // is cream gravy on sourdough, blood sausage, and coffee"—but he tempers the flavor of this regional satire with an abiding love of the surrounding natural world that borders on the numinous. Baker—in opposition to Wright, whose vision of the ice-fretted limestone plateaus and refulgent dogwood blossoms of Martins Ferry, Ohio, is essentially redemptive—endows the landscape of the Midwest and its wildlife with a cosmic radiance that renders it almost wholly other. Thus, he sets up what Harold Bloom termed in *The Anxiety of Influence* (1973), a "counter-sublime" to his immediate precursor.

"Starlight," a poem selected from Baker's first volume published by the University of Arkansas Press, *Sweet Home Saturday Night* (1991), amply demonstrates his uncanny knack for figurative language and exuberance of diction within the context of a haunting winter night. The poet is ice-skating on a frozen starlit pond that could as easily be William Wordsworth's Lake Windermere as a glacial surface in Missouri or Ohio: "Tonight I skate on adult ankle across the blue pond / sifted with snow, back and forth across ice lit / as if from underneath by moonlight and many stars." The repetition of sibilants in "skate," "sifted," "ice," and "starlight" awakens readers to Baker's searing lyric acumen, while the blue glaze that the speaker skims doubles the twinkling firmament and effaces the boundaries between heaven and earth, setting up the poem's genuine pathos, which inheres in the dramatic situation: the poet imagines he's skating with his beloved maternal grandmother who is terminally ill:

> Like melting ice
> the fluids drop down trickling to their tubes.
> When I take her hand, and off we go, our skates slice
> lightly in the rippled ice, her hair blown-frost
> and tangled. She tugs my arm and sings *I wish.*
> Brittle tree limbs crackle in sudden gusts.

The IV drip, like an icicle bleb, resolves itself into a life-giving infusion—note the marvelously onomatopoeic "drop," "trickling," "tube" in the second line above as the poet and his grandmother launch into an enchanted *danse macabre*, the incantatory rhythms of which are implicit in the deftly enjambed "our skates slice / Lightly in the rippled ice." Her hair disheveled—"blown frost / And tangled"—the poet's mother's mother is the ecstatic *genius loci* of this place, which bristles with a kinetic pitch and timbre: "Brittle tree limbs crackle in sudden gusts." But here the poem turns as Baker reflects ruefully on how he and his siblings took for granted and sometimes rebuffed their grandmother's nurturing overtures:

> Once I watched her
> pile of precious scraps become a quilt.
> Once she pulled it to my chin and in my first sickness
> I kicked it off. The fragile ice, blue-floured ice
> we cut across, groans and gives, grows weaker.
> Each time we pass in time. Once she wept when
> her child's children, sullen in their hand-me-downs,
>
> scuffed early home and wouldn't speak.

Baker manipulates a continuous parallel between time past and time present as the thread of his narrative comes together like the "precious scraps" of cloth his grandmother stitched into a quilt. Then, he knew nothing of love's austere and lonely offices; now he regrets the callow indifference of his youth, a sullenness captured in the brusque cadence of "scuffed early home from school and wouldn't speak." Now, in a *tableau vivant* both tragic and lovely, she is beyond all pettiness and slight, leaving behind even the poet's rueful in memoriam intoned against the backdrop of starlight: "On she glides when I have stopped. On she sails when I have / Laid me down under starlight and closed my eyes."

Baker's sixth volume of poetry *Changeable Thunder* (2001)—and arguably his finest—extends and consolidates his obsession with the twenty-first century's slow but inexorable encroachments on the landscape and townships of the American Midwest: "the scene you loathe, the sheer fervor, the speed / of dangerous cabs—the city street / in oil, and spray when they pass" ("Postmodernism"). However, his vision expands to include seminal figures from the nation's shaping past, encompassing such theological, philosophical, and aesthetic forbears as Edward Taylor, Cotton Mather, and Walt Whitman. Baker retraces the origins of his preoccupation with closely knit communities, especially through his engagement with the lives of leading Puritans. Indeed, the founders of the Massachusetts Bay Colony conceived of their enterprise as a first-generation effort toward religious corporate self-definition, thus Baker's interest in the inhabitants of the small "city set upon a hill."

Baker derives his title for "Preparatory Meditation" from Edward Taylor's posthumously published volume of poems titled *Preparatory Meditations before my Approach to the Lord's Supper* (1937). Foremost among the poets of colonial America, Taylor was born near Coventry and immigrated to the Massachusetts Bay Colony in 1688, but not before attending Cambridge University, hence gaining a familiarity with the poetry of John Donne and George Herbert. Upon completing his education at Harvard, he accepted an appointment at Westfield, Massachusetts where he served as pastor and physician for fifty-eight years. Baker opens his poem with his protagonist torn between ministering to the body or the spirit:

> No preparation, no participation.
>   Thomas Doolittle's treatise *Treatise Concerning*
> *the Lord's Supper* lies on Taylor's table,
>   braced open next to pots of sugared teas,
>   his writing tools, and cups of poultice-herbs
>   to treat the ill parishioners come so
>
> recently to Westfield and still beset
>   with scurvy from poor provisions aboard
> *The Good Hope*—or was it *Sanctity*? No
>   matter. The detail's rich in the waiting.

Baker endows rhythm, syntax, and diction with a mellifluous play of assonance and consonance, sonorous *t* sounds ringing like porcelain among locutions such as "pots," "teas," "tools," and "poultice." Even as he contemplates his herbal medicines, Taylor's listing imagination yields almost imperceptibly to the microcosmic / macrocosmic conceits of sacred metaphysical poetry:

> He needs a pinch more of Saint Johns-wort, as
>   for each stomachic *Oyle of Spike most sweet*
> *May muskify thy Palace with their Reek.*
>   How like a holding hand of God is his
>   white antimonial cup, he thinks. How
>   his grinding pestle's His Fury. His Club.

Baker enters into a dialogue with his seventeenth-century precursor. Highly generative parallel emblems conjoin the sacramental chalice with the apothecary's mortar and pestle, which Baker likens in turn to "His Fury," and "His Club," intimating that God's love is compounded of passion and compassion. The cumulative tropes underscore Puritan theology's comparison of Christ to the bridegroom and human soul to the bride: "Huswifery is / a fitting figure to depict the true / alliance of God and all His peoples." "Footfalls" and a "soft knocking" recall Taylor to his immediate task. The meditative poem in preparation for his sermon must wait for those ailing in the flesh:

> His work will wait for his work to finish
> —as his poem will lie packed, right, prepared
> for print until nineteen thirty-seven.
> When the sickly spirit comes beseeching
> There is so little time to get ready.

Orthographic expedience—specifically the retention of arcane spellings—helps to sustain Baker's tone.

In "The Puritan Way of Death," Baker employs a structure at once lyrical and elliptical to portray the response to the burgeoning mortality rate among children in Cotton Mather's New England. The doctrine of Predestination deemed salvation the seemingly arbitrary gift of an inscrutable God, and most Puritans believed that the requisite signs of election seldom manifested themselves in people under the age of twenty-one. Thus Puritan children, polluted with the residue of Adam's fatal transgression, knew a surfeit of sin and corruption from the very onset: *"They go astray as soon as they are born. They / no sooner step than they stray, they no sooner // lisp than they ly,"* mourns Cotton Mather. Baker opens his poem with a bleak scenario, the burial of a child beyond the reach of grace:

> How hard this life is hallowed by the body.
> How burdened the ground where they have hollowed it,
> where they have gathered to set the body back,
>
> handful by handful, the broken earth of her.
> They have gathered to sift back the broken clod
> of her body, to settle her, now, back down.

Anaphora, internal near-rhyme, balanced repetition, and the ominous juxtaposition "hallowed / hollowed" lend these stanzas a haunting incantatory effect. Moreover, the metaphor "broken earth of her," knocked down to the metonymic gloss "broken clod," implies the young girl's return to unregenerate clay. This mounded plot is not, in the words of Wallace Stevens, "the porch of spirits lingering." And yet the Puritan community, for all of its austere spirituality, never cultivated a *contemptus mundi*, and unlike medieval plague victims often left to shift for themselves, those afflicted with smallpox in New England were tended with sedulous care:

> They do what they can. Long days and nights they stand
>
> with her, through her fevers and ague, and clean her
> gentle Vomit, and try to soothe the Pustules
> and her Eruptions, until there grow Hundreds,

and neither a common poultice of Lint
dipt in Variolous Matter, nor warmed
   Leaves of the Cabbage laid to her rapid heart,

nor prodigious bleeding, nor prayer, can save her.

Baker evokes tenderness through aural devices, a crooning sympathy implicit in the long *u* sounds of "ague" and "soothe." The emphatic repetition of plosive *p* mimics the hellish seething and festering of pustular eruptions. The scenario becomes a psychomachia or "soul battle," eliciting both pity and fear. Baker clarifies the dichotomies inherent in a culture that yearned for assurance of salvation and thus considered all children hostages to an uncertain fate. Of Cotton Mather, Baker remarks, "he himself is father to / fifteen, and loves them, suffering their afflictions." Indeed, Mather and Boston physician Zabdiel Boylston introduced smallpox inoculation into America, and the Puritan divine's lengthy *Angel of Bethesda* (unpublished until 1972) remains the only comprehensive medical work from the colonial period. In "The Puritan Way of Death," Baker engages a receding historical milieu with chilling linguistic acumen: "So the lamplighter takes up his grim vigil, / torch in hand, and together we walk the slick path // through the centuries."

    In "Romanticism," Baker further pursues the evolution of American literary history by exploring an extraordinary notation found in the journals of Ralph Waldo Emerson: "March the 29th, / 1832, of an evening strange / with dreaming, he scribbles, I visited / Ellen's tomb & opened the coffin." Ellen Tucker, Emerson's bride of less than eighteen months, succumbed to tuberculosis at the age of twenty; she had been dead scarcely a year when Emerson walked from Boston to the family vault in Roxbury and broached the locked casket with a gleaming brass key. What he saw is not recorded, but his strange gesture doubtless arose from a nascent sense that the individual must trust his powers of intuition, discovering by dint of personal experience a harmony with nature and the "Oversoul" immanent in nature. Baker imagines Emerson struggling with his as yet unarticulated transcendentalist philosophy: "Half angel, Emerson wrestles all night // with his journal, the awful natural / fact of Ellen's death." But Baker participates in his fellow poet's terrible confrontation, devising an elliptical lyric structure that manipulates a continuous parallel between Emerson's loss and Baker's own recent brush with mortality: "Months of hard freeze have ruptured the wild fields / of Ohio, and burdock is standing / as if stunned by persistent cold wind." The speaker and his young daughter roam acres of brittle fescue thawing in the morning sun:

I have come out for the first time in weeks
still full of fever, insomnia-fogged,

to track her flags of breath where she's dying
to vanish on the hillsides of bramble
and burr. The seasonal birds—scruff cardinal,

one or two sparrows, something with yellow—
scatter in small explosions of ice.
Emerson, gentle mourner, would be pleased
by the physical crunch of the ground, damp
from the melt, shaped by the shape of his boot.

In the second line above, smoldering fricatives and sibilants intimate how Baker's fever refuses to abate, even after weeks of illness. Nevertheless, an almost otherworldly evanescence still clings to the landscape barbed with hoarfrost and bramble. As his daughter's ecstatic cavorting calls to mind Emerson's love of nature, Baker envisions the Concord sage pacing off his own aesthetic and philosophical tract of ground, printing the rimed and oozing sod with a deft, sure-footed measure. The paths of the two poets converge abruptly, somewhat to Baker's chagrin:

Kate has found things to deepen her horror
for evenings to come, a deer carcass tunneled
by slugs, drilled, and abandoned, a bundle
of bone shards, hoof and hide.

The child beholds the tined sovereign of meadow and thicket reduced to a dried carcass reamed by gastropods until just a few tufts of hide and cleft hooves remain. Of course, only Baker perceives the analogue between Ellen Tucker Emerson's desiccated corpse and the slug-riddled deer. But he must witness the moment when his daughter is bereft of joy and innocence, no longer the "six years Darling" of Wordsworth's "Intimations" ode. Will she be able to adopt, a decade hence, Emerson's Neoplatonic credo: "I believe in the existence of the material world as an expression of the spiritual or real?" Baker seems to demur on this point, rendering Emerson's coffin key metaphorical: "Dreams & beasts are two keys by which we are / to find out the secrets of our natures." Several factors conspire to remove this poem from the typically narrow strictures of a journal entry. Baker's ability to embody more than one vessel of consciousness, his gift for appropriate but striking imagery, and his knowledge of the myriad phonetic connotations inherent in poetic diction suffuse "Romanticism" with an aura of immediate experience.

In "Simonides' Stone," Baker dramatizes certain affinities between the fifth century B.C. poet from Keos—best known for eulogizing with stoic eloquence the Spartan hoplites who fell defending the pass at Thermopylae against an overwhelming host of Persian invaders—and inner-city aficionados of rap music and tenement graffiti. Baker describes Simonides carving verse epitaphs into quarried stone: "He tapped his chisel lightly. He lined his words / horizontally as well as vertically, shaping them into grids 'like ranks of men in / military uniform.'" The speaker opts for compression, capturing Simonides's meticulous precision in the consecutive trochees of "chisel lightly." If each character is indelible, the residue proves ephemeral as motes in a sunbeam: "Puff / of dust. A verse." Baker then crosscuts to a tableau wherein young gangbangers mark their territory like prowling tomcats: "The kids are spray painting / the alley with their names, their tags / swirling shadow-mark, // meaning it's their neighborhood, stay out or die." As the aerosol pigment bleeds down the bricks, the youths move to the percussive rhythms of a street anthem, a mock-elegy of youthful bravado: "They rap / a song, a rhyme, no // time to live, no time to die: one dances off / with a can until the others chase him back." But their spree comes to an abrupt halt:

> They are laughing and then they are not. They stop
> where the man's bedded
>
> down, stone-cold, covered in leaves. They paint the stairs.
> They spray some thick, blue lines and shadow them with
> red around his form. They do not write on him.

Derelict as the neighborhood where he perished of drug addiction and exposure, the man lies inert, his very being circumscribed by the dead metaphor "stone-cold." Struck dumb by stark reality, the tattooed roisterers enact a scribal gesture of their own. They trace out the victim's shade in a primal blue then illuminate this tribal glyph with a rich carnal mist that dries hard as lacquer. Thus the police corner's yellow tape becomes superfluous, and Baker's closure lifts a human shape clear of the pavement by proxy of Simonides's concise, well-turned line: *"Man's dirge is praise."* Through the adroit agency of visual and aural tropes, Baker enlivens contrapuntal scenarios depicting such disparate historical entities as a canonical Greek elegist and street rhapsodes of the present century. In the process, he effaces momentarily the lines of demarcation between paean and lament, comparing patient craftmanship to the inspired improvisations of the heart.

In "Midwest: Ode," Baker once more focuses on the ideal of community and his beloved Middle America, but the poem also serves as an in memoriam for the late William Matthews, perhaps the cleverest and most cosmopolitan poet of his generation. Baker's mode is one of direct address as he relates to his fellow-poet the beyond-belief rusticity of market day in rural America: "Each Saturday morning the meeting point / of many worlds is a market in Charm." Baker assures Matthews that the name, at once real and allegorical, embraces something rare and genuine:

> You could believe a name so innocent
> it is accurate and without one blade
> of irony, and green grass everywhere.
> Yet, how human a pleasure the silk hairs
> when the corn is peeled back, and the moist worm
> curls on the point of an ear like a tongue—
> how charged the desire of the children
> who want to touch it, taste it, turn it over
> until it has twirled away in the dust.

Baker resorts to an idiom relaxed though scarcely colloquial. Matthews would appreciate the sensuality of the corn's "silk hairs," the subtle delectation implied in the sensual metonyms "tongue" and "ear." If the speaker indulges in the evocation of culinary largesse, sure tokens of artisanal mastery also wax abundant: "There are black buggies piled high with fruit pies. / There are field things hand-wrought of applewood / and oak, oiled at the palm of one man." But here Baker's engagement with local history reveals the inevitable inroads that time imposes on a mutable world as he cites the nearby corporate farm's blithe and culpable subsidy of the latest genetic technology: "its means of poultry production / faster, makes fatter hens, who need no sleep, // so machinery rumbles the night through." Indeed, such "progress" bodes ill for "the whole strange market of Charm, / Ohio, where we weekly come, who stare / and smile at each other, to weigh the short / business end of a dollar in our hands." Ultimately, destiny is not altogether unkind, as the poet observes in "Humble House":

> Soon enough we will go to our places
> down the road, where the creek cuts through the graves.
> The whole family waits there, passing toward home,
> worm and mole, creeper and clod, humus, loam.

The visionary scope and linguistic acuity of *Changeable Thunder* marks a watershed in Baker's poetic career.

Baker has expended many years developing an idiom distinctly his own, a voice others will hearken to with steady attention, poem after poem. *Never-Ending Birds,* his ninth book-length collection, signals the culmination of those efforts. His subjects range from personal loss and the raising of a daughter to the wonders of the natural world and the poet's contemplation of his own place within the larger cosmos. In language by turns taut and expansive, he unremittingly seeks the recondite truths that invariably seem to elude us: "That's us pointing with our delible whorls / into the faraway, the trueborn blue- / white unfeathering cloud of another year" ("Never-Ending Birds").

"The Rumor," a poem comprising sixteen quatrains, provides a salient example of Baker's meticulous method of composition. The speaker muses on a secluded clearing in the woods—specifically a birch tree—beneath which lie the scattered remains of a whitetail deer: "Consider thus / the tufts and tail piece / hooves cleft from the legs, the legs / what's left of them." The repetition of *u* sounds in "thus" and "tufts," not to mention the fricatives in "cleft" and "left," bestows on these sinewy lines a haunting resonance. Only a protein heat and a whiff of the predator's scat linger, crawling the raw nostrils: "aureole of deer guts, bitten / skin, bone." Indeed, one never sees the big cat, rapt with hunger, land in hail of claws on the hapless herbivore's back. The speaker remembers rumors: "deputies spotted / something— / 'buff deer or maybe a Dane running // loose in the corn.'" But the catamount has moved on when Baker introduces a superb irony:

> Consider the beech
> *the lovers' owne*
> *tree,* this one, yes,
> hearts scored in
>   and someone's and someone else's, initials
>   so swollen
> they're unreadable and
> more-than-head-
>   high-up the trunk.

The killing tree was once a living memorial to love, the bole carved with initials a generation ago; now the "scored in" scars are healed over so as to be illegible. The comingling of Eros and Thanatos proves both primal and bestial. This is Eden after the Fall.

Enlarging on the meditative moment, "Posthumous Man" initially appears somewhat lachrymose in tone. The title derives from John Keats's reference to his own "posthumous existence" when he lay dying in a tiny second-floor room overlooking the Piazza di Spagna in Rome. Indeed, were not the opening couplet also attributable to the desperately ill young poet of the Romantic Triumph, it would seem to some readers at once petulant and unearned: " I hate the world. / I have come to the edge." The speaker, dog leashed fast to his wrist, ponders "a neighbor's white / bean field in the snow fog." Baker delves deep into the foul rag and bone shop of the heart for an arresting image: "gray coat / rising now // —scuffed like a bad / rug, scruff eared." Up from the white acreage in a gradual thaw, the strange apparition "Shake[s] // off a night's sleep." Thus the poet resorts to a strange bit of delayed coding. *Genius loci* of the snowy terrain, the disheveled coyote lopes off into the woods. Structurally contrapuntal, "Posthumous Man" plies between terse unrhymed couplets and blank verse paragraphs. In the ensuing passage, one learns of the speaker's growing estrangement from his wife; nevertheless, he takes solace from the coyote's plaintive crying on nights sprent with stars:

> The long married abide in privacy
> longer and longer. That's one irony.
> After hearing the coyote crying
> a week, ten days, maybe more, late at night
> through the glassy air, crying like a bird
> his song among the billion stars, we saw him
> sunning asleep in the neighbor's old field.

This passage is richly sonorous, especially the liquids and nasals in the phrase "among the billion stars," and confirms Baker as a poet in command of an idiom uniquely his own. He returns to couplets, establishing an intertextual resonance between Keats's immortal nightingale and his own speaker's canine outlaw: "he's writing to Fanny// a few weeks cold after the nightingale," // He hears it sing in lone full-throated ease." To Baker's surprise, the coyote eventually proves as ethereal and elusive as the Old World thrush:

> He's a reel of fog unspooling
> toward the far, half-shadowed rim of trees.
> Uptick of grackles more wrens.
>   He's loping.
> Now he's running through the field toward the woods.
> By the time he is halfway he is gone.

The coyote vanishes in slow dissolve. Like Keats, Baker almost invariably triumphs in an encounter with nature when he invests it with an aura of the numinous.

Baker parlays his obsession with the flora and fauna of the Midwest into language of exceptional depth and loveliness. Consider this brief passage from "One Willow": "Crack willow, its name. The ice broke / the top branches down until it was stripped, / a glassine mass of shards shining fire in the morning's hard light." Baker reminds us that the basic function of poetry often lies in calling things by their right names. Moreover, the harsh sibilants in "glassine mass" play off the slurred *s* sounds of "shards shining" to kindle a prismatic blaze that suffuses the entire landscape. Indeed, the poet's subsequent trope recalls the lustrous bough that lit Aeneas's progress through the Underworld in Book VI of Virgil's *Aeneid*: "Whip willow / —a thing being its name—or torch to light / the way, to bury the dead by the path." But Baker is not loath to engage in an occasional witticism and does not shirk the citation of authority: "Its leaves 'convolute— / i. e. rolled together like the bud, like / a scroll of paper,' tapered to the points." These lines are wonderfully fraught with mock erudition. On the other hand, nuggets of bona fide wisdom—conjoined with imagery both diamond hard and deliquescent—occur throughout "One Willow."

An avid gardener, Baker's outlook with regard to nature is in some measure custodial. In "Clean Blade" he adopts a Frostian tone that begs reader participation in the most emphatic way: "My rawhide gloves, hard machete, I have / my tall boots on, heat like fever crying—you know // where we're heading—deeper in the splayed woods." The poet extends the decasyllabic line characteristic of his voice by as much as a metrical foot, hacking his way through dense foliage with measured precision: "ivy vines like forearms wrapped along trunks, helix // of cilia and sinew; cut them in half, else / the hairy stuff will clutch and haul down more." These lines breathe with aspirates and fricatives, as Baker heaves his machete with increasing fervor, heedless of the growing stain on his sweat shirt. But the inevitable that attends all hubris brings his labors up short:

> Bramble everywhere, clots in the last season's path.
> I'm swinging clean, cutting on the bias, pull—
>
> then the heron knows, spray of creek water,
> and the mole under my foot, and then my foot
>
> knows, blade slant-cut in the boot. You knew
> all along, didn't you? I'm—blood now—last to.

The blade is whetted so keen that the poet's breath never catches in his beard until the blood seeps through the leather. One suspects that he takes all this with a wry, albeit tight smile. Perhaps the most affecting entry in *Never-Ending Birds* is title poem. As Robert Lowell said in his "Epilogue": *"The painter's vision is not a lens / it trembles to caress the light."* A close look at "Never-Ending Birds" provides a case in point. It contains both elegiac and pastoral elements and while tinged with an ineffable sadness, it is essentially life-affirming:

> That's us pointing to the clouds. Those are clouds
> of birds, now see, one whole cloud of birds.
>
> There we are pointing out the car window.
> October. Gray-blue-white olio of birds.

If the poet adopts a pedagogical tone, his auditor happens to be his daughter Katherine, now older—perhaps aged 10—but then still a little girl agog at the natural world when the shutter tripped and the camera trapped her image. Typically mindful of how he metes out rhythm, syntax, and diction, Baker opts to let all run on a metaphor in what seems a secular rendering of Anglican Bishop Launcelot Andrewes's Nativity sermon preached on Christmas Day, 1622, before King James I in Whitehall: "The text is a star, and we may make all run on a star, so that the text and day may be suitable, and Heaven and earth hold a correspondence." As in "Starlight," Baker blends tenor and vehicle, as he points to himself, his wife, and Katherine pointing out the car window at thronging birds on a leaf-strewn autumn afternoon. The fourth line proves most compelling: "October. Gray-blue-white olio of birds." The poet uses the palette knife without stint, layering a smear of "gray" that deepens to "blue" then glows an incandescent "white" before mellowing to the vowel-rich "olio" of migrating birds. The ensuing couplets are touched with an arid bliss:

> Never-ending birds you called the first time.
> Years we may say it, the three of us, any
>
> two of us, one of those just endearments.
> Apt clarities. Kiss on the lips of hope.

"Never-ending" would smack of a love-smitten teenager's hyperbolic avowal—as in a popular love song—did it not spring from a child's sense of wonderment and delight. While Baker recognizes the worldly cynicism regarding such "endearments," over time they fade and lose their original meaning—uttered within the bond of the nuclear family, they become "just," "apt clarities," "kiss on the lip of hope." Yet, in the midst of this tempered optimism, the metaphorical "clouds of birds" that opened the poem stand in ironic contrast with the family unit:

> I have another house. Now you have two.
> That's us pointing with our delible whorls
>
> into the far away, the trueborn blue—
> white unfeathering cloud of another year.

The speaker has been displaced, the family unit torn asunder, presumably by divorce. His daughter now dwells in two separate households. The "delible whorls" suggest an erasure of identity; the fingerprints that mark us as individuals are ephemeral, have become metonyms for human mortality. The white "unfeathering clouds" are apparently cirrus: composed of ice crystals, their slow effacement at the wind's hand precipitates the encroachment of winter and the gathering of the flock, not its dispersal. Baker's closure is poignant indeed:

> Another sheet of their never ending.
> There's your mother wetting back your wild curl.
>
> I'm your father. That's us three pointing up.
> Dear girl. They will not—it's what we do—end.

The birds undergo another permutation and emerge as a "sheet" or cloud cover, but perhaps also a mort cloth, more commonly referred to as a pall. The last couplet is a recapitulation of the first, but embodies a salient difference: it hints at the generative impulse that is erotic love, but this love is no longer a possibility because the initial bond between the adults has been severed. In retrospect, the poet sees his wife's gestures of parental affection as act of loving solicitude—"There's your mother wetting back your wild curl"—hinting at a transformative erotic love. The final line also offers hope, though that optimism is decidedly not free of thorns: "Dear girl. They will not—it's what we all do—end." The gathering flocks connote the endless cycle of renewal that has no terminus—as did the seemingly eternal bond between her parents to the very young Katherine. Just as relationships have an end, so do we all. But the seasonal cycle of death and renewal continues, and there is a harsh joy in this prospect.

Those poets who would bid for a secure place in the canon must contend with the most formidable poets on a particular subject matter, and in the case of Baker's most recent volume titled *Swift*, "Osprey" affords him the opportunity to so. The poet engages immortals such as John Keats ("Ode to a Nightingale"), Emily Dickinson ("A Bird came down the walk"), Gerard Manley Hopkins ("The Windhover"), William Butler Yeats ("Leda and the Swan"), and Wallace Stevens ("Thirteen Ways of Looking at a Blackbird'), as well as more recent luminaries such as Robert Duncan ("My Mother Would Be a Falconress"), John Haines ("If the Owl Calls Again"), Ted Hughes ("Hawk in the Rain"), and Sylvia Plath ("Black Rook in Rainy Weather"). "The Osprey" consists of seven deftly patterned stanzas and an orphaned last line, its variable syllabics mimicking the ecstatic glide and graceful dip of this fisher-bird over the blue estuaries, salt marshes, and inland lakes of its natural habitat. Baker's beginning appears bookish, almost pedantic, before he arrests our attention with an abrupt tonal shift:

> [the] sea-eagle,
> what the guidebook says is
> white, grayish brown, and "possessed of weak eye-
> masks" in its non-migratory island
>
> instance, is blue.

The poet need only consult a guidebook to gain access to the marvelous Old English kenning "sea-eagle"; indeed, he limns its various attributes almost verbatim from a text, "white" shading off into "grayish-brown," and appropriates almost word for word that the osprey's eyes are not hooded against the frost like an owl's but instead are masked with a dull black. But here Baker arrests our attention with the aforementioned tonal shift, which amounts to an intercession of the truly numinous:

Blue, riding thermal bands
so low over the water it picks up
the water's color, reticulate

tarsi tipping
the light crests; and picks up
one of the silver fish cutting the surface
there, so the fish is blue, too, flapping-gone-

slack in the grasp
of its claws—as only
the owl shares an outer reversible
toe-talon, turned out for such clutching.

The osprey glides on an updraft as it skims the water's surface, its sleek
white-feathered underside reflecting the water's blue. Note the exquisite particularity of Baker's diction, how the glyptic *t* and short *i* within a three-
word span—"reticulate // tarsi tipping"—implies the raptor's lethal intent.
Once caught, the bright-scaled "silver fish" is a creature literally out of its element—the description "flapping-gone—// slack in the grasp / of its claws"
conveying a dying fish's convulsive seizure when the talons meet in a terrible
grip—but it too becomes imbued with the osprey's signifying blue:

as the water,
in turn, picks up the sky-
depth reflective blue sent down from ages
beyond, into which the osprey lifts now

without a least
turning of wing-chord though
"they are able to bend the joint in their
wing to shield their eyes from the light"; what I

mean is, by the
time I tell you this it's
gone: fish and bird away, "bone-breaker,"
or gray, "diurnal raptor," back into

the higher trades. Someday, too, this blue—

Before the fierce bird returns to its nest of woven sticks to rend and slake,
Baker leaves readers to ponder the sea-eagle's niche within the larger cosmos.
Color motifs are key to the meaning of this poem, and Baker uses blue to

bind bird, prey, the surrounding natural world, and the speaker himself, and here it becomes a signifier of the ultimate: "the sky- / depth reflective blue sent down from / ages beyond." Baker's osprey with wings as swift as the spoken word, picks the trade wind's high thermals out of sight into the redeeming blue, and readers are able to trace its going in every linguistic nuance and gesture so that they are left to stand agape, with the speaker, at the mystery of this spectacle. Particularly adroit is the double-noun combination "wing-chord" indicative not of ligament or tendon or of the bird's every breeze-riffled feather, but rather the subtle orchestration of all those components into a pleasing coherence that offers a hint of the ineffable. "The Osprey" is the best of the new poems in Baker's *Swift: New and Selected Poems*, and if it does not quite equal Robinson Jeffers's "Hurt Hawks," it is nevertheless a remarkable achievement.

Eric Pankey: The Crisis of Faith

Eric Pankey received his baccalaureate degree from the University of Missouri and earned his M. F.A. from the University of Iowa Writers Workshop. His first volume, *For the New Year* (1984), was selected for the Walt Whitman Award by Mark Strand. He currently teaches poetry workshops in addition to courses on modern and contemporary poetry at George Mason University where he serves as Professor of English and Heritage Chair in Writing. His honors include fellowships from the National Endowment for the Arts, the John Simon Guggenheim Memorial Foundation, and the Ingram Memorial Foundation. Jane Hirshfield has cited Pankey as a poet of "precise observation and startling particularties," a telling assessment of an aesthetic singular among today's poets.

An exquisite tempora on wood depiction of the Trinity by fifteenth century Russian painter Andrej Rublyov adorns the jacket of Eric Pankey's *Apocrypha* (1991), and an inner flap offers an interpretation of the volume's title: "various religious writings of uncertain origin regarded by some as inspired but rejected by most authorities." Even if we put aside for a moment the time-honored maxim about the futility of judging a book by its cover, a certain irony prevails. Surely the survival of any text for several millennia would seem eloquent testimony to its inspiration, whether the capricious ogres of the canon have bestowed their blessing or not. We should therefore view Pankey's title as more aspiring than self-deprecating.

Pankey is essentially an elegiac poet who has a sense of continuity more far-ranging than most poets of his generation. He treats subjects from the Creation to Last Judgement with a felicity and loveliness so desolate that he occasionally feels compelled to provoke rather than suspend our disbelief. Several poems loom larger than life because they are so emphatically staged and dismantled before our eyes. Here is "Tenebrae" in its entirety:

> How can we doubters explain the midday dark
> When such an elaborate system of spars
> And crossbeams propped it up? Though scaffolded,
> Dark fell like heavy canvas, slack, unfolded,
> A weight no wind could alter, a torn mainsheet
> Tenting the sinking deck. Underfoot
> The land is a wreck of wheel ruts and gravel,
> Crazed with aftermarks, a hill that levels
> Here where the killing's done. His body, unbroken
> And lifeless, tackled down under the open
> Shadows, seems in their arms a drowned man's,

> Except for the wash of blood on his feet and hands.
> How can we believe his tomb will stand
> Emptied, a cenotaph to a god and man?

Pankey's use of a variation on the sonnet imposes a tentative order on this chaos of figurations, while its rhythms mimic the visual phenomenon so graphically depicted. For example, an unstressed syllable follows a spondee at the end of line five, "torn mainsheet," so that we see (and by implication hear thunder) lightning flap like a shredded tarp on the horizon. By rendering a cosmic disturbance in deliberately contrived images, Pankey creates the sense that "we doubters" are common folk gaping at a pageant wagon in a medieval mystery cycle, an impression underscored by lines six and seven: "This land is a wreck of wheel ruts and gravel, / Crazed with aftermarks." The gnomic closure aligns what seem contradictory terms, "tomb" and "cenotaph," thus resurrecting the Greek originals, *kenos,* (empty) and *taphos* (tomb).

Pankey concerns himself less often than some poets with the strictures of form, but "Tenebrae" demonstrates that he is a genuine adept when he is inclined to do so. Of course, there are times when he is not even concerned with the logical ordering of events that typifies narrative verse. His methodology proves as much one of evocation as it is one of denotation and description. In "Provision" he bluntly declares that

> Clarity is not precision, the particular
> Intersection, the crude x.
> It is what the tools cannot measure:
> The gap, the lack, the verge of arrival.

Elsewhere, he seems to belie this notion, implying that the word can be an incarnation, a mysterious embodiment even in nature: "The whippoorwill echoes its name, // A compensatory music for one / Who is drawn to it, for one called back" ("At Dummerston Bridge"). In "The Holly and the Ivy," Pankey enshrines the paradox, both in language and the natural world. His speaker broods on the paucity of green the landscape puts forth during a season T. S. Eliot's Magus declared "the very dead of winter." He then notices the frost-seared ivy entwining a maple pruned earlier in the year: "That high branch I lopped off / Left an oozing stump—cross-cut and pale amber—// That oozed until the cold clamped down and sealed it shut." Burnished with frozen sap, the "cross-cut" branch waits silent and enigmatic as the tomb in Palestine for the radiant reawakening. Indeed, the cold weather and long nights presage a miraculous beginning:

> It is Christmas time and the Christ child is born.
> Yes, I have left the holy unacknowledged,

> As if to undercut the evergreen world,
> As if to say this is the end, beyond hope.

The holly is a paradox in nature; it stands perennially outside the cycle of death and renewal, though the blood-red berries and crown of nettled leaves also recall the Crucifixion and our redemption. By pointing so intentionally to his omission of the holly bush, the speaker accentuates rather than undercuts its symbolic significance. The qualifying phrase, "As if," signals the exact opposite of the despairing statement of the last line. Far from being "an end, beyond hope," the season marks a beginning that surpasses all expectation.

Pankey can also consider the prospect of death and continuity in terms that ring more personal than mythical or historical. The speaker of "Milk Glass" contemplates an heirloom endowed with "pricelessness," a bowl of translucent pressed glass stolen by his mother, "a child's act of theft," on the day of his grandmother's funeral. Here we have a compression of syntax and diction singularly appropriate to the object described:

> What was left to her she now leaves to me:
> Milk glass, a near-flat bowl with fluted edges,
> A trifle that sits on the sideboard
>
> As her sole marker. Its blue translucence
> Is translunary, an overcast:
> Ice has no ancestor in ember,
>
> But is a source and receptacle of light,
> The morning's light and the blue of backlit clouds.

The "translunary" artifact is imbued with an occult, almost Dionysian beauty, implying that the speaker traces his psychic origins along lines distinctly maternal. However, line six reminds us that his "inheritance" is far from being the crystal of a precious stone nurtured in fire for eons. It is actually a "gift of contraband," the token of a stealthy act perhaps not associated with love: "The bowl sits on the sideboard, its cold beauty / As welcome as frost on the window, hard frost / That daybreak will not melt away." This closure reveals how precise Pankey's locutions are when deftness fits his purpose. If we substitute a word such as "dawn" or "sunrise" for "daybreak," the poem loses much of its impact. As it stands, the idea of continuity takes on a brittle, numbing luster.

The dominant philosophical concern of *Apocrypha* finds its most succinct expression through the speaker of "In Memory," an elegiac piece that opens with a conscious debate about the relationship of *Logos* to the world around us:

> If the world is created from the Word,
> What can I hear amid the noise of that one
> Assertion and all that rattles and diminishes
>
> In its wake: the mockingbird's trill and grate,
> The sluice and overlap where the creek narrows,
> The dragonfly needling through the humid air?

The speaker goes on to address his mother's remains as "ash-that-you-are," which in the lyric of a writer less earnest than Pankey could just as well be a sardonic comment on the method of inhumation as a metonym. Risky, perhaps, but modulation of tone and breadth of vision rule out the possibility of double entendre: "If I can believe that Christ / Is risen, why can't I believe that we too / Will be risen?" By proxy of his speaker, Pankey here voices a sense of continuity based ultimately on the contemplation of a divine principle. For him, "veiled and silenced" are solemn attributes of the Engendering Word:

> I take comfort in your silence,
> In the absence of the voice that voiced your pain.
> The body apart from the spirit is dead
>
> But that does not mean the spirit is dead.

In a symposium on writing and spirituality titled "To Repair the Material of Experience," Eric Pankey posed the following question about the validity of the Judeo-Christian mythos for a poet living near the end of the second millennium since the Star of the Nativity blazed over the hayricks and outlying stables of Bethlehem: "What does it mean for writers to participate in the myths of their culture and to hold those myths as truths. What does it mean to disbelieve and participate nonetheless?" The question of how to negotiate in mythic terms the gap between belief and disbelief is the crux of Pankey's fourth volume, *The Late Romances*. For Pankey, myth and poetry have similar objectives, both focusing on humankind's unity with the cosmos: "poems themselves are pilgrimages between Eden and this green world." The dualities inherent between death and resurrection, renunciation and celebration, flesh and spirit, provide the catalyst for poetry: "The invention of perfection was The Fall. / Still one longs for discord and accords the flaw // Dominion over the whole" ("Two-Part Invention"). As in his previous book, *Apocrypha*, Pankey questions the dichotomies of existence within the framework of Christianity.

Unlike many contemporaries, Pankey often deals with overtly Christian themes in a mode of direct address reminiscent of John Donne and George Herbert. "Homage" celebrates the conditions of mythology, the rift between physical and spiritual realms, in a language both austere and sensual. Here is the first stanza entire:

> O my God, looming and rough-hewn,
> Forge me with rage. If this is the purge
> Ferret out and scald the cold grub
> Burrowed in my heart. Let havoc
> Consume its nest and larder.
> Let your gold cauter stanch the wound.

Pankey invokes both the divine Christ and the big-knuckled carpenter from Galilee. Through implied metaphor, the speaker becomes raw material: adze and gouge strive with the wood's rough grain in "forge," "rage," and "purge." The phrase "cold grub / Burrowed in my heart" recalls the "invisible worm" of William Blake's "The Sick Rose," thus evoking the image of heartwood peeling away in concentric petals as the augur bores deeper. The "gold cauter" is sticky amber that rises in the spring, so pungent that a whiff burns. The second and concluding stanzas couple grief and joy:

> Fall, inviolate the sledge, and be known.
> Blast away the sawdust and matchwood,
> The ash-fall and rusted filings.
>
> Let me be your wedge, let that edge
> Gleam from use, burnished as it divides
> The flawed from this hammerdressed world.

If "matchwood" is nothing more than the detritus of plane and chisel, the locution seems volatile, even incendiary. Pankey employs a misnomer for the sake of interior rhyme: a "wedge" would actually be driven by an iron-ringed maul, a hardwood block with a long handle, rather than a "sledge." In an abrupt turn, the speaker implores Christ to let him be the "burnished" instrument that divides the perfect from the imperfect world. The wedge also conjures the lance-head that pierced Jesus's side, releasing ichor and blood, water and wine. Here Pankey recasts William Butler Yeats's assertion: "nothing can be sole or whole / That has not been rent." The spilt between the "flawed" and "hammerdressed" world—between rude timber and the finished Cross—provides the motive force behind Pankey's longing for mythic unity. With its vigorous syntax and muscular diction, "Homage" echoes visionary poetry from the Old English "Dream of the Rood" to John Donne's "Batter My Heart, Three-Personed God."

In "The Phrase of Thine Actions," Pankey decries the remoteness of the Engendering Word from the present age: "What I know of the sacred is gloss, / Word that will not translate into flesh." In the ensuing lines, the concept of transubstantiation lapses into a quaint metaphor: "The bread he broke was not his broken body, / But is a vernacular and homely trope." What troubles Pankey most is the ineffable nature of the religious experience:

> I expected the audacity of bliss,
> But was given the figures of sacrament.
> The heavy curtain of allegories,
> Words and acts that articulate his absence.

The dwelling in absence that words betoken no loner suffices. In "late summer just before the harvest," the poet delves into the repository of language and memory for the appropriate emblems: "the gate—a trellis really for vines—is closed. / The way through covered with floury dust. / What is dust that he would think to reshape it?" The allusion to the Garden of Eden offers mythic resonance, but the gate is an entrance seldom frequented, a "trellis" choked with vines and jungling briars. The adjective "floury" implies a kneading or reshaping of "dust," a trope for human mortality and resurrection. Still, the poet desires "the audacity of bliss," a leavening of the spirit without which the Bread of Life loses its savor. The metaphorical properties of language—tropes, figurations, allegories—remain mere sign and symbol, inadequate to embody transcendent experience.

But nowhere in *The Late Romances* does the problem of belief receive such devastating treatment as in "The Grave of a Woman":

> All the flesh left is a patch of leather
> Where the skull hollows. Each vertebra
> Like an ancient fish with an open mouth
> And ragged fin, holds its place in the line.
> The pelvis could be a worn mortar
> And the scattered finger bones, gimcrack.
> Do all who lie down expect to wake?
>
> Consider the remains of this woman,
> Buried in the gesture of sleep—
> Her knees drawn up, one hand as a pillow.
> Long ago the worms abandoned this trough.

Pankey assails us with a numbing array of metaphors from the dessicated tissue patching the woman's skull hollows to the exquisitely articulated "gimcrack" of her fingerbones. Each vertebra, once a gaping socket and conduit, now resembles a bony-lipped piranha forever fixed in the age-old hierarchy of predator and prey. When we remember that the fish was the original symbol for Christ, Pankey's figurative symbol becomes all the more harrowing. The pelvis is a "worn mortar" sans pestle, a battered vessel empty of life's ferment. "Trough" denotes the ravaged body rather than the grave. The poet turns to scripture in his brusque, bitterly ironic closure: "Behold the kingdom that comes, / The earth that the meek shall inherit."

In his quest to reconcile the opposing ardors of flesh and spirit—and thus achieve the mythic unity he desires—Pankey adopts the persona of Mozart's Don Giovanni, the archetype of the rakehell and whoremaster. In "Don Giovanni in Hell," the dubious protagonist ponders his life of sin after the fact. Part two, titled "The Body," proves a singularly arresting piece: "The calipers pinch as they close on / This slack form, this vehicle of lust, / Still addled with use and so other." How can "calipers," a cold metal instrument for measuring anatomy, gauge a man's abiding passion for women? Indeed, Don Giovanni archly compares sexual arousal to an altogether different awakening: "What did I expect, my God, from you? / The resurrection of the body?" A born sensualist, he is at once enthralled and jaded by the compulsions of the flesh:

> The wax, the oily ichor, spills down
> The candle's length. I cannot not
> Touch my finger to the hot liquid
>
> And when it cools, I peel it away.
> If only flesh were so easily
> Disposed of. But I am bound to it
>
> Like a worn horse to a whippletree.
> Who will untie the leather harness?
> Who will pull the pin from the clevis
>
> And let me drag my burden away?

In the adjective-noun combination "oily ichor," Pankey renders indelibly the nacreous texture of molten wax. An ethereal substance suggestive of carnal pleasure, the "hot liquid" seems a sticky commodity once it cools. Pankey's libertine reverses the classical conceit of the lover as a stallion, instead likening himself to a drayhorse eternally shackled to fleshly toil. His prodigious sexual appetite notwithstanding, Don Giovanni scorns the excesses of the glutton and winebibber in another poem, "Ode on a Beet": "This pauper's diet is all that's needed, / A bloody show to sate the gut and heart." He expresses his "Nostalgia" for stealthy seduction in a passage that combines Christian sacrament with pagan ritual: "I miss the face of each who gave in. / The bleached bodice in place but unstrung. / The host like a coin on my tongue." Here "host" ostensibly refers to the communion wafer, but also connotes the ceremonial drachma meant to pay Charon for ferrying the souls of Roman noblemen across Stygian waters to Hades. Sacramental bliss and the culmination of coitus—in

Old World parlance, "the dying away"—become one and the same: "The moan of pleasure. The muttered *amen*. // I was a ghost made flesh in women."

Pankey's evocation of the Judeo-Christian mythos through Shakespeare's Prospero is perhaps the most intriguing element of *The Late Romances*. Both benign magician and master of revels, Prospero longs in *The Tempest* to transcend time through magic and mortality through art, but ultimately acquiesces to the encroaching realities of what is past, passing, or to come. Pankey's protagonist in "Confession on the Island" betrays a sense of historical belatedness: "Romance conceals a dark tragedy / Played out long before the play begins." Prospero admits failure, forswearing his attempt to reconcile the flaws of human nature: "I've lived out my life in Eden / / Believing it to be the World, / Believing I could reclaim the lost, / All that was forfeited to greed." A subsequent poem, "In Sienna, Prospero Reconsiders the Marriage at Cana," underscores the sorcerer's lachrymose mood after his return to Italy:

> What else can be made of signs and wonders
> But close readings and a display of awe?
> What is left when the waited upon is fulfilled?
>
> After the standoff Jesus conjures a trick.
> Should such an act be enacted knowing
> The *next* and the *next* will be demanded?

By proxy of his speaker, Pankey would dismiss any substantive difference between Jesus the miracle worker and Prospero the magician. A bold assertion, to be sure, but the dark allusions and paradoxically numinous language of his closure seem to confirm the analogy:

> As if in confirmation of a miracle,
> A twisted olive bears the wind's history,
> A gnarl that handles the brisk disorder,
>
> Renders it as the unmoved here and now.
> Skittish pigeons clatter up in the air.
> Into shadow. Out of shadow. And then back down.
>
> And no one, not even God, lifted a finger.

The "twisted olive" conjures not only the Mount of Olives and the Garden of Gethsemane thereon, but also the tree of the knowledge of good and evil and the cross etched against the low skyline at Golgotha. The incorporeal air lists and tacks in bare branches, each gnarl a slipknot in time's rigging. Pigeons "clatter up" and resettle, as sibilants—"brisk" and "skittish"—trace the spirit's progress from light to shadow. Thus, Pankey's speaker discerns the miraculous in the ordinary, and his multiple tropes bear a mythic weight greater than "the wind's history." Indeed, these lines invoke Christ's words to Nicodemus shortly before the crucifixion: "The wind bloweth where it listeth, and thou hearest the sound thereof, but canst not tell where it cometh, and whither it goeth; so it is with everyone that is born of the Spirit." Prospero has abjured magic and drowned his book of incantations; henceforth, he must seek cosmic unity in the mundane significations of the natural world. Unhappy in the old dispensation, Pankey's necromancer yearns for the days when, in Shakespeare's phrase, "I made shake and by the spurs plucked up / The pine and cedar; the graves at my command / Have waked their sleepers, oped and let 'em forth / by my so potent art."

Just as Pankey's Prospero poems remind us that English Renaissance drama had its origins in the morality and miracle plays of the medieval period, so "In Arcadia" traces Greek theater back to its roots in the cult of Dionysius. Here, as elsewhere, the poet awakens mythic resonances amid the fractured remains of an ancient civilization:

> Half-buried in scrub and red poppies
> And half-exhumed, the barren half-moon
>
> Of the threshing floor, fissured and chipped
> Is bleached the white of lime, of the moon
>
> Itself, full last night, instructed in light,
> In chapters of light as wordless as
>
> The owl's wing. Not yet noon, the sun hangs,
> Worn and burnished with use, like a heart
>
> Made of glare and ember. The mint spreads
> Its mineral flame down the hillside.
>
> Amid the green, the lizard's tongue flicks
> A Y of blood divining the air
>
> There and gone. There and gone. There.

The "threshing floor" is a limestone relic half-sunk, buckled and crazed by roots. The ecstatic hymns sung here in praise of Dionysius are silent, eclipsed by the passing centuries. But why is the moon "instructed" (as opposed to *versed*) in light? The former locution suggests a deliberation antithetical to the irrational and orgiastic nature of Dionysian revel. The phases of the moon—the Yeatsian echo is unmistakable—occur in "chapters of light," hushed as the buffeting of an "owl's wing." Dionysius no longer presides over dithyramb and tragedy, over the seasonal death and resurrection of the vine. But Pankey does not end here. If the lizard sheds its nocturnal lethargy in the sun's Apollonian "glare and ember," its tongue—"A *Y* of blood"—interrogates the tranquil air. The cool crevices of the "fissured and chipped" threshing floor are its true sanctuary, and its forked tongue winnows the brilliant landscape for intimations of the divine. Pankey may be assailed with what Harold Bloom called a sense of historical "belatedness;" nevertheless he pursues arduously a mythic unity within our chaotic milieu: "What do you love better: the ruin or its repair? / Desire's affliction or fire's harsh sacrament? // The stone wall of the orchard or the open gate out / Into this reliquary world?"

Cenotaph is Pankey's fifth full-length collection of poetry and the central panel in a triptych that includes two previous volumes, *Apocrypha* (1991) and *The Late Romances* (1998). His visionary aesthetic bespeaks the desolation of the individual in a postlapsarian world that blithely abjures redemption; indeed, Pankey mourns the passing of others and the slow erosion of his own faith. In a ten-line prologue titled "See That My Grave Is Swept Clean," he compares language inscribed on ancient tablets to raw earth gouged by shovel or back-hoe: "Words are but an entrance, a door cut deep into cold clay." Pankey likens writing to the enigmas of the grave, then proceeds to debate the efficacy of lyric utterance: "I say, *A Late sky flagged with jade; ice on the pear blossoms.* / I say, *A thrush of cinnabar in a lily's throat.*" / Behind each assertion, each gambit I could place a question mark." Initially, the interrogation yields images of evanescent splendor: "Behind each question a residue of longing half-assuaged, / An argument of brine-edged light the moon, your stand-in, doles out / Grain by grain." But the moon's particle dissolution evokes an ineffable dolor, and the speaker accentuates the self-reflexive nature of his quest for meaning: "Behind each question a hook blackened with rust." The question mark becomes the gleaner's hook that gathers the grain the reaper missed. In the final stanza, the poet briefly switches to the imperative mode: "Begin with a clay bank, / A chill wind's insufflation. / Begin with thumb-flint, a fever, some sticks to fire the kiln." The speaker would transform the deeply scored clay to a kiln fired by fricatives in "thumb-flint" and "fever," a crucible for body and spirit fed by "the wind's insufflation." However, in "See That My Grave Is Swept Clean," the speaker declines to invest words with the force of ultimate transcendence: "Are words but an entrance? *Words are but an entrance.*" Thus the poet's engagement with language, its power to recast the phenomenal world in figures that compel belief, comes under vigorous scrutiny.

In his desire to impose a singular vision on the universe, Pankey never ceases to ponder the nature of reality or the innate potential of words to embody experience. Here are the first five couplets of "Sacred and Profane Love":

If it is indeed more fitting
To say the world is an illusion,

Does it matter if what I behold is a gold braid
Inlaid upon ebony, or the wind-tousled jackstraw

Of salt hay that edges the marrow of the mudflats?
Does it matter if the gift the cicada leaves behind—

Hollow, dawn-enkindled, paper-thin—
Is the hieroglyph: *to begin again,*

Or the embodiment of the cold light's sealed and sepia pallor
Beneath the ice floes of Europa?

For Pankey, the issue is not what the eye perceives, but rather what the imagination conceives. If language is the poet's medium should he privilege the aspirate vigor of "wind-tousled jackstraw" over the ornamental braid embedded in ebony and brimming like an ear of wheat? Is the larval blister the locust sloughed a fossil word, a frail "hieroglyph" for life's renewal or a husk of light frozen beneath the planetary cold of Europa? As each metaphor subsumes its predecessor, Pankey turns to the plastic arts for an answer: "In Titian's Sacred and Profane Love," / One woman is unclothed, exposed and naked, // And the other is wrapped, decked, and bejeweled." Adorned or unadorned, neither depiction exists as a Platonic ideal: "Each the image of the image of an idea. // Not an illusion, but an illustration." Reluctantly, the poet embraces the shifting figurations inherent in poetic speech: "Sometimes I can feel my heart in my throat. // Sometimes I can swallow nothing I put in my mouth." The locution "heart" serves as a synecdoche for both fear and desire, echoing the third stanza of William Butler Yeats's "Sailing to Byzantium," wherein the speaker enters eternity through the refining fires of art. But Pankey's is a voracious heart that feeds on its own passion: "What is a heart that consumes and is consumed?"

In "How to Sustain the Visionary Mode," Pankey continues his quest to master the protean qualities of language, offering the aspiring poet a simple admonition: "Whenever possible avoid predication: *the night sea, the dark river, this rain.*" However, to avoid predication is to sunder words from any meaningful context:

As in a dream, where the door opens into a cedar grove, and
the haze conjures a screen of sorts onto which an ill-spliced
film is projected, and the words, poorly dubbed, seem mere
trinkets in a magpie's nest, let each object be itself.

Objects a magpie might hoard.

Words become objects, "mere trinkets" gleaming in a magpie's secret cache. The dream scenario takes on a double meaning when we recall that a magpie may hoard and reiterate words, a treasure trove of the human intelligence; however, the glossy little bird has no glimmer of understanding. Pankey regales us with series of gorgeous constructions enlivened strictly by participles: *"The blown dusk-smoke of flies above the sacrifice: The flames / inlaid and lacquered: The horizon, a single graphite line on rice / paper."* Richly evocative, these lines might appear self-indulgent in another context, inasmuch as they lack sequential ordering; but Pankey clarifies his yearning for such numinous imagery with a passage from the apocalyptic verses of St. John: "Revelation is and will remain the subject: 'Behold, I come / quickly: hold that fast which thou hast, that no man take thy / crown.'" Thus Pankey hankers for the benefit of inner light, the unfettered incantation of the true visionary. Moreover, he desires a poetry untainted by any sense of historical belatedness: "The moment present and full: thyme-sweetened honey, a / New World of Gold, quick with what made it."

A cynical reader might trace Pankey's crisis of faith in *Cenotaph* to a foiled attempt to infuse his own poetry with the potency of s Scripture: "The Word is what I heard and cannot replicate" ("The Unstrung Lyre"). But this disclaimer is fraught with an irony that anticipates and dismantles criticism. In spite of his disavowal, Pankey's lexicon actually *does* attain the resonance of Scripture. Pankey's finest efforts conjure a landscape of doomed beauty, a vision startling in its evocation of Last Things. Here is "Dream Landscape with the Old Brick-yard Road Creek and Blind Willie Johnson":

> I have returned to the creek, the current-scalloped sand,
> The mud bank that gives and gives against the onrush and backwash,
>
> To the gust-cobbled surface sun-flecked with amber, the sky
> As bright as ice-melt, or blue, in deep shade, or buttermilk,
>
> At times more depth than surface, black as charred fircones or rain,
> Rain at night and a slide guitar troubling an old hymn
>
> That I have no voice to sing, but still discern from the hush
> Of water oaks and willows, the full reservoir of wind,
>
> The nighthawk and the field mouse. A voice calling from the porch,
> And having returned to the creek, to these oxbow shallows
>
> I wait hell-bent, as one waits for Judgment Day, knowing
> With one or two steps, he can ford the depth and distance home.

Pankey opens with an independent clause recalling the voice of the preacher in Ecclesiastes ("I returned, and saw under the sun, that the race is not to the swift, nor the battle to the strong"), an appropriate resonance when we remember that Blind Willie Johnson was a "sanctified singer" whose antiphonal technique reverberated with a meetinghouse fervor. Pankey's seven heptameter couplets, comprising a single run-on sentence, describe water as "sun-flecked" and gravid as "buttermilk." Other times, the creek reflects the sky and runs blue as "icemelt," the slick glissando of a "slide guitar troubling an old hymn." Never once do we see Blind Willie Johnson working the ache of those strings into callused fingers, but we sense the current narrowing in the crosshatched texture of charred "fircones." As in Ezra Pound's theory of the Vortex, images defy logical sequence, become radiant nodes and clusters, systems in dynamic interplay. Pankey's language is both sensual and austere, and as he takes his soundings, the poem gathers momentum as swift and sure as the Jordan.

Notwithstanding a recent tendency toward doubt, Pankey's ongoing engagement with the Judeo-Christian mythos lends at least one personal narrative the gnomic flavor of a New Testament parable. "From the Book of Lamentations" belies the promise of its first line with a series of arresting and disjunctive images:

> We all have a story to tell. Mine begins
> With the gift of a knife. With a rod of sand.
> With bees like haze above a field of the thistle.
>
> Light falls silverpoint on a parchment of straw.
> Snow dusts the wings of a crow. Rude at its edges,
> The season is the season-between-seasons.
>
> I hear my father mumble through his dreams.
> The hailstone placed on his tongue turns each curse to song.

The flinty diction of stanza one combines fricatives and sibilants—"gift," "knife," "sand," "field," "thistle"—as though a blade were being sharpened to a glowing edge. At once volatile and suggestive, the dissonant images give way to the diminutive glitter and amber hues of the fourth line. Even the crow's wing is lit by a particle brilliance. But what strange impulse places a hailstone like a caramel on the father's tongue, a delectation turning "each curse to song?" Pankey unfolds a story of poverty and family strife: "No, we were never poor, my mother counters. // When she died I went through her closet and found / Five hatboxes, each stuffed with unopened bills." Although the tone remains nightmarish—wolves lurk about the door and hornets swarm in the eaves—the poem contains moments of poignant humor, as when the patriarch repudiates and disinherits the speaker's brother, leaving him bereft of the opportunity to turn prodigal: "My father left my brother a heart of rain / And the back of his hand. *Here, all this is yours: // This cold heart of rain and the back of my hand.*" Indeed, grief converts to joy as Pankey underscores the paradox at the heart of lyric mourning:

> Unless the stone melts and the tongue is cut clean
> A voice goes on singing a song of exile.
>
> *So long,* he sang in lamentation.
> The gift of a knife is bad luck, but this blade,
> Well-edged, sharp to the point, has been my fortune.

Pankey's haunting imagery and elliptical narrative converge in his closure. According to folklore, the gift of a knife severs a friendship, unless the recipient offers a coin in return. The poet lets his father go on nurturing a hailstone like an obol on his tongue. He refuses to wait "until the stone melts or the tongue is cut clean" but departs with his own legacy, the gift of song, well-honed, incisive, "sharp to the point."

Perhaps Pankey performs best when he allows his ample and well-schooled imagination to mediate successfully between words and the variable contours of the living universe. "In Divination at Chapman Beach," he stands where Cold Spring Brook "runs to salt," marveling at the gritty resplendence that swift water shears from a clay bank: "sandstone, raw sienna, and native umber," / And the light changes (or so I'll remember)—// Jade, a transparency of shadows." But he cannot forbear to meditate, however obliquely on the creation myth set forward in Genesis: "How the world began / I couldn't say, but no one was looking on." Once again, he questions the power of the Engendering Word to wrest order from chaos: "What I meant to say has to do with light, / How, though divided from the dark, it shifts // Mote by mote to the weight of its absence—/ Unstable, volatile, a confluence." Indeed, the capacity for doubt endows Pankey's vision with a plangent loveliness:

> If the world were to begin at this moment,
> Here, where the freshwater brook runs to salt,
>
> God would behold a flat *S* of gray,
> Not dovetail or pewter, but of the bank's own clay.
>
> Then more blue than gray, like a nick in pewter,
> Like a dove's blurred flight. Then a blue like water.

NOTE FROM THE AUTHOR

I would like to thank the following individuals who made the publication of this book of critical essays possible. I should begin with Kimberly Verhines, editor of the Stephen F. Austin State University Press whose receptiveness to this project and timely advice facilitated the process at every turn. I must also acknowledge the editors of the following literary journals—Barrett Warner of *The Free State Review*, Gerald Maa and Stephen Corey of *The Georgia Review*, Mark Drew and Peter Stitt of *The Gettysburg Review*, David Baker and David Lynn of *The Kenyon Review* and Andrew Ciotola of *West Branch*. I am furthermore indebted to managing editors C. J. Bartunek, Emily Ruark Clarke, Mindy Wilson, and Lauren Hohlen whose skills lent a certain refinement and polish to those articles originally appearing in the aforementioned periodicals. Special gratitude is owed to Father Thomas Zahuta of St. Peter the Rock Catholic Church as well as parish members Nelda Allen, Robyn Hiatt, Bernadette and Kenny Luger, and Dr. Richard Schmude. Finally, I wish to thank Caroline Wellman who generously served as my first reader and amanuensis for over three decades.

CPSIA information can be obtained
at www.ICGtesting.com
Printed in the USA
LVHW090353020921
696501LV00004B/12